LIT UP

LIT UP

ONE **REPORTER**. **THREE** SCHOOLS.
TWENTY-FOUR BOOKS THAT CAN CHANGE LIVES.

DAVID DENBY

HENRY HOLT AND COMPANY   NEW YORK

Henry Holt and Company, LLC
Publishers since 1866
175 Fifth Avenue
New York, New York 10010
www.henryholt.com

Henry Holt® and 🛡® are registered trademarks of
Henry Holt and Company, LLC.

Copyright © 2016 by David Denby
All rights reserved.

Library of Congress Cataloging-in-Publication Data
Names: Denby, David, 1943– author.
Title: Lit up : one reporter, three schools, twenty-four books that can change lives /
   David Denby.
Description: First edition. | New York : Henry Holt and Company, 2016. |
   Includes bibliographical references.
Identifiers: LCCN 2015029973| 1SBN 9780805095852 (hardback) |
   ISBN 9780805095869 (electronic book)
Subjects: LCSH: Literature—Study and teaching (Secondary)—United States. |
   Teenagers—Books and reading—United States. | High school students—Books
   and reading—United States. | BISAC: LITERARY CRITICISM / Books & Reading.
   | EDUCATION / Philosophy & Social Aspects.
Classification: LCC PN70 .D46 2016 | DDC 807.1/273—dc23
LC record available at http://lccn.loc.gov/2015029973

Henry Holt books are available for special promotions and
premiums. For details contact: Director, Special Markets.

First Edition 2016

Title image based on cover photograph by George Baier IV.

Designed by Kelly S. Too

Printed in the United States of America

1 3 5 7 9 10 8 6 4 2

I have sometimes dreamt, at least, that when the Day of Judgment dawns and the great conquerors and lawyers and statesmen come to receive their rewards—their crowns, their laurels, their names carved indelibly upon imperishable marble—the Almighty will turn to Peter and will say, not without a certain envy when he sees us coming with our books under our arms, "Look, these need no reward. We have nothing to give them here. They have loved reading."

—Virginia Woolf, novelist, 1926

Where is the wisdom we have lost in knowledge?
Where is the knowledge we have lost in information?

—T. S. Eliot, poet, 1934

You don't have to burn books to destroy a culture. Just get people to stop reading them.

—Ray Bradbury, novelist, 1993

A reader lives a thousand lives before he dies, the man who never reads lives only one.

—George R. R. Martin, novelist, 2011

Books smell like old people.

—student, age 15, New Haven, 2014

CONTENTS

INTRODUCTION

Well, maybe not on the way home from the hospital. Maybe when the baby is six weeks old, or when she begins smiling. That might be a good time to pull her into your lap, or prop her up between you and your spouse or partner. Turning through pages, you read aloud a picture book. She won't remember the words or pictures, but an impression of being held and read to will remain—a familiarity with the experience, an emotional reminder of pleasure, especially when it's repeated hundreds of times. Second part of the deal: you talk to your baby constantly, from birth, telling stories, pointing out the things of the world, defining words, asking questions, and gently demanding answers when she's old enough to give them. Like a child in a fairy tale, she will possess an unknown power, which, sooner or later, will burst forth. The reading ego, and the speaking ego, need thousands of little victories before they assert themselves without fear, and she will be ready. A child held, read to and talked to, undergoes an initiation into a useful life; she may also undergo an initiation into happiness.

Everyone agrees that establishing reading pleasure early in a child's life is a monumental achievement (and you do it, the pediatricians say, with books, not with screens); and everyone also agrees that the gap between those children who grow up loving books and active conversation and those who don't—with troubled school performance and restricted career opportunities likely for those who don't—is a gap that gets set early and may be hard to close. Hard, but of course not impossible. It can be done in grade school and middle school. But what about high school? How do you establish reading pleasure in busy, screen-loving teenagers—and in particular, pleasure in reading serious work? Is it still possible to raise teenagers who can't live without reading something good? Or is that idea absurd? And could the struggle to create such hunger have any effect on the character of boys and girls?

A few years ago, I was thinking about these issues, thinking in a nonproductive, desultory way, and wondering, too, about high school reading lists (Does anyone read *The Catcher in the Rye* anymore? Is Hawthorne gone? Did anyone care?), when a stranger came up to me on the street. This sounds like an Upper West Side joke: "Guy comes up to you on the street . . . and starts talking about a school." The stranger was a teacher, Samuel Abrams, a dark-eyed, well-knit man in his middle forties with an intense way about him. For years, he had taught history and economics at a public school he loved, the Beacon School, on West 61st Street in Manhattan. He was on leave in 2011 (and, as it turns out, would not go back); he was writing a book on the economics of education. (His book is now finished: *Education and the Commercial Mindset*, by Samuel E. Abrams, director of the National Center for the Study of Privatization in Education at Columbia's Teachers College.) Sam told me about the school, a cramped, ridiculously overcrowded place with a gym so intimate that a jump shot launched from fifteen feet would scrape the ceiling. Beacon inhabited a cruddy old building never intended as a school. Yet the place had spirit, Sam said. It had interesting students, ambitious teachers, a decent library, dozens of computers. It was a "progressive" school but hardly a slack, feel-good place. The students worked hard.

Yes, but how much were the students reading—in school, and on their own? And how much of it was quality of one sort or another? General information on such issues is not easy to come by. A Pew Research reading survey, conducted by telephone in 2014, reported that 46 percent of teens sixteen and seventeen said they read a book, including books for school, every day or almost every day. Since almost all the respondents at that age are students, 46 percent is not an impressive number. A recent summary of studies cited by Common Sense Media indicates that American teenagers are less likely to read "for fun" at seventeen than at thirteen. The category of reading "for fun" is itself a little depressing, since it divides reading into duty (for school) and gratification (sitting on a couch, beach towel), as if the two were necessarily opposed. The category reinforces the idea that an assigned book—literature, usually—can't be fun.

A more recent Pew survey, issued on April 9, 2015, reported that "aided by the convenience and constant access provided by mobile devices, especially smartphones, 92% of teens report going online daily—including 24% who say they go online 'almost constantly.'" Apart from statistical studies, the testimony of teachers and parents is overwhelming; the evidence of one's eyes is overwhelming. In general American teenagers may be reading more sheer words than ever, but they are reading mostly on screens; they certainly aren't reading many serious books. Most of them are incredibly busy. School, homework, sports, jobs, parents, brothers, sisters, half brothers, half sisters, friendships, love affairs, hanging out, music, and, most of all, screens (TV, Internet, social networking, games, texting)—compared to all of that, reading is a weak, petulant claimant on their time. "Books smell like old people," I heard a student say in New Haven.

When they were very young, teens may have read *Harry Potter*, and later they may read dystopian and science-fiction novels, vampire romance, graphic novels (some very good), young adult fiction (ditto), convulsively exciting street lit. By the time they are fifteen or sixteen, however, reading anything more demanding and time-consuming threatens to cut off their smartphone sense of being in touch with everyone and everything at once. Suddenly, they are not everywhere, they are *there*, on that page, in that time, moored, limited, and many are glum

about it. Talk to them, and you will find out: being unconnected makes
them anxious.

As they get older, many don't see why reading seriously should be
important at all. "Everyone knows how to read and write. Why do we
need a whole class for it? That's just stupid," a fifteen-year-old said to his
teacher in Mamaroneck, New York. He was referring to English class.
If students are thinking of college, they may have been told by their elders
that a liberal arts education and the humanities in particular are a waste
of time. In an economy demanding "skill sets"—defined narrowly as
technical and business skills—that stuff won't get you anywhere. But
this is actual nonsense. We are producing more college graduates skilled
in science, technology, engineering, and mathematics (the STEM subjects) than the economy can absorb. At the same time, employers have
repeatedly said that they want to hire people with a good liberal arts education, people who can think, judge, and express themselves; they want
people who can follow complicated instructions, talk in a meeting,
understand fellow workers. They can always *buy* robots.

The demand for better-educated workers is only one part—and maybe
the lesser part—of the issue. Sometimes, as Orwell said, the restatement
of the obvious is a duty. So the obvious, then: the liberal arts in general,
and especially reading seriously, offer an opening to a wider life, the
powers of active citizenship (including the willingness to vote); reading
strengthens perception, judgment, and character; it creates understanding of other people and oneself, maybe kindliness and wit, and
certainly the ability to endure solitude, both in the common sense of
empty-room loneliness and the cosmic sense of empty-universe loneliness. Reading fiction carries you further into imagination and invention
than you would be capable of on your own, takes you into other people's
lives, and often, by reflection, deeper into your own. I will indulge a
resounding tautology: every great civilization, including ours, has had a
great literature and great readers. If literature matters less to young people
than it once did, we are all in trouble. Speaking for myself, my life
would be a poorer, weaker, duller thing without Jane Austen, Walt Whit-

man, Ralph Ellison, Saul Bellow, Raymond Chandler, John Le Carré, Zadie Smith, Elena Ferrante; without John Grisham and Stephen King, too. Together and alone, we need literature as the California valleys need rain.

Electronic utopians say, "Calm down, nothing has been lost. If anything, the opportunities for reading have become much greater. Plenty of books are being sold, and even if books as physical objects are doomed, reading will survive, even expand. After all, you can get *anything*." In the literal sense, this is true. You can find almost any book you want *somewhere.* Those who know what they are looking for can find it on a computer, a Kindle, Nook, iPad, tablet, or smartphone; the electronic library goes on forever, and the volumes will not get moldy. What technological utopians don't and can't explain, however, is this: How does the appetite for serious reading get created in the first place? A baby held in happy attention to books and stories has a good chance of loving reading as an adult. What about the others?

School was the place to find out. And students in tenth grade, I thought, were the right kids to look at. Recent work by neuroscientists has established that adolescence, as well as early childhood, is a period of tremendous "neuroplasticity." At that age, the brain still has a genuine capacity to change. Fifteen is a danger spot and a sweet spot. Tenth-graders are going through a period of adolescent turmoil before they begin to grapple the next year with college admissions, the military, or a job. Many are figuring out who they are and what they want to be, sexually, professionally, and in all the other ways that matter. They can be reached. Their moral education as well as their literary education is at stake; the two may be inseparable. They may even learn to read good work "for fun."

To write a nation-spanning report, or any kind of large, well-researched study was out of the question for me. Even a regional study, a city or school district report was impossible. I wasn't qualified to do it. I could only make an arbitrary selection of teachers and readers, and then observe and describe and judge, using every element of my subjectivity as well as my sense of how the world works and how life was going—and would go in the future—for the students I followed. By common standards, a classroom is hardly a dramatic subject, but the drama is clear enough if you listen to the patterns, the revelations, the spurts of engagement, and the pall of boredom. It's all there in the fumbled or lucid remarks, the cross talk, the moments of silence and enthusiasm.

After considering other schools, in New Jersey and Pennsylvania, I came back to Sam Abrams's school in Manhattan. He made Beacon sound interesting, and he was right. I scouted the place in the spring of 2011, and, in the following academic year (2011–12), I settled in with a single tenth-grade English teacher, a dynamo named Sean Leon. I wanted to see as well where some Beacon students might wind up a year later in their high school careers, so I paid periodic visits to two eleventh-grade classes, taught by Mary Whittemore and Daniel Guralnick. As kids banged off one another in the hallways, I scanned posters, collages, computer projects, and everything else on the walls. I walked up and down the single narrow stairway as students, hurrying to their next class rushed past me ("Sorry, *sorry!*"). In a dreary green-walled lunchroom, I sat down with some of Mr. Leon's tenth-graders and tried to talk to them above the din.

I had done something like this before. In the eighties and early nineties, many people teaching humanities in the universities were debating such questions as, "Should the Western canon be imposed on kids descended from Latin American or African families? Was the 'hegemonic discourse' of the West empowering white elites and disempowering everyone else?" And so on. There was much else in "the curriculum wars," but I do remember wondering, back in the late eighties, how anyone could be hurt by reading a good book. Curious to find out, I worked on a hefty tome that was eventually titled (with great invention) *Great Books*. For a full academic year (1991–92), I sat with students and teachers at

Columbia, my alma mater, and read the College's required selection of Western classics—pretty much the same books I had read as a freshman thirty years earlier.

Great Books, which came out in 1996, was a mixture of elements—my own feverishly happy reading; teachers at work on Homer, St. Augustine, Rousseau, and Virginia Woolf; students struggling with the books, sometimes reading them brilliantly, sometimes not. *Great Books* was something else as well—a physically placid, middle-aged adventure story. Lucky and generally content as a movie critic, I was nevertheless jangled by too many media images rattling around in my brain. I wanted my head to rattle with other things as well. I needed to go back to school. The ceremony of teaching and learning charmed and fascinated me a great deal.

Some of the same things are true for this book, which, in the event, has turned into a kind of prequel. Again, I wanted—needed—to see students and teachers; I needed to read and make a report on my reading. I would sit, listen, keep my mouth shut, talking to students and teachers outside of class when I could. And I would try to be faithful to my impressions and reflections, wherever they led. The billionaires throwing money at such education fixes as smaller schools or charter schools have, many of them, spent little time in classrooms. I am not a teacher, but I have been taught, and I have had some success watching teachers and reporting on what they were doing. As before, I wanted to work from the bottom up, with teachers and students, not from the top down.

The earlier book, in part, became a search for myself, a movie critic who was feeling lost in a welter of media images and needed to read and think seriously again. It was something of a reclamation job. But the point of view of this book is frankly parental. I wanted to see what the students were like and how they were doing intellectually. I decided not to suppress my feelings about them. I would describe them physically (or else they would never come alive on the page) and commit the sin of "judging," always bearing in mind that they were very young. Fifteen-year-olds, through an academic year, develop stems and roots, their cells divide. In particular, I wanted to see if readers could be born—what happens when a nonreader becomes a reader?—which meant necessarily recording the students' mistakes and awkward moments as well as their insights and breakthroughs as they struggled into life. *If* they struggled into life.

Beacon is the setting for much of the book, but not its subject. Reading is the subject, and I read all the books, stories, and essays assigned to the students. As I sat in classes, I continued at my regular job— reviewing movies for the *New Yorker*—so that something like a normal working life would flow in and out of what I read and saw. Sitting down to write, I resolved not to quote Bacon, Montaigne, Emerson, de Tocqueville, or even John Dewey. Then, and later, I read such well-researched and powerful recent studies as *The Knowledge Deficit* (2006) by E. D. Hirsch Jr.; *Proust and the Squid* (2007) by Maryanne Wolf; *Alone Together* (2011) by Sherry Turkle; *Present Shock* (2013) by Douglas Rushkoff; *Book Love* by Penny Kittle, and other works about the intersection of technology, education, and reading. My debt to these authors and many others (I have listed them in the bibliography) is considerable, but in the end I relied principally on my eyes and ears as a limited but still useful set of tools.

As I wrote up my year in school, friends expressed some doubts. Wasn't Beacon a special school with a special New York population? How well would it "scale"? That is, how much of what I found could be used (if anyone wanted to use it) by other public schools in other parts of the country—schools with different values, different students? My initial response was that there weren't any typical high schools in America. What would they be—suburban schools, country schools, inner-city schools? They are all different. Any generalization you could make about American education, even one heavily backed with statistics, could be refuted by a contrary generalization, a contrary example. America isn't Finland; it's a big country, enormously diverse, and you could tie yourself in knots trying to typify and generalize while not learning much of anything that mattered. Therefore I would do better to observe a single place where literary education seemed to be working.

My resistance to the idea of scale was tied, I realized, to my distaste for the increasingly dominant American notion that only those things that could be quantified mattered in national life. Assertions that cannot be backed with statistics and probabilities—metricized, in tech-world jargon—create at best shrugging indifference, at worst disgust and ridicule. The demand for quantifiable results has created a desperate obsession with test scores. In the view of opponents like education historian Diane Ravitch, the obsession with scores has denatured education's function as cultural enrichment, as citizen making, as soul making. Let's put it this way: you don't have to be John Keats to realize that the soul and what used to be called sensibility—a combination of knowledge, taste, judgment, wildness, respect—can never be quantified.

As I got into the writing, however, I discovered that my friends had a point. Beacon's Sean Leon had an unusual reading list—existential classics, including Huxley, Orwell, Hesse, Vonnegut, Dostoevsky, Beckett, but not Twain, Dickens, Jane Austen, Toni Morrison, or even Shakespeare. He grabbed his students by the throats and shook them into life. He challenged them constantly, asking them to define themselves and take hold of their lives. He was clearly trying to shape character with the books he assigned, the discussions he led. Other teachers could perhaps learn from parts of what he did, perhaps use parts of it, but they couldn't replicate the entire experience. They couldn't *be* him. And certainly no one could say that his was the only way to talk to teenagers. There is, of course, no ideal reading list, no perfect syllabus, no perfect classroom manner, but only strategies that work or don't work. In a reading crisis, we are pragmatists as well as idealists.

So I came around. Typicality and comprehensiveness remained impossible to achieve, but variety was not. I delayed finishing the book, and, in the academic year 2013–14, I visited tenth-grade English classes in two other public high schools—shuttling up many times during the year to the James Hillhouse High School, an inner-city school in New Haven with a largely poor African American population; and five times in the spring to a school in a wealthy New York suburb—Mamaroneck, a "bedroom town" in the language of the fifties, where people sent their kids to good schools (and paid as much as $30,000 annually in taxes to do so). Hillhouse had multiple troubles, including many transients, dropouts, low-performing kids. At the beginning of the year, the tenth-grade students refused to read the assigned texts at home; they weren't openly rebellious, but they seemed puzzled by the assignments. What was the point? At a school like Hillhouse, only the most dedicated, passionate, and inventive teachers can help students surge forward, and I think I found one. But Mamaroneck High School was worried, too. The administration and the English Department were alarmed to discover that some of their kids were not reading the assigned books. The nonreaders and grudging readers consulted the online "study aid" SparkNotes and threw back what it had to say about *The Great Gatsby* and *Macbeth*; they listened in class, picked up what they could, and brazened it out. Acting on its disappointments, Mamaroneck was attempting something new with parts of its English curriculum. Pleasure in reading was the key issue for them. They needed to create it.

People read for all sorts of reasons, and at all levels of difficulty and art. (Only prigs read demanding books all the time.) A minority, perhaps, read not only to enjoy themselves but to understand the world, and, ultimately, to know how to live and die in it. That kind of reading is a special good. If saying so amounts to an elitist assumption, I accept the charge—as long as it's understood that this is an elite anyone can join. Those who assume that serious recreational reading is bound solely by class (the upper middle class and those who would join it) may be overvaluing their own pessimism. The entranceway is not as narrow as that. The first premise of American public education is that the door is wide open. The question always is how many will walk through or get pushed through. That entranceway is where teachers matter more than the rest of us.

To argue that reading is *good* seems as silly as arguing that sex, nature, and music are good. Who could disagree? Yet, implicitly, many teenagers do disagree. This book, I hope, will provide something better than an argument; it will perhaps offer a small demonstration—not a proof, certainly, but a small demonstration—of why literature should be central to the moral, spiritual, and pleasurable life of young people.

A NOTE ON TEACHERS AND STUDENTS

The teachers appear under their own names. The students are real people, and I have taken down their words faithfully. Teenagers, however, should not be tagged by an outsider at a vulnerable time in their lives, and I have made up names for them. I have called them "boys" and "girls." They were fifteen going on sixteen.

A NOTE ON CHRONOLOGY

As I earlier noted, I visited Beacon one year, Hillhouse and Mamaroneck in another. Most of the book was written after the reporting was done, and I realized, as I wrote, that the practices of one school, or one English class, challenged, contradicted, played on the practices of another. So I have raised these issues in what I wrote, at the end of my experience, regardless of when the classes took place in time.

A NOTE ON PRONOUNS

I'm not crazy about writing "his or her" to describe a group mixed by gender. Those locutions kill the rhythm of nearly every sentence they appear in. At least they kill *my* sentences—other writers may be shrewder in getting around the problem. Therefore I have used, as a generalizing pronoun, "she" in some cases and "he" in others, "hers" in some cases and "his" in others. Nothing should be inferred from the use of one pronoun or another. It's just a compositional strategy to avoid bad prose.

A NOTE ON UNIONS

I went looking for good public-school teachers. It was only after I found a few that I realized they were all members of teacher unions.

A NOTE ON THE SUBTITLE

The number twenty-four refers to the books, stories, and plays discussed in the text. The complete reading lists for the classes I visited can be found in appendix 1.

LIT UP

CHAPTER ONE

BEACON, SEPTEMBER:
THE FIRST DAYS OF ENGLISH 10G

- ➤ Naming
- ➤ Everywhere in Chains
- ➤ The Beacon School
- ➤ Azar Nafisi on the Strengths and Pleasures of Literature
- ➤ Themes Are Brought Up

A teacher was speaking.

"As we develop a community here, and I see you thinking about a text, your voice is as important as my voice. What you say is as important as what I say. *I'm standing above you. You have to sit there quietly as I fill the receptacle—you.* That's how it goes in large parts of the world. That's not how it goes here. Nino, I'm interested in what you have to say about the text, but back up your points with evidence. And when you refer to each other"—he looked at the others—"don't say 'him.' Say Nino."

Nino looked up. He was a handsome boy with curly black hair, a good smile, and large hands. It turned out he was a carpenter, a catcher, and did magic tricks. He liked doing things with his hands. Nino was a nickname. He was Antonio Ferrante, with an Italian American father, a legal proofreader, and a Jewish mother who had been a teacher.

The teacher went on: "When someone is talking, you will look at him or her, because not looking is a lack of respect. I will not tolerate any disrespect. I will push you hard, but I will not disrespect you. Do not disrespect me. I will take it as a personal affront if you are late."

It was the first class of the year, on September 9, at the Beacon School, on West 61st Street in Manhattan, and the teacher, Sean Leon, seemed to know everyone's name. How was that possible? It was an ordinary tenth-grade English class, not an "elective," a special class that students signed up for (Mr. Leon taught such a class in twelfth grade). Their pictures were on the school website, and he may have scanned the faces. Or perhaps he was just very quick. A few minutes earlier, he had gone through the class list and asked the students to introduce themselves. It's possible he remembered the names from one glance. Later he told me, "It's really important to them that you know who they are."

Clear enough. Identity was the first step toward respect and self-respect. A teacher needed to fix a student's identity, for himself, for the entire class. They would know one another and address one another personally. He did some cold-calling, asking students to name other students. Most of them stumbled and guessed wrong. For some reason, no one remembered the name of Lauren, a girl of mixed Latino and Asian background with long dark hair and a soft smile, who was sitting on the side of the room.

In English 10G, there were eighteen girls and fourteen boys—not an unusual breakdown for Beacon or, for that matter, for many American schools. Girls were generally doing better than boys and staying in school longer. In any case, thirty-two students were a lot, I thought, for an English class. They were ethnically mixed and members of every economic class in the city—from poor families in East Harlem and the Lower East Side; from middle-class families in Queens; from such upper-middle-class precincts as Park Slope in Brooklyn and the Upper West Side of Manhattan. Every social class but the rich, who often sent their kids to private schools. At the moment, they were more than a little abashed.

"How are you feeling right now?" he asked.

"Shy and a little nervous."

"Curious and a little excited."

"Anxious, excited—you seem like a great teacher."

"By the way," he said to the Hispanic girl who blurted this out, "I've heard great things about you as well." Had he really? I wondered. There was a pause. "I know I sound like a suck-up," she went on, and he stopped her. "How long have you been in class already?"—"Twenty minutes"—"Okay, I know you, I can read you already. I know you are not a suck-up."—"I'm not," she said.

That's the way English 10G began, with command, with candor, with embarrassment and reassurance. We were to be introduced to the difficulties and ardors of literature. The class would be a cross between boot camp for readers and the anteroom of paradise. Our teacher was a slender man in his late thirties, about five feet ten inches, taut and trim in a pink, long-sleeved shirt rolled up on his forearms, a brown vest, a dark gold tie. He had thinning brown hair, a short, pointed beard. Sean Leon smiled a great deal. His voice was dry, a little hard in tone, penetrating, and he said what he wanted to say, without hesitations or false starts. The accent, however, was hard to place. He had been born in Northern Ireland—a member of the Catholic minority in the city of Derry. His father was an American—a navy guy—his mother Irish, and the family had moved to Louisiana, near New Orleans, where he grew up. But his accent was neutral, certainly not Irish, and I couldn't hear a trace of the American South in it.

Mr. Leon's classroom, room 332, was located on an inner corridor at Beacon. A room without windows, good-sized but closed in on itself. The desks were nothing like the separate oak units with black iron frames, arranged in parallel rows, that I remembered from my own high school decades ago. They weren't really desks at all. They were dark brown rectangular wooden tables, with room for six students, and they could be moved about, arranged into any configuration. At that moment, they were arranged in a squared-off U-shape with an opening in the front. Mr. Leon would step forward into the opening at times, but he was restless, and he moved around to the sides of the room or to the back, standing behind the students as he talked. On the walls of his classroom there were pictures of his favorite writers, including a large poster-photo of Franz Kafka, eyes wide open, looking haunted, as if he had seen a ghost (his own, no doubt). Old student projects hung on one side of the room—collages, mostly, with pieces of cellophane and string, maybe some glitter, all mounted on wooden boards or construction paper. The style was student Chagall—everything seemed upside down, determinedly antirealistic, symbolic. Pop culture and classic-lit references were joined together in mixed tonalities of derision and respect.

Mr. Leon asked the students about their passions. Some played the guitar, some did photography, some played baseball or basketball, some were obsessed with friends and family.

"I'm also passionate about my family," he said. "I'm passionate about teaching. I love what I do. When I come in, I will never not be here. I will bring it every day. I want to laugh because I laugh a lot. I'm a cheese-ball. I've been a cheeseball my entire life. I don't take myself too seriously. I take what I do very seriously."

Suddenly, he darted to an empty chair and sprawled out, legs apart. "*Whatever, asshole,*" he said in mock boredom. He addressed us from the chair. "There are times when you're here physically, but you're not really here. You're in la-la land. You think you'd rather be somewhere else. I find that disgusting. I will always be here every day. I'll stay in this damned building until seven if I have to. I will never fail you. I will set the bar high—very high. Anything else would be bullshit. By the way, I don't favor students who just play for the grade, for the A."

They were silent. Some of them, I imagined, wouldn't mind knowing how to play for an A.

He told them what would be expected of them. There would be quizzes on the reading and essays in class. They would keep journals, noting their responses to what they were reading, and they would hand in those journals every week. When he gave them printed versions of stories, he wanted them to take notes right on the printout, and he would read those notes when the students handed the stories back. The school would give them copies of the novels they were reading; they would attach Post-its to the pages with their questions and responses. Again, when they handed the books back, he would read the Post-its. They would be free to say what they wanted, but they would be monitored; at liberty, but judged.

When it came time to write papers, he told them, they would first do an outline and then go through multiple drafts, handing in each draft before the final one. Writing, writing, writing, there would be no end of writing. And talking, too. They would stand on their feet and make presentations in class. Class participation would be graded, but he warned them against raising their hand merely to talk. "How many of you have been in a class in which people simply say the same thing as other people? Cat B says the same shit as Cat A. If that becomes your M.O., it's a problem. *Add* something! Disagree!"

"Plagiarism is academic suicide," he suddenly announced with a mournful look, as if he had smelled a dead cat.

And then: "What was the theme of last year's reading, in ninth grade? Self-discovery? This year it's the individual and society." He turned and pointed at something he had written on the board:

MAN IS BORN FREE, AND EVERYWHERE HE IS IN CHAINS.

"That's Rousseau, Jean-Jacques Rousseau. Please write it down. I'd like you to talk for about seven minutes to one another about what that might mean."

There was a momentary pause, a few panicky looks, and then, shyly, slowly, they turned toward one another. I was sitting on the side of the room, to Mr. Leon's left, perched on a table laden with books (my rear pushed against Camus's *The Stranger* and Herman Hesse's *Siddhartha*).

Some of the students had their backs to me, but I could see that at each table one or two did most of the talking. As the conversations started and then sputtered, Mr. Leon walked around the room, crouching now and then at one of the tables, his face at the same level as the students' faces; he asked questions, pulling a few blank-faced kids out of silence. The room volume hit a high buzz and stayed there.

After seven minutes, he led them through a short discussion about authority and conformity. He agreed that he, too, was an authority, that the school was an authority, that they would have to define their freedom all year. And then he summed up: "You are going to read books that make you uncomfortable. I will make it very hard for you to find yourself. I hope you get lost. If a character suffers, don't be afraid to suffer with him. If you're confused by *Slaughterhouse-Five*, don't be afraid to be confused. I have been, and I've read it many times." And then: "Listen. Finding yourself is not conforming to what others expect of you." This was a Rousseau-like sentiment, a possible plan for action. He wanted to strike off chains.

He turned to the girl whose name no one had remembered. "Lauren, I think you have an awesome presence," he said.

The class was over. They walked out of the room, a little dazed.

Beacon was started, in 1993, as a small "alternative" high school. The founders, Ruth Lacey and Steve Stoll, two New York City teachers, wanted to create a good public high school on the Upper West Side—there wasn't one, except for LaGuardia, a school for artistically gifted kids a few blocks north of Beacon on Amsterdam Avenue. In American education lingo, Beacon is a magnet school, which means that it draws on the entire city, not just the neighborhood kids, and it has a "screened" (i.e., competitive) admissions policy. Finally, it offers a special focus. To get into Beacon, you have to have good grades and score in the top half of the tests in math and English taken in seventh grade by all New York public school kids (the top *half*; not the top quarter). You have to submit a "portfolio"—a paper written as schoolwork, and also a statement of personal dedication to technology, the arts, a particular academic subject, or public service. The student gets interviewed at the school by a Beacon teacher. It helps if you can write a report on a science project, design a website, dance a little, sing, play an instrument, take pictures. Beacon has science requirements and labs (it offers courses in immunology and tropical ecology as well as in chemistry, biology, and physics), but it was known informally around the city as a humanities school.

In 2011–12, the year I was at Beacon, the national enrollment in public schools, divided by ethnic groups, was 52 percent white, 24 percent Hispanic, 16 percent African American, and 5 percent Asian. Beacon's breakdown that year was actually quite similar: 52 percent white, 23 percent Hispanic, 15 percent African American, and 9 percent Asian. But Beacon's ethnic enrollment was very different from that of New York public high schools as a whole. Overall, the city breakdown was 12 percent white, 40 percent Hispanic, 32 percent African American, and 16 percent Asian. Putting it bluntly, from the point of view of an elite New York private school, like Dalton or Horace Mann, Beacon was just another public school. But from the point of view of an ordinary New York public school, Beacon was an elite place.

Charter schools are public institutions financed by public money and sometimes by private money, too. They can hire nonunion teachers, and fire them pretty much at will. Beacon, a magnet, not a charter, was an all-union shop. It belonged to a consortium of thirty schools in New York state whose students were exempt from the Regents exams that other high school students took. In the humanities courses, instead of exams Beacon required, from each student, a stand-and-deliver presentation for a teacher or a panel of teachers—an exposition and defense of a specific topic that was independently researched. The paper was joined to a project of some sort, and the entire effort was called a PBA—a Performance-Based Assessment. As part of the consortium, Beacon gave its teachers considerable freedom to shape their curriculum, and the principal, Ruth Lacey, insisted on that freedom, which was one reason intellectually ambitious teachers wanted to work there. Mr. Leon's tenth-grade reading list, for instance, was his own, not like other tenth-grade lists. He shaped it; Miss Lacy approved it. "Teachers don't leave here. It's a talented staff," she said to me.

By the aughts, Beacon was increasingly popular with students and parents. It was a good school, perhaps a rung below New York's top public high schools, Stuyvesant, Bronx Science, Hunter, Brooklyn Tech, and a few others, all of which, however, were far less diverse than Beacon. Virtually everyone graduated, and more than 95 percent of the graduates went to college. They rarely went to Harvard, Princeton, Yale, and Stanford, but they went to respected places—small private colleges and the great state universities and the many campuses of the State University of New York (SUNY) and the City University of New York (CUNY). (I have appended at the end of this book a list of where Mr. Leon's students in English 10G went to college.)

Silence, absolute silence. They were bent over their tables, writing. It was eight in the morning—awfully early, I thought, to be writing anything, much less writing about literature. (Could I write at that hour? I could not.) Many of the other Beacon kids hadn't arrived at school yet, so the building was generally quiet. Yet I could hear, from the hallways, a vagrant laugh or curse, the repeated sound of an overstuffed locker being slammed shut (*wham! Wham! WHAM!*—that sucker was *closed*); and, from deep within the building, obscure low rumblings, strange knockings and groans. It was mid-September and still very warm, so the noise couldn't have been a heating system kicking into to life. Air-conditioning, probably. These school buildings had their inner lives and mysteries; they weren't haunted, exactly, but not every sound you heard was strictly accountable.

In the second week with English 10G, Sean Leon drew on some remarks by Azar Nafisi, the author of the wonderful book *Reading Lolita in Tehran*. In the 1980s, Nafisi, a professor of English literature at

Tehran University, became disgusted with the constant monitoring of her academic life by the authorities. She retired in 1995, and then asked some of her former graduate students—women in their twenties and older—to come to her apartment, once a week, and discuss literature. The book, written in English and published in 2003, was an account of a flourishing cabal. Away from men, the women talked over their lives; they discussed Nabokov (*Lolita*, of all things), F. Scott Fitzgerald, and Jane Austen, while all around them a reactionary theocratic administration controlled almost everything. Their reading and talking became an act of liberation and self-creation.

Mr. Leon did not tell his class much about *Lolita in Tehran*, but he had provided for the students—as part of his printed syllabus—some of Nafisi's general ideas about literature. Among them:

A great novel heightens your senses and sensitivity to the complexities of life and of individuals, and prevents you from the self-righteousness that sees morality in fixed formulas about good and evil.

I explained that most great works of the imagination were meant to make you feel like a stranger in your own home. The best fiction always forced us to question what we took for granted. It questioned traditions and expectations when they seemed too immutable. I told my students I wanted them in their readings to consider in what ways these works unsettled them, made them a little uneasy, made them look around and consider the world, like Alice in Wonderland, through different eyes.

In all great works of fiction, regardless of the grim reality they present, there is an affirmation of life against the transience of life, an essential defiance.

Fiction was not a panacea, but it did offer us a critical way of appraising and grasping the world.

These sentences could be called the elements of humanist creed, a high-minded roster of literature's strengths and satisfactions, and therefore, necessarily, an entry point to a better world—at least to a better inner world. If you were women living in a restricted society like Iran, literature was not just an escape from orthodoxy but an opening to yourself. Sean Leon's students were fifteen, they were not politically oppressed, yet they lived in a highly competitive society that squeezed them hard. He obviously wanted literature, in the long run, to work for them as it had for Nafisi's women. Right now, Mr. Leon made practical use of her statements.

The previous summer, as the students were working and playing, they also read—at least they were supposed to read—Khaled Hosseini's *The Kite Runner*. Hosseini's popular 2003 novel (made into a decent movie in 2007) was devoted to the adventures of a Kabul boy who lives through the Soviet invasion of Afghanistan, the exodus of Afghans to the United States and elsewhere, and the rise of the Taliban. Since the first day of school, the students had been writing things down about *The Kite Runner* in their notebooks—the melancholy old speckled white-and-black school notebooks they all used for keeping journals. Mr. Leon had already collected the notebooks. Now he asked them to write a three-paragraph essay in class, applying Nafisi's general ideas to specific passages in the *The Kite Runner*.

I could see the beginning of a strategy. He assumed that fifteen-year-olds hadn't read much literature. Faced with a complicated book, they would likely flail around in a sea of intuitions and feelings; he wanted to give them something to hold on to—some fixed posts in the shifting sea of impressions. Nafisi's remarks may have been lofty, but the connections to *The Kite Runner* had to be very specific—the students needed to nail specific passages, actions, bits of dialogue at crisis points. "The point is," Mr. Leon said, "to see whether you *really* read *The Kite Runner*, and didn't just do a bullcrap reading of *The Kite Runner*."

As they wrote, I scanned the bent heads. The boys wore T-shirts, or sweatshirts over T-shirts; a few wore shorts, the rest jeans or khakis.

They all had simple cuts—nothing street-trendy. Two of the girls had long silky burnished hair falling in soft curtains, which they brushed back from their faces every few minutes. The rest gathered their tangle at the back of their necks with rubber bands or scrunchies; a few had earrings or some sort of band at their wrists. In all, the students dressed plainly, without the Day-Glo, tie-dyed madness and vaguely anarchic defiance of the sixties and seventies, the style and attitude of the eighties. A few of the girls had tattoos at their ankles, but—no doubt about it—the age of flamboyance was long over. Plainness was the style. Dress wasn't a big issue for them, at least not in tenth grade. Perhaps they adopted a somber way of facing the world because they knew, even then, that getting a good job would not be an easy affair. Self-expression was a less pressing matter than just staying in school, getting into college, getting ahead, moving on. How, I wondered, would literature fit into these perfectly sensible ambitions?

Sitting by the side of the room, I picked up a student essay lying on the table. It was from 10A, Mr. Leon's other tenth-grade section.

"Themes are big part of *The Kite Runner*. In all great works of literature, themes are brought up." I summoned my courage and continued reading: "*The Kite Runner* is a great example of this, bringing up the themes of truth/realization, friendship, and manhood, which is brought up a lot in Azar Nafisi's five quotes."

A pang of despair. They were fifteen, they lived in a hyper-media age, and they were not, I was sure, *easy* with literature or with writing. Still, these sentences were a misfortune, a way of turning the devices Sean Leon had given them into lame tautology. He had brought on this kind of gibberish, and he would have to clear it out of their heads. He had his work cut out for him. They all did, the English teachers of America.

CHAPTER TWO

BEACON, OCTOBER:
FAULKNER AND HAWTHORNE

- "A Rose for Emily"
- The Neighborhood, the School
- Ruth Lacey
- "The Minister's Black Veil"
- Social Conformity and Sin
- Baby Doll
- *The Scarlet Letter*
- A Hard Read

A few days later, section 10G was working on the first readings of the year, the stories "A Rose for Emily" by William Faulkner and "The Minister's Black Veil" by Nathaniel Hawthorne.

Faulkner's "A Rose for Emily" was published in 1930, the year after *The Sound and the Fury* and the same year as *As I Lay Dying*. Unlike the two great novels, it has always been considered "easy" Faulkner—accessible, straightforward, readily anthologized. A ghost tale of sorts, the story looks back, in shifting planes of time, at the life of Emily Grierson, a genteel southern woman who dies in the 1920s. By then, her fine old house from the 1870s was overwhelmed by garages and cotton gins. A spinster, an emblem of faded aristocracy, she had lived with her father when she was young; all we know about the father is that he repelled her suitors. When he died, Miss Emily lived with the corpse until the town took it away. Soon after, she allowed a northerner doing work in town to pay court to her. They were seen together a lot, but he was a swashbuckling type, not a marrying man, and, at a certain point, he disappeared without a trace. After that, Miss Emily became haughty, indifferent to everyone, a tax cheat. Accompanied only by a silent Negro servant, she lived in virtual isolation.

The story is written in the first person plural—a catty, malicious "we," apparently made up of crass townspeople, who wonder at and enjoy Miss Emily's oddities and miseries for decades. "When we next saw Miss Emily, she had grown fat and her hair was turning gray." At the end, the busybodies get their comeuppance: after the old lady dies, a group of women from the town enter her bedroom and find, lying in Miss Emily's bed, the emaciated corpse of her old beau. "The body had apparently once lain in the attitude of an embrace, but now the long sleep that outlasts love, that conquers even the grimace of love, had cuckolded him." A thread of Miss Emily's iron-gray hair lies beside it on a pillow. A ghastly image, laced with morbid and hostile irony. The entire story, with its heroine living among floating dust in her odiferous house, carries suggestions of the sinister, the inadmissable, all of it rendered by Faulkner in quiet, rather dry prose that occasionally rises to eloquence.

Miss Emily was both a murderer and a necrophiliac, dislikable in many ways—an arrogant presence seen only at the windows. Yet the students found her sympathetic. As Sean Leon culled their initial responses, they said she was a victim—a victim of rigid social conventions. Saul Ramirez, a Latino boy, silent, intense, his face almost masklike, looked up and said, "It's a story about abandonment," and others agreed, noting that Emily had been betrayed first by her father, who chased away her suitors, and then by the northerner who wouldn't marry her. "It's not her fault she turned to necrophilia," someone said, which I thought at first was a joke, but apparently was meant as a sympathetic remark. No one protested. The students, it seemed, had a rather broad idea of sex. Jordan Richardson, a girl with a frank, appraising stare and strong shoulders (I later found out she was a rower), raised her hand: "I think that her relationship with her father was sexual, and she didn't think there was anything wrong with it."

Things had come to a strange pass. We had taken up perverse love before having even a minimal discussion of ordinary romantic relationships. Mr. Leon paused for an instant, then said, "I've taught this story for six years, and I've never had a student who saw that relationship with the father as sexual. It's a contentious reading. Are there grounds for this interpretation?" A few of the other girls offered mild agreement with Jordan, but Mr. Leon, acknowledging their agreement, quickly moved on to firmer ground.

Mr. Leon had earlier asked them to work up presentations on such things as setting and character, and now, John Gruen—a large, blond boy with a rather bluff macho manner, an athlete who grabbed girls in the corridor and lifted them off their feet (sometimes they protested; sometimes not)—stood up at a whiteboard in front of the room, and, with a slight smile on his face, called on people to talk about the town, its changing culture, the South. Mr. Leon, meanwhile, sat down in John's empty chair. He raised his hand a few times and made comments, steering the conversation gently one way or another as John spoke, at the end of which Justin, a large, shapeless boy with an acned face and a mop of hair, suddenly looked up and said, "If the story had been told from Emily's point of view, it would have been a very different story." This was a shrewd literary remark—the first, I thought, of the year. Understanding point of view and how it affects the meaning of a story—how it *is* the story in some cases—escaped many readers, for whom a story, more often than not, was simply *told*.

Mr. Leon concluded by giving the class a little talk about "southern gothic," the genre of writing associated with Faulkner, Carson McCullers, Flannery O'Connor, and many others. "They believed that literature could reveal some of the dark side of who we are, especially those like Emily pushed to the margins."

Many of them nodded. From *Star Wars* they knew about "the dark side" well enough; they knew it was part of what any human being might become. And many American teenagers love violent horror films—the thrill, the dizziness, the near nausea, and then the release from the spell. Mr. Leon now pushed us forward to Hawthorne's bizarre and difficult tale "The Minister's Black Veil," a kind of intellectual horror story.

Amsterdam Avenue behind Lincoln Center was a stony and blank part of the West Side, a stolid institutional passageway between the bounding theater and commercial districts to the south and the comfortable upper-middle class neighborhood—the Upper West Side—to the north. On Amsterdam, moving north from 57th Street, you faced Roosevelt Hospital; John Jay College of Criminal Justice, which was part of the City University of New York; a variety of enormous apartment buildings set well back from the street, fortresses against the unwelcome; the rear of the Metropolitan Opera, where large sets and props were constantly being unloaded out of trucks; the gloomy-looking public housing development, Amsterdam Houses, across from the Met; a variety of public schools with bluff cement facades. The streets were created by proud cultural and institutional plans, by greed and benevolence, all of which worked together to produce an extraordinary architectural deadness—a rare case of a New York Nowhere.

Beacon was located not on Amsterdam itself but down 61st Street, west of the avenue. The block sloped to West End Avenue, with its big, expensive apartment complexes along the Hudson River. Walking rapidly downhill (momentum wasn't hard to sustain), you could stride right past the school without realizing it *was* a school. The building was almost comically ordinary—dim and yellowish, a low-rise commercial structure that for much of its life had been a warehouse. An American flag flew over the entranceway, a square aperture cut into the building; at some point, the aperture must have been a loading dock. Entering the door, you were immediately plunged into school; there was no more than a minimal lobby, and kids streamed and swirled past the entranceway. Between classes, they were all over each other in the narrow corridors, hugging and gossiping and singing bits of songs. Beacon had good basketball, soccer, and track teams, but it did not have a football team, which meant, among other things, that strapping young men did not barrel down the hallways and set the social tone of the school as mini-celebrities. Even without football players the noise level was challenging, though far from unpleasant—easier to take, certainly, than the racket in a crowded New York restaurant. The stairway going to the upper floors, however, was a problem, so badly clogged that you couldn't stop for a second to talk—you had to keep moving, and when you reached your floor, you spilled into a hard-flowing river of students and teachers.

The farcical gym had a low ceiling crisscrossed with structural beams that made the ceiling still lower. There was small, square, mirrored dance studio, a tiny recording studio, and several other places within classrooms for music. The arts room ran long and deep. Computers in rows filled three large rooms, one on each of the main floors. The kids from poorer families—or maybe kids who had two working parents—stayed late at school and did their homework on a computer until they got kicked out. The library was good—stocked with recent fiction and public affairs books, and students often hung out there between classes. Where else could they go? In good weather, they could walk up 61st Street to Amsterdam and stand at the dead corner of the housing complex. At lunchtime, the wealthier kids wandered down Amsterdam for a slice of pizza, which they ate on a stone ledge across from the school. Everyone else crowded into the lunchroom, outfitted with long tables and benches, green walls, and fluorescent light. That was about it for social space. The neighborhood was an alien place, the school cramped and uncomfortable, but, as far as I could see, everyone wanted to be there.

"Ruth Lacey is the spirit of that place," Sam Abrams had said to me on the street. She had been sole principal since 2004, commanding the school from a sizable office just to the left of the entrance. Miss Lacey was unattended by the usual staff of secretaries and assistants guarding a school principal's office. Her door was often open. If you wanted to see her, you walked in and saw her. She was a short, intensely vivid person in her sixties, hardheaded, funny, at times unnervingly direct. She wandered restlessly around the office or stood outside in the hall, greeting and chaffing students—"Why aren't you in class?" Teachers dropped by for a minute to share a joke or confer on some matter. Students would wander in, sit down on a couch to the left of her desk, and air their problems. Others came in and worked on computers on the opposite side of the room; a few even worked on the principal's computer at her desk when Ruth was wandering around. The office was both a command center and a den. When I wondered at the informality of the arrangements, Ruth told me that "high schools should have the same warmth as elementary schools."

Her father, a German Jewish refugee, a lawyer, arrived in the States in 1939, and was assigned by Immigration to a dairy farm in the tiny town of Deposit near Binghamton, New York (just north of the Pennsylvania border). In her office, Ruth had some aerial photographs of the property, which she showed to students who couldn't believe she grew up on a dairy farm in a town called Deposit. After the war, her mother, also born in Germany, opened a camp on the farm for the children of German Jewish refugees. But the family was pushed off the land by a big state highway (Route 17), and they moved to Manhattan, where Ruth went to public school—to Music and Art, the *Fame* school—and then to the University of Wisconsin. She began teaching in the city in pre-K. Eventually she taught every grade up to the fourth, and then became an art teacher for all grades. She was teaching in middle school in the early nineties when the city asked her to start a school.

"It was the farthest thing from my mind!" she exclaimed. "I like leading from behind, I like complaining, but it was the time of the small schools movement"—the belief that students functioned better in schools of limited size—and she asked another teacher, Steve Stoll, to join her.

When it opened in 1993, Beacon had one hundred students; it now had a population of almost 1,300 crowded into the disused warehouse. Despite the larger enrollment, the place was harder and harder to get into. In the fall, on Open House day, anxious parents, arms draped around their children, came to visit, and the line snaked up to Amsterdam and well around the corner. "I don't know where I'm going to fit everyone next year," Ruth Lacey said to me in her office.

Again, a kind of ghost story. Hawthorne set "The Minister's Black Veil" in the 1730s—some forty years after the Salem witch trials and persecutions, but well before the more genial late-colonial era of Benjamin Franklin and Thomas Jefferson. Mr. Hooper, a handsome young minister in Milford, a small New England town, shows up for his Sunday sermon wearing a black veil. The congregation is astonished. What is he hiding? He offers no comment, but just smiles sadly (the veil leaves his mouth visible). As days pass, he continues to remain veiled, and, by degrees, the entire town becomes obsessed with him. Cloaked, he sees more, not less, of his congregation. He gazes into people's souls; sinners on their deathbeds cry out for his aid and solace. He is judgment itself, a kind of ambulatory dark god among them, his presence so menacing that he kills the life of the town, spilling wine on the floor of an attractive couple just married—cursing, by implication, the sexual pleasure of their marriage.

It's a great and strange story, and difficult, too—not difficult from line to line, but slightly opaque and rather subversive in its meanings. A secret malice plays through it—the "sad smile" on the minister's face lasts until his deathbed, and though he says over and over that he is miserable, we wonder if he isn't partly gratified by the town's absorption in him. Hawthorne finished the story in 1835, when he was thirty-one, and published it, along with such tales as "My Kinsman, Major Molineux" and "Young Goodman Brown," in collections that, along with Edgar Allen Poe's gothic-ghoulish fantasies, amount to the birth of imaginative literature

in this country—no fiction with this spiritual intensity and malevo-
lent power had been written in the colonial and immediate post-
colonial age.

Mr. Leon told the class a few things about puritanism, about the
unrelenting consciousness of sin, the sense that one could never be good
or clean enough; and then he asked them to research the subject online.
He gave no more context than that. He wanted them to experience the
strange story in an unmediated way. He asked the students to mark key
passages and to focus their responses on those points, and then to read
passages aloud. Tina Hsu, a quiet Asian American girl, who giggled and
covered her face with her hands before she spoke, picked up the first
paragraph in its third sentence:

> Children, with bright faces, tript merrily beside their parents, or mim-
> icked a graver gait, in the conspicuous dignity of their Sunday clothes.
> Spruce bachelors looked sidelong at their pretty maidens, and fancied
> that the Sabbath sunshine made them prettier than on weekdays.

Like other students who had read aloud in class, she read efficiently,
without hesitation or stumbling—they were all fluent, "good readers"—
but she read without emphasis, too; indeed without expression of any
kind, as if reading aloud were simply an exercise, a duty that had to be
got *through*. They all read that way, flatly, barely above a monotone, and
I thought I knew why: they didn't want to reveal any of themselves by
giving one phrase or another extra emphasis. Not personal strengths or
weaknesses, not sexual feelings—not anything. They were shy, and
they read defensively, and I felt a traditionalist pang for earlier America
schoolrooms in which public reading and even memorization had
been a central part of education.

Mr. Leon didn't urge any more out of their public reading. Instead,
he asked, "How many have had the feeling when you dress in your Sunday best that you're *good*? For those who aren't raising your hands, I
would suggest that you're lying."

No response. "Why does Hawthorne refer to God as 'the dread being'?" Mr. Leon asked abruptly. "Why fear God?"

Marco Perez was a slight, willowy kid who liked to fool around. A couple of times, he had called Mr. Leon "Bro," which was not well received by his teacher. Marco the class clown now blurted out, "He's the one who condemns you to eternal hell." Which of course was the right thing to say, but some of the others ignored this remark. They thought that "being," in the phrase "the dread being," referred to the social collective, the massed opinion of the town itself. After all, the theme of the course was "the individual and society." They were taking the cue. To my amazement, they saw Mr. Hooper as an individualist who had provoked the enmity of the town. Many of them thought the story was about social conformity, about distaste for a man who is merely different or odd. A girl named Vanessa, who had dark eyes and a slightly plaintive way about her—she seemed close to tears at times—now said, "It's the community that has judged Mr. Hooper as bad."

Mr. Leon didn't correct what was wrong; at least, not immediately. If the conversation was rolling, he let it roll, but sitting on the side of the room I said to myself, "They're not getting it. This is what *they* fear— society as the great dread being that was always evaluating them, with nothing but college prep and endless job pursuit ahead of them." In the wildly successful *Hunger Games* books and movies, the authorities set teenagers against one another in competition to the death. The students felt they couldn't escape society's judgment. The demanding "society" was their dark God. Just outside of Mr. Leon's classroom, on a bulletin board, a drawn poster showed students being fed into a hopper.

Suddenly, a girl named Marina broke into the conversation, and right away she began to make sense: "Hooper brings evil to the wedding; he brings down the bride. The veil represents the darkness we don't show in our appearance." She had a purple streak in her thick dark hair, a tattoo on her right shoulder, and a brazen way about her. Every day, she bustled into class, spilling in different directions—books, purse, clothes—and plopped herself down. She was ready to rock. Her remark was more like it, and when Vanessa, the social-conformity obsessive, stated her theme again, Marina came right back at her: "He is saying to the pure people, 'You aren't so pure,'" and I felt relieved, because she had nailed it.

After wearing the veil for years, Mr. Hooper draws close to death, and the members of the community gather around the old man; they beg him to remove the veil at last. Marco, prompted by Mr. Leon, began reading Mr. Hooper's impassioned last words, but Marco the joker had trouble getting angry—it wasn't in his nature. So Mr. Leon stopped him and read what another minister says to Hooper: "Dark old man! With what horrible crime upon your soul are you now passing to the judgment?" Marco started again, and this time, in a Bronx accent, he read Hooper's final speech with surprising emotion.

"Why do you tremble at me alone," cried he, turning his veiled face round the circle of pale spectators. "Tremble also at each other! Have men avoided me, and women shown me no pity, and children screamed and fled, only for my black veil? What, but the mystery which it obscurely typifies, has made this piece of crape so awful? . . . I look around me, and lo! on every visage a Black Veil!"

Hawthorne, as great as he was, often had a dreadful ear for dialogue: "the mystery which it obscurely typifies" never passed the lips of a dying man or even a living man. But at last, in this devastating final scene, Hawthorne cleared things up—somewhat. The story wasn't about nonconformity and the power of society, it was about the individual consciousness of sin, the guilt of each man and woman before God and his neighbors. Mr. Hooper and his mysterious veil amounted to an accusation of himself and others. He was an ironist of sorts—that "slight smile" was more like death's head grin. He wears a veil because *they* are veiled, hiding their sins behind Sunday clothes and proper manners.

Henry James, who wrote a short study of Hawthorne in 1879, when he was twenty-six, thought that his predecessor in fiction was playful, even mischievous. "The old Puritan moral sense," James wrote, "the consciousness of sin and hell, of the fearful nature of our responsibilities and the savage character of our Taskmaster—these things had been lodged in the mind of a man of Fancy, whose fancy had straightaway begun to take liberties and play tricks with them—to judge them (Heaven forgive him!) from the poetic and aesthetic point of view, from the point of view of irony and entertainment." In other words, Hawthorne made use of the Puritans' extreme consciousness of sin as an outmoded religious faith—used it (repeatedly) as richly eccentric material for fiction. Puritanism was irresistible in its oddity, its convergence of the human and the uncanny.

In an essay written in 1964 called "Hawthorne in Our Time" (and included in the collection *Beyond Culture*), critic Lionel Trilling rebuked Henry James, arguing that whatever Hawthorne himself believed—his religious sentiments were cloudy—he took sin and guilt very seriously. He was descended from Puritans—descended from one of the three judges in the Salem witch trials of 1692. And Trilling described reading Hawthorne through the lens of modern literature, through Kafka's work in particular. Mr. Leon didn't mention Kafka, but there he was, the man with haunted eyes staring at the kids from the back wall of the class-room. Mr. Leon didn't teach Kafka to tenth-graders (he had a twelfth-grade class for that), but, for me, sitting in that room, Trilling's evocation of Kafka was hard to miss. You wake up one morning, and you've turned into a bug. Or you've been arrested for a crime, and you never find out what it is. That was Kafka—"Metamorphosis" and *The Trial*. In Kafka's work, we are objectively guilty without having done anything—a trans-position of the religious sense of sin into a psychological and political condition. Hawthorne built on religious traditions, but he anticipated modern consciousness. He was one of us; that was Trilling's point. Mr. Hooper hasn't done anything wrong, but he can never, in his own eyes, be cleansed, and neither can anyone else.

"The whole time, it's been about *you*, Jane," Mr. Leon said, turning to a pale-faced girl who looked a little frightened. She opened her mouth but said nothing. "The minister is saying, 'You're looking at me, never inside yourselves.' This story is tragic for us, in terms of what it says about us."

In the end, he moved them to the "right" interpretation, but he never simply laid down the law. If they were going to talk candidly in class, they needed to be free to make mistakes, to head off in strange directions. He played off pairs and groups of students against each other, teasing and cajoling, and he ruled out nothing categorically. When he wanted to straighten things out, he asked a student to read from the text. At a certain point subjectivity had to end. *Read from the text*: The conversation was free, and sometimes loose-limbed, but it had to come back to literature.

"The Minister's Black Veil" was hard for tenth-graders, hard for everyone. Hawthorne! Was there any point in continuing to ask teenagers to read him? What about his masterpiece, *The Scarlet Letter*? Some of my friends loved it, others recalled reading it as a slog interrupted by moments of excitement, even exaltation. In any case, it had become notoriously hard to teach in high school. The book was passionate, almost anguished, fantastical, shot through with intimations of the supernatural entering everyday life, but for American teenagers it was also stiff, awkward, and distant. As it happened, an eleventh-grade class at Beacon was taking up *The Scarlet Letter* at the same time as Mr. Leon's class was reading "The Minister's Black Veil." I had to find out. How do you teach this extraordinary book? Many high school teachers had given up on it.

At the beginning of her classes, Mary Whittemore, an attractive woman in her late thirties, with light brown hair and gray-green eyes, pushed the desks out to the far walls and lined up the abandoned chairs in rows. The class had become an auditorium. Suddenly, from the corner behind her, a student emerged from a supply closet. She was holding a bedraggled baby doll, and she was wearing on her chest a large *A*. The other students giggled and sighed. An instant of suspense: Would the *A* fall off? No, it was felt with an adhesive back. She climbed onto a chair in front of the class, and everyone began hissing and jeering.

Thus the first scene of Hawthorne's novel, in which Hester Prynne, the book's magnificent heroine, emerges from a "beetle-browed and gloomy" jail and stands on a scaffold before a good part of seventeenth-century Boston. In her arms, she holds her illegitimate baby, Pearl. Miss Whittemore then handed out pages of script to different students who played the handsome young minister, Arthur Dimmesdale, Hester's former lover; the decrepit elderly doctor, Roger Chillingworth, her cuckolded and coldly enraged husband; the town officials and divines, the harpies and ordinary citizens. She chose still other students to read the narration. The script was the students' first introduction to *The Scarlet Letter*. Reading aloud, they stumbled over words like "contumely," and they laughed at the intentional period formality of Hawthorne's prose—the "hithers" and "haths" were a problem.

D. H. Lawrence, in *Studies in Classic American Literature*, teased Hawthorne as "a blue-eyed darling" who nevertheless "knew many disagreeable things." Among the disagreeable things that Hawthorne knew: prurience, social cruelty, sadism masquerading as concern, moral weakness disguising itself as sanctity. Hester has not, in her own eyes, done anything wrong; Dimmesdale, in his own eyes, *has*, and he suffers terribly from agitation, physical weakness, despair—all the symptoms of a man in psychological torment. But his sin is not so much lust as hypocrisy. Like Mr. Hooper, the hero of "The Minister's Black Veil," he must lead his congregation, yet he feels himself an impostor, and his torment is only increased when Chillingworth, who keeps his identity hidden, moves in with him under the guise of helping him and sticks the knife in and twists it. Nasty solicitude is perhaps the most disagreeable thing that Hawthorne knew.

Miss Whittemore's students, like Sean Leon's, had trouble understanding a society suffused with the presence of God, and still greater difficulty accepting extreme punishments dealt out by a godly people. They were baffled by the moral logic of the story. One girl, exasperated, burst out: "I don't get it. If she's married, and she's got a baby, what is the problem?" There speaks the twenty-first century! Her scorn produced a ripple of amusement. Other students voiced similar discontents. They felt that the emotions of the story were overwrought in relation to what was actually at stake. Why was an entire community obsessed with an adulterous woman? They judged Hester by modern standards, and by those standards, in which sexual pleasure was a right for women as well as men, she was certainly not innocent, but she was not terribly guilty, either.

As she worked her way through the novel with her students (they read it at home as well as in class), Mary Whittemore was calm, encouraging, friendly—her face mild, her eyes flashing when a student said something especially interesting. Yet she was extremely persistent, with hints of an underlying fire beneath the warmth and equanimity. The students responded to her, especially in those moments when she cast away mildness. For four weeks, she alternated an increasingly detailed discussion of character, atmosphere, and motive with additional performances in the reading theater. After a while, the idiom became more familiar, the difficulty of the prose easier to handle. When Miss Whittemore caught a student reading Dimmesdale weakly, she asked, "What does that mean? What did you just say? Do you know what you just did, Dimmesdale?"

"Let me think," the reader said shyly. A few minutes later, when the conversation came back to him he said, "I just made a lot of excuses and contradicted myself," which caught Dimmesdale's confusion; the reader had fallen into the character without quite realizing it. So did the others. A tall, pale, intellectual boy, dry and earnest, with a bony nose and parchment voice, read Dimmesdale a few times and then seemed more like Dimmesdale every time he made a comment. A blustering boy lowered his voice to insinuation as Chillingworth. A girl who spoke a great deal, her words normally a thicket of "likes" and "sort ofs," read Hester's refusal to relinquish her child: "God gave her into my keeping. I will not give her up!" She read it with passionate anger, and, after that, her classroom comments became leaner, more to the point, less self-conscious. Whatever the students' resistance to the novel, Hawthorne's defining strength cleared away their adolescent vagueness.

As the weeks went on, the students admitted that they were surprised by the power of the fable. Hawthorne suspended the three adults and wicked little Pearl—a child associated with nature, amoral, irrepressible—in a physically vague but psychologically dense thicket of fear, guilt, pride, and vengeance. At first, the students thought Chillingworth might be sincere, even helpful in his advice to Dimmesdale. A worldly, knowledgeable man, plausible, sensitive to the nuances of personality—Chillingworth's ruthless subtlety did not fit into their moral universe. Understanding what he was up to was an introduction, for many of them, into the nature of perversity, a stage in their moral education and their perception of character. The girls in the class, initially baffled by Hester's situation, warmed to her power, her indifference to contempt. Hester becomes a repentant Christian woman, yet there's something brewing in the fervency of her pride. "She was patient—a martyr, indeed—but she forebore to pray for her enemies; lest, in spite of her forgiving aspirations, the words of the blessing should stubbornly twist themselves into a curse."

Mary Whittemore not only got the students to embody the characters as much as possible, she made them see the fable as shaped around certain choices, conditions, changes in character. She kept shifting the classroom routine, even the shape of the room, rearranging the tables for debates over Chillingworth's character. She kept the *apparatus* of reading constantly in motion, so the students could never settle or allow the book to fall away from them. She made the book possess them, so that, eventually, they would possess the book.

All along, they had been quizzed on the reading, and near the end of the unit there was a full-length test, followed by a final assignment: they wrote papers extending the narrative, in the voice of one or another of the characters. The tall, bony boy whose Dimmesdale was so effective wrote, of Hester, "Her hair was a beautiful black, like the night's sky, that flowed down her face like rain, like the flow of water down a stream"—a lover of women wrapped in parchment and uncertain grammar. The girls were bolder, more in the spirit of Hester. One girl wrote about a young woman going back and forth between two lovers—Hester unleashed. Another wrote a utopian fantasy of old New England under the domination of women, with some of the gender roles reversed—Dimmesdale is a woman married to Chillingworth, and Mr. Hester Prynne is a man, with whom Dimmesdale has an affair. That sent my mind spinning.

In the final class on *The Scarlet Letter*, Mary Whittemore showed up wearing a twenty-dollar black Cher wig and holding a baby doll in her arms—the same baby doll that a student had held earlier. It was a return to the scaffold, where Hester had faced the jeering students. Miss Whittemore sat on a high stool. "The teacher Mary asked me to talk to you," she said quietly. "She asked me to answer your questions for your test tomorrow. I will answer any of your questions about my behavior." The students settled down and peppered her. They were with her, longing on her behalf for the happiness which they accepted she would never have. They all agreed, for instance, that Hester Prynne could not run away with Arthur Dimmesdale even if he had the strength to take her off. In the end, the moral complexities of *The Scarlet Letter* made sense to them. Taught aggressively and flexibly, with humor and dramatic power, Hawthorne's difficult book lived in high school.

Back in Mr. Leon's tenth-grade class, the students were launched, however uncertainly, into reading literature. In both the Faulkner and Hawthorne stories, a town is baffled by a willful, aberrant individual. In the first story, the students judged the town's response as malicious and intrusive; in the second, they were presented with the idea of sin and judgment, even the notion of judging themselves. The story is "about *you*, Jane," was a remark that came close to a taunt, but Mr. Leon meant it for all of them. Why shouldn't they read something hard? And why shouldn't they be troubled by it? As Azar Nafisi said, literature unsettles the reader. Mr. Leon's was no placid, feel-good approach to tenth-grade English.

"Tremble also at each other!" the minister says as he's dying. Well, that was a stern command, and an exciting one, too. Mr. Leon had been setting them up for something—but just what that was became clear only in the following week.

CHAPTER THREE

BEACON, OCTOBER: SYLVIA PLATH AND CONFESSIONS

→ "Daddy" and "Lady Lazarus"

→ Confessions

→ Are There No Happy Adolescents?

→ Telling One's Story

Just before class, Mr. Leon often stood at the doorway, naming the students as they passed by, nodding, smiling, shaking hands, congratulating Justin on his sneakers, Vanessa on her sweater. Today each student gave him a couple of sheets of paper. "*Gracias*," he said. "*Gracias, Gracias, merci, merci* . . . thanks, awesome, thanks."

He asked them to rearrange the tables, and they quickly formed the pieces into a large rectangle that took up the entire middle of the room. Then he asked them to move to the inside of the rectangle. They sat shoulder to shoulder, a tight fit, boys and girls packed together in no particular order. On the way into the room, it turned out, each student had handed Mr. Leon two identical sheets, one with his name on top, one without. A poem was printed on each sheet. He put the signed sheets away, in a folder on his desk at the back of the room, and he climbed over a table and squeezed in with the students.

In his hand, he held a sheaf of anonymous poems, which he now distributed randomly. He asked them to read what they were holding, and one student after another around the inner rectangle became a reader, reciting not her own poem but the work of some unknown student. "Don't forget," Mr. Leon said. "There's another person on other side of these words. No applause after each one. No comment. If there's language that you're uncomfortable with, I'll give it to someone else."

> *Exhale*
> *I'm more than nothing*
> *You leave me bone dry*
> *Sometimes I just want to die*
> *You're a dictator*
> *Without your foot in my face*
> *I wear my skin like a cage*

The reader was Maud, tall, slender, pretty, well-dressed Maud, who had an almost regal air. The lines might have been written by any other girl or boy—or by herself, for that matter, if she had drawn her own poem. Actually, I was quite sure they were not written by a boy. The tone and snap of those words sounded like female rage. And the anger wasn't exactly a surprise. The previous week, as we were discussing "The Minister's Black Veil," Mr. Leon had asked the class to read at home two poems by Sylvia Plath, "Daddy" and "Lady Lazarus." Plath wrote "Daddy" in the famous burst of creativity before she died in 1963, a suicide at the age of thirty. The poem begins as follows:

> *You do not do, you do not do*
> *Any more, black shoe*
> *In which I have lived like a foot*

For thirty years, poor and white,
Barely daring to breathe or Achoo.
Daddy, I have had to kill you.
You died before I had time—
Marble-heavy, a bag full of God,
Ghastly statue with one gray toe
Big as a Frisco seal.

In a break from Hawthorne, we had briefly discussed such poetic devices and conventions as diction, rhythm, dramatic monologue, and so on. Mr. Leon spoke of an author's "toolbox," which provided the students with a set of tools, too—a way of talking about poetry and fiction that went past mere impressions. He went through "Daddy" and "Lady Lazarus" with the students, pointing to the short, rippling lines, the shock effect of violent imagery, the anguish and contempt. But Plath's words were so calamitous that talk of "tools" felt trivial—at least to me. Back there, the week before, we had briefly discussed the morality of Plath's killing herself by sticking her head in an oven while her two little children were sleeping in the next room. The students were not awed as many of their elders have been for years by Plath's suicide. They were appalled. Moving away rapidly, Mr. Leon returned to poetic devices, and he said, before giving them an assignment, "The literary devices are just as important as a conversation in which we're talking about ourselves."

At the time, I was puzzled. *Talking about ourselves?* But that, it turned out, was precisely what we were going to do. He asked them each to create a confessional poem over the weekend. At the door, they had handed over their effort, as if paying a toll.

A student named Ike Pressman, a round-faced boy, trembling slightly, now read as follows:

There is constant monitoring
Of what I say or do,

Because they're right
They always are
And if they're always right
Then I'm always wrong
Yet if I'm always wrong
I could be wrong about them being right.

A nice turn there at the end, a bit of proud irony that suggested the writer suspected he was not wrong at all.

I could see where this was going. They had been cued by the brilliant, ferocious Plath poems—primed to accuse, to complain, to vent. They read, one after another, and the mood in the room was hushed, even solemn; no one snickered or even smiled. Lodged inside the building, without a window, Mr. Leon's classroom was like a sanctum, an interior space devoted to books and reading, and Mr. Leon took advantage of the closed-in quality. He was pushing them to reveal themselves, anonymously and collectively—to bind them together and to make them trust one another by exposing how vulnerable or angry they felt. Each student read someone else's poem, but for that moment it seemed to become his own story, her own story. Latisha Hornby, an African American girl from Brooklyn, read this one:

I've lied, I've stolen, I've cheated
Who hasn't
I've been lied to, stolen from,
Cheated on. Who hasn't.

The poetry recitation was like one of those trust games at summer camp or at an office retreat in which you fell backwards and prayed that someone else would catch you. Or maybe it was closer to sitting around a campfire and telling ghost stories. Shiver my timbers. Whatever it was, it was working. I felt a kind of mute solidarity growing among the students as the poems were read—often intoned—aloud.

People think I'm happy
I'm wealthy, I'm this, I'm that
That I've got it good
Judgments
Assumptions
You don't really know me
You don't really know what I go through
Coming to school each day with a smile is hard
It's a lie.

My God! Were there no happy poems by fifteen year-olds? Yes, Mr. Leon had pushed them in a definite direction, but did they all need to sound like mad, mean, brilliant Sylvia Plath? There's such a thing as being too good a student. A number of poems, I noticed, complained of absent or overly demanding fathers: "He screamed so loud / With his veins popping out of his neck / You're a bitch / You're a brat." Plath had licensed the aggrieved tone, but I was still surprised. These kids were the *winners* in the public school system. They had faced a competitive entry and gotten into a good school, and most of them were heading to college, even very good colleges, and I grumbled to myself that their fathers' toughness may have been one reason for their success until now. Kids with absent or indifferent parents or guardians rarely made it this far. The pressure on Beacon students may have been unpleasant; it may have worked, too.

But all of that was beside the point. The poems may have made me squirm, yet in some way or other they were bitterly true. Anyway, I was an idiot for expecting a balanced view. They were *fifteen*. The point was they were propelled into self-expression, even anonymous self-expression. For Sean Leon, literature enabled students to tell their own stories, to fix the beginnings of an identity out of the chaos of fear and desire. Teenagers have a talent for morbidity and dramatized self-pity, emotions that, ten years later, they might laugh off. But if they didn't go through this complaining now, they might not have anything to relinquish later.

"I have a great deal of respect for the courage to share, even anonymously," Mr. Leon said at the end of the class, and I thought to myself, imitation Plath or not, "I wear my skin like a cage" was a powerful line. I couldn't have written anything like it at fifteen. No one asked me to, but I doubt I could have done it if someone had.

BEACON, NOVEMBER:
NUTS MATTER, AND BOLTS, TOO

Mr. Leon stood before his class holding up a student paper—one of his own, it turned out. "I thought of myself as a good writer," he said, turning it over in his hand as if it were some sort of alien object, then turning it back again. "I was a student at Louisiana State, and I was nailing it on paper after paper—A, A, and A. I wrote an essay on Walter Lippmann, the journalist and political thinker. My professor said it was one of the best essays he had received, but he gave it an F." He paused. "I had misspelled the author's name throughout the essay. I was purporting to criticize this guy Lippmann, and I misspelled his name. Over time, I've become a more humble person."

He was saying what he had said before in one form or another. If the students didn't care for precision in writing, they wouldn't write anything anyone wanted to read. The soul expresses itself in speech, in words, in writing, but craft has to come first, or the soul would be stunted or mute. Nuts and bolts—grammar, syntax, vocabulary, and "thesis statements"—were as much part of tenth-grade English as literature.

"Writing and instruction can be pretty boring, but I get revved up about it, so don't try to figure me out. I love this stuff," Mr. Leon exclaimed. He was wearing a pink shirt, a yellow tie pulled down from the neck, and a blue sweater. He was festive. Excitement ahead! Thesis statements!

Sean Leon happily slipped writing and language instruction into literary discussions, or inserted it at the beginning of a class, or saved it for the end, as if it were champagne, a reward for hard work. At home, the students punctuated pages of run-on prose that he distributed on sheets. They also turned the passive voice to active in such mishaps as "My books were stolen by someone yesterday." In class, they rearranged dependent clauses, set up parallel constructions, transferred qualifiers from one place to another. They were forever moving words around, for a sentence was a malleable thing, and writers of sentences were either dynamic or inert.

He read some sentences generated by another class. They were intended as thesis statements—jumping-off points for an essay: "Mark Twain's *Huckleberry Finn* is a great American novel." Pause. "That is shite," he said. He drew the word out contemptuously. For the first time, and only briefly, he sounded Irish. "Shite. Meaningless. How about this? 'Mark Twain's *Huckleberry Finn* develops a contrast between life on the river and life on the shore.'" The class was quiet. "Well, that's better, isn't it? But where's it going?"

The students were working on their first paper, a comparison of "The Minister's Black Veil" and "A Rose For Emily," and Mr. Leon was easing them into writing a step at a time, starting with a statement of what the paper was about. He had asked them to email him their statements, and now some of them read the sentences in class.

Nino: "In 'The Minister's Black Veil,' Hawthorne uses symbolism to show the fallibility of human behavior."

Vanessa, who wouldn't let go of the idea that Hawthorne's story was about conformity and individualism: "In 'The Minister's Black Veil,' Hawthorne uses symbolism to relay the essential message that people should be authentic rather than crack to societal pressures."

Justin: "In 'The Minister's Black Veil,' Hawthorne uses foil to express . . ." No, no more. *Uses foil?* They were plugging literary terms like flagsticks into the middle of sentences. "You've got to show," Mr. Leon said gently, "how symbolism is used to make those points about society." He asked the class to score the thesis statements according to the following criteria: Is it clear and concise? What are you analyzing? What are you arguing? And also: So what? That is, why does it matter?

He was tough on them, making them do things that would have caused me to freeze. He asked individual students to go to the board, write their sentences, and call on others for comment and criticism. In effect, they would lead a discussion that could tear apart their own work, a daunting exercise. They had to man up, woman up. Some of them looked a little scared, but they did it. Mr. Leon remained quiet, though when energy flagged, he said, "Let's go, let's go! Time is short in my world." The class revived and roundly criticized most of the statements on the whiteboard as vague and rudderless. "I don't see an argument in it," was the common sentiment. They were hard on one another, though ragging and sarcasm were forbidden.

For Mr. Leon, grammatical, syntactical, and usage questions had their spiritual implications. He wanted to shake his students out of safety and lethargy, to make them energetic, even effervescent. Writing was a way of being. The British had ruled an empire with boys educated in Latin declension and syntax, and he set out the modern equivalent, rules for the active life.

Wordiness—that was the other thing he got the students to criticize in one another's writing. They could hear the meandering in other kids' writing, however, without necessarily knowing how to cut it out of their own. "One way we address wordiness," Mr. Leon said, "is to get rid of all versions of 'to be.'" A few classes later, as they brought in a complete first draft of their essays, he asked them to swap the pages with one another and to mark forms of "to be" in the writing in front of them. "If you wind up with ten, not bad; twenty, worse; thirty, stomach-turning." Most of them, looking at other writers' papers, counted about fifteen.

I had mixed feelings about Mr. Leon's disapproval of "to be." Yes, it was weak: "is," "are," "were." What are you saying? That something *is* something else. It's just a way of identifying one thing with another. Much of the time, the first part of the sentence predicts the second half, eliminating surprise. *Weak*, as Mrs. Thatcher would say, definitely feeble compared to the vibrant activity of those bold Anglo-Saxon athletes *break, bend, fight, yield, sing*—expressing force or at least energy. All true, yet who didn't use various forms of "to be" again and again? I used it myself in this paragraph. And I sympathized with any fifteen-year-old who depended on it thirty times in a three-page paper. I made a guess about them: They were just coming into an identity of their own, and the kind of will expressed by ax-wielding Saxon activity might have scared them a bit. They weren't ready to act upon the world. More likely they wanted to find a place in it, and so, instinctively, they said one thing equals another. They identified the world as a state of being, often, apparently, a hostile state of being. The world *was*.

Mr. Leon taught as a vitalist, that much was clear. You had to will yourself into activity, using the active voice in words and deed. They had no trouble demolishing a ridiculous sentence he wrote on the board. "An amended declaration shall be filed with the IRS office with whom the original was filed, even if you move to another district." He said he would tell them later that the passive voice had its uses, but right now he wanted them active.

This normal reliance on "to be," however, was linked to something else, something that puzzled me at first. I noticed it not so much in Mr. Leon's

class but in other Beacon classes. It was this: the students had trouble saying the name of the author. Until the teacher spoke the words "Fitzgerald" or "Hawthorne" or "Hesse" about twenty times, students said things like "It says that Nick lives in a house right next to Gatsby's mansion." Or "Even though it's not telling you the story, I think it's very beautiful—I like the full descriptions." Or, even more strangely, "They say that Siddhartha ate very little for days." But who in the world are *they*? The fifth or sixth time I heard this, I thought to myself that the French critic Roland Barthes, when he announced "the death of the author," didn't go far enough. It now appeared that the author had never lived. I was amazed. What's so hard about remembering "Poe"?

They had trouble acknowledging authorship. But why? One obvious reason: Like most American high school students, Beacon kids are given the books by the school. They make them their own, taking notes on yellow and pink Post-its, which they attach to their copies—some of the books were so flapped and colored they looked like exotic birds incapable of flight. They customize the school copies, but they eventually give them back. Officially presented and then retrieved, the books possess authority but, for many, no particular author.

There may be some other commonplace reasons. My son Thomas, who was then twenty-four, reminded me that the students had seen a lot of textbooks. Didn't I remember textbooks? Many of them had multiple authors. "Dad, no one remembers who wrote them." Okay, the boy was right. Writing often came to students impersonally, produced by authority without any particular identity. Another commonplace reason: fifteen-year-olds were used to seeing TV series and movies made in collaboration. The best-informed knew who David Chase and Matt Weiner were, but TV was always there, always a feast, and as for who made individual shows—did it matter? It wasn't important for most people.

All this made sense, but I was a little sore (I was taking this personally in some way), and I wasn't prepared to let up on them. There had to be less innocent explanations. Many of these kids don't have favorite authors, I said to myself. That's why they don't care about who wrote

the books they were reading in school. But that can't be entirely true. When they were younger, many had read the *Harry Potter* series; many were now reading the *Twilight* and *Hunger Games* series, which certainly demonstrated loyalty—if not to J. K. Rowling, Stephenie Meyer, and Suzanne Collins, then at least to a common setting, a common destiny, a familiar pace and style. But did they know the authors' names? Or were the books something that hit them anonymously, propelled out of the whirlwind of media noise?

I gave Mr. Leon's students a questionnaire, asking them to tell me what books they read on their own, what books were most important to them. One of the girls said Camus's *The Stranger* and a couple said Sylvia Plath's *The Bell Jar*; the elegant Maud said *Go Ask Alice*, the sensation of 1971, which purported to be the diary of a teenage drug addict but was largely concocted by the therapist Beatrice Sparks, who signed herself "Anonymous." Jordan of the strong shoulders liked Kurt Vonnegut and Ian McEwan; she had read McEwan's great *Atonement*. She was one of three real readers, three out of thirty-two students. The others were Nino and Latisha Hornby, the one African American student in the class, who mentioned books by Toni Morrison and Maya Angelou's autobiographical writing. Several boys read sports bios like Derek Jeter's *The Life You Imagine*. James Patterson's fiction had a couple fans. Again and again, *The Hunger Games* and *Twilight*. Several said they hadn't read *any* books recently on their own, and none of the answers were ambitious or wild or obsessional.

No doubt I'm asking too much: I know perfectly well that there was never a Golden Age of Teen Reading—let's say fifty years ago—in which more than a minority read on their own J. D. Salinger or Joseph Heller or Charlotte Brontë; or, forty years ago, Kurt Vonnegut or Ray Bradbury or Allen Ginsberg. Obsessional reading is always a minority taste, and now such readers are even a smaller minority. But, unfairly or not, I was sorry that among Mr. Leon's students there were no mad enthusiasms, no crazy loves, no compulsive reading of every book written by a single author, no stretching and reaching—not for Dave Eggers nor

for Anne Tyler nor, except for Latisha, for Toni Morrison. For a hundred and fifty years, *Jane Eyre* has been an emotional favorite of girls this age, but it did not turn up. A thing about Grace Paley, perhaps, or Emily Dickinson? I didn't find it. No, most of them did not relish *authors*. Except for Latisha and Jordan, no one named an actual writer. Salinger and *The Catcher in the Rye* were gone as teen reading, at least at Beacon. When I asked, they told me that they had heard that Holden Caulfield was "whiny."

They all said they read on the Internet, which meant, like the rest of us, they read not just signed articles and parts of books but fragments and summations and borrowed text in which the words came from everywhere and nowhere—the words aggregated but seemingly not authored (even when they were). Writing on the Internet, with some exceptions, is manifold, accumulative, highly interwoven, repetitive, associational. It may be good writing, but much of the time it has no obvious *source*. "Isn't the World Wide Web a new ether, in which we are all haunted by ghostwriters"? asked the Scottish novelist and essayist Andrew O'Hagan. The Internet really was a "they."

All right, cool down. They were young—isn't that mainly what I am saying? They were students, tenth-graders, uncreated readers, or half-created, and their unwillingness to name authors may have been related to their dependence on some form of "to be" seventeen times or thirty times in a three-page paper. They lacked confidence, as I did at fifteen. If they recognized a strong personal voice in writers, they might wonder if they didn't have to create a voice for themselves, which is hard at any age. At the moment, a lot of their speech was a way of putting off clear declaration. Like using "like" again and again. "I thought he was like saying you like face up to what you had done"—this about *The Scarlet Letter*. "Like" is a kind of spontaneous punctuation—a verbal tic setting off units of meaning. But it's also a way of suggesting that the opposite of what one says may be true. "I offer this now, but I may take it back." The word *like* is suppositional, a minor down payment upon assertion, a way of showing other people that you don't take yourself any more seriously than they do. Eventually, as we get older, "like" fades away and gets overtaken by real punctuation, by need, want, hope. But give them time, for heaven's sake.

Initially, I was startled when Mr. Leon introduced the blunt question "So what?" into a composition lesson. Of all the compositional criteria "So what?" was the hardest for fifteen-year-olds to meet. To say why something—anything—mattered, or did not matter, required knowledge of the world, experience in all varieties. They would have to read and observe a great deal, and probably get knocked around, too, before they could answer well. But they would have to answer some day. We all have to answer, at any age. *So what?* is the common skepticism of the world. Is what you're doing or saying interesting? Valuable? Original? Of any use? Does it make money for anyone?

America is a supremely utilitarian society, and a derisive one, too. The Internet is spangled with words, ideas, proposals, jokes, so many of them that the most determined young person could be climbing up someone else's tailpipe, choking on the exhaust, without even knowing it. Then they find out: the teasing irony and snark of professional entertainers is the common style of anyone who wants to boast that he knows something that others don't know. The Internet has created a generation of information snobs and put-down artists. And even in the best of times, the world—the professional world—little feels it needs to make room for another ego, another claim on its attention, and the easily discouraged could be cowed by indifference or hostility. That the students had to be interesting as well as grammatical seemed paramount among the many things Mr. Leon wanted to teach them. *So what?* was an unpleasant question, but it toughened them up.

At the end of the composition talk, Mr. Leon turned to a thesis sentence that had been on the board all along. It was a kind of matrix with missing words. "Sylvia Plath uses [blank] and [blank] to illustrate psychological tumult wherein each 'death' empowers her to rise above the ashes of her life."

"Is it perfect?" he asked. Someone in the other section had written it. The 10G students could fill in the blanks and make it better. Perfect, no, they said, but they all liked it. The sentence was active; it didn't depend on some form of "to be"; it was interesting. "It's heading in the right direction," Mr. Leon said. "This student is trying to connect the themes of suicide and rebirth and resurrection."

He had asked them to tell their own stories in rude little poems, and, in his composition lessons, he was trying to pull them out of adolescent tentativeness and create them as bold young men and women, forcing them to put their entire being into words. It was a utopian goal, an English teacher's goal.

CHAPTER FIVE

BEACON, NOVEMBER: HUXLEY

- *Brave New World*
- Digital Fast
- Need
- False Happiness
- Maryanne Wolf and Deep Reading
- What Is the Soul?

Aldous Huxley's dystopian *Brave New World*, the satirical shocker of 1932, is not a great novel, as Huxley himself seemed to know. Huxley created the characters as vehicles for whatever attitude or temperamental quirk that he wanted to define them by. The story moves intermittently, in odd fits and starts. As fiction, it feels arch and a little thin—remarkably clever, but repetitive, pedantic in its scandalous way, even a bit self-satisfied. Yet *Brave New World* still has power; it still feels like an accusation that has to be answered. I remember reading it decades ago in high school, paired with Orwell's *1984*, just as it would be paired now in Mr. Leon's class. And I remember getting into an argument with the best English teacher in my school, a staunch anticommunist, who insisted that Orwell's dystopia, ruled by constant surveillance and pain, was much closer to the current truth than Huxley's futurist nightmare, which was ruled by biological engineering and pleasure (i.e., sex and drugs). I thought he was wrong—that Huxley's vision was closer to our reality. I wasn't much of an arguer, and anyway, back in the sixties, we were talking about two different things—he of the USSR, me of America, with its tranquilizers, its Muzak, its avid hedonism and incessant advertising for goods not always needed. Fifty-odd years later, the Soviet Union is gone, though the iron fist hasn't disappeared in Russia and elsewhere, while America is still its pleasure-seeking, consumption-addled self. If anything, much more so. Which novel better predicted our current world?

That old question—a high school chestnut that still glowed—couldn't have been the only thing that interested Mr. Leon in *Brave New World* as a book for teenagers. The theme of tenth-grade English was "the individual and society," which could be called a serious teenage obsession. All right, an obsession of serious teenagers. Dystopian fiction in which the individual had to fight to survive had become pop culture. *The Hunger Games*, with its starving American teenagers manipulated by corrupt, media-wise elders (they have tinted hair, and they *smirk*), is certainly the ultimate in teen paranoia, an emotionally satisfying metaphor for the kid-crushing demands of "society." *The Hunger Games* was actually assigned in some American schools, but when I asked Mr. Leon about it, he said, "What is there to teach?" Clearly, there was something in Huxley's eighty-year-old book, or something provoked by it, that mattered more to him.

Reading *Brave New World* again, I was amused by how much Huxley relished his own naughtiness as he laid out the repulsive social structure of a future civilization. In the World State, as he calls it, babies are created in hatcheries, and enclosed in a caste system, ranging from Alpha Plus overlords at the top, down through Betas to Deltas, Epsilons, and Gammas. The masters look after administration and ideology; the lower orders do menial, agricultural, and industrial work. Art and religion have been banned; instead, people go to the "feelies"—pornographic movies whose tingling joys pass through the chair armrests into the audience's flesh. Heroism and nobility have been rendered irrelevant; strong loyalties and love do not exist. Suffering doesn't exist, either, and no enemy looms on the horizon. It is a *world* society, always at peace, tranquilized by sex, which you enjoy as often as you want and with whomever you want, for everyone belongs to everyone else. Anger and discontent, insofar as they exist at all, get washed away with a feel-good drug called Soma and with ritual gatherings that begin with incantation and end in orgy. Those few Alpha dissidents who find the lack of freedom intolerable are sent off to remote islands. For most people, life is very pleasant.

Mustapha Mond, the Resident Controller for Western Europe (the local overlord), holds forth on the subject of past civilizations for ardent students in the London hatchery:

> He waved his hand, and it was as though, with an invisible feather whisk, he had brushed away a little dusk. . . . Whisk. Whisk—and where was Odysseus, where was Job, where were Jupiter and Gotama and Jesus? . . . Whisk, the cathedrals; whisk, whisk, King Lear and the Thoughts of Pascal . . .

And so on. It had all vanished, and no one cared. Only a few people, like Mustapha Mond, hoarding a library of vanished books, knew about such things—the old religious and artistic glories, the product of suffering and hope, two states that were now impossible to imagine.

As Mr. Leon was introducing his students to *Brave New World*, he suddenly said, "I want to ask you a question. In what ways have advances in science negatively affected the individual?" That was a mouthful, and not easy to answer. No immediate response. And then he asked, "How many of you sit down for a family dinner every night?" The students looked a little puzzled, and about half of them slowly raised their hands.

"There was a time," he said grimly, "when most families did that." He left the question hanging as the class ended. The two questions made an odd pair. I wondered where he was going.

When we returned, the questions were still hanging. He began by asking the students about certain characters in *Brave New World,* especially Bernard Marx, a diminutive and cranky Alpha Plus who initially seems to be the book's dissident hero. Bernard finds much of life in the World State inane. In search of variety, he goes off with Lenina, a conventional but beautiful and shapely woman—"highly pneumatic," as all the men say, which is one of Huxley's least amusing naughty jokes. Together they cross the Atlantic and visit the Savage Reservation in New Mexico, an area that has been left "uncivilized." They are shocked by a part of the world in which parents conceive and raise children, and sexual desire leads to possession, jealousy, competition. But Bernard sees an opening to make himself more important. He will bring back a savage with him—John, who grew up in a hut but has read, again and again, the only book available to him, a filthy one-volume edition of Shakespeare's complete works left behind by an earlier visitor from the World State. John's head is full of passionate nobility expressed in extraordinary language. Literature, and nothing else, creates the novel's single fully alert human being, alive to pleasure and pain; literature provides the only resistance to technological utopia. A naïve idea? Extreme? False? I was still stirred by it.

Mr. Leon asked them to break into groups and talk over Bernard, and, as always, he patrolled, the room crouching next to one table or another, asking questions, urging them on, pulling silent students into the conversation. Almost every class had some small-group discussion. The groups allowed some students to loosen up and talk openly, take some risks, without the pressure of an audience of thirty-two. For instance, Tina Hsu, who was mostly silent in class, and covered her face with her hands when she did have to speak, talked aggressively in groups. She wasn't timid, but a public performance was not her style.

When the group sessions were over, Nino led off by observing that

"Huxley makes Bernard out of his image of how he himself would fit into the Brave New World," which was probably true. Latisha said, "If he had a mother, he would feel secure," which may also have been true, but no one in the World State has a mother. At one point, Bernard, who is infuriated by Lenina's vapid ways, suggests that she have a child— something forbidden in the World State, where women wear Malthusian Belts, which prevent conception. In Mr. Leon's class, the girls seized on Bernard's overbearing remark. The plangent Vanessa said indignantly, "It's not his business to tell her she should be a mother," and Maud joined her, saying, "He talks as if he were above her," which, as it happens, is literally true—Lenina is a Beta Plus, Bernard an Alpha Plus.

Would the students get *Brave New World*? Did they understand that the World State was a tyranny ruled by biological caste and by pleasure? They weren't reading the book; they were reading themselves in the twenty-first century—Bernard was a *sexist*. Marina, who had been so impressive in the past, said, "I find him unpleasant, and if I were living there I would slap him. He constantly makes fun of the teaching. He's trying to be unorthodox, to rebel against what others say." The trouble, alas, is that the highly conscious and critical Bernard lacks the courage to rebel against "the teaching," an ideology that controls virtually everyone so thoroughly that almost no one can imagine any alternatives to it. The students were right about Bernard, who was a worm, but no, they weren't getting the book, and it occurred to me that Mr. Leon's fifteen-year-olds, born after the totalitarian era in Germany and the Soviet Union, might not know that such a thing as complete control had ever existed. In Huxley's itchy dystopia the atmosphere is openly erotic, happiness is mandatory, suffering forbidden, but even in satiric form, his tyranny is just as powerfully coercive as that of Nazi Germany and the Soviet Union.

I thought Mr. Leon was going to straighten them out about history, but that wasn't his way. He asked the students to read up on totalitarianism on the Web, just as he had asked them to read up on puritanism earlier, but he had something more pressing on his mind than history. *Brave New World* was a book for now.

"How many hours a week do you spend using electronic media?" he demanded in class. He turned and made a list on the board: television, computer, cell phone, radio, iPod or iPod equivalent, video games. Then he totaled up his own consumption. Television: one to four hours. Computer: fifteen to eighteen hours. Cell phone: three hours. Radio: zero. iPod: seven hours. Video games: zero. The total: twenty-six to thirty-three hours a week.

"Huxley's primary fear," he said, "was that technological advancement endangered the individual. Okay, if you go down this list, how much time on average per week do you spend doing each of these things?" At last, his odd question about the students having dinner with their parents made sense. Nods, smiles: they understood the implicit charge. They were addicted to electronic media; they didn't sit down to family dinners because games mattered more than chicken, texting more than family conversation. They were amused, but they didn't think the charge was important. Their time spent texting and the rest was central to their lives.

At Mr. Leon's request, they wrote down their own totals. Some watched TV three hours, some twenty-one. Justin haughtily said that he didn't watch at all. An angry kid, Justin, less accommodated to his life than the others, and someone to watch—everything he said was interesting or strange ("My grandmother has ten dogs. Two of them bit me," he noted one day). In the entire class, the highest total was forty-two hours a week, which produced a derisive round of applause. The boy who watched that much TV was Hasan Azim, a heavyset, extremely amiable fellow who was born in Bangladesh but raised here. His father, a chef, had died in 2001, his mother had never remarried, and he took his responsibilities as the male in the household seriously. The family, including Hasan's two sisters, was Muslim, and Hasan practiced his religion faithfully, praying every day; he intended to make a pilgrimage to Mecca. Yet he was an Americanized Muslim, a New Yorker, and a ravenous media consumer.

Mr. Leon turned next to social media—to Facebook, the self-publicizing diary of the age. Four of five said they weren't members, but then Mr. Leon began asking them to state both their Facebook time and their total media time. Nino said zero for Facebook, but his total media time was a staggering 174 hours a week—he listened to music constantly. John Gruen's total was forty-two hours on Facebook, his total media time 135 hours a week; Latisha's grand total was ninety-seven, Vanessa's fifty-four, Hasan's an unimaginable 238 hours a week, Marco's two hundred. He said it with a grin.

How was this possible? Two hundred hours? Two hundred *thirty-eight* hours? Hasan was a busy guy, looking after his family, but he somehow had time to experience over two hundred hours of media a week. I stared at them all in disbelief. The entire week was only 168 hours long. Mr. Leon was baffled, too, but they laughed. "Overlapping! Multitasking!" they shouted. They were merry. Didn't he get it? They did their homework with music or TV on, or with Facebook nestled on one side of the computer screen. Those who truly loved Facebook had it on from the time they got home in late afternoon until they went to bed hours later. Or they texted all day and into the evening. (This was just before Instagram became popular and well before Snapchat caught on.) For those who were hooked, social media coexisted with time itself: Facebook and texting were the mediums within which life took place. The students lived on Facebook and on smartphones as earlier kids lived with their friends in the streets, in backyards, in parks and playgrounds, in suburban game rooms. Some of them said they didn't love Facebook. It was mean, it was intrusive, kids acted out on it, someone was always making use of the information you put on it. Still, except for the few who scorned it altogether, they didn't turn away.

"If you're doing media one hundred hours a week, how do you have time to talk to your friends?" Mr. Leon asked. Well, they listened to music and watched television with friends. They were socializing as they watched. But as they said such things, they were on the defensive, and several bridled at Mr. Leon's aggressive questions. "We need it to live," said Susanna, a dancer with golden hair and a big smile. Jose, one of the quiet and somber Latino boys, said, "It's your own choice." They may have been rueful about the time spent, but they were not about to be shamed out of it. They *chose* it.

Mr. Leon persisted. "What if I say we're just wasting time? Our self-worth and self-esteem is connected to how many notifications on Facebook we have. If someone comments on your photo and says you look handsome, you feel good. When we're on the cell phone all the time, we no longer look at people the same way. We no longer have compassion for other people, we're spiritually adrift. We become concerned with *this*." He held up a phone. "My mom and her friends in Louisiana spend a lot of time with each other talking. They just *talk*. But texting gives us a lot of time to filter our thoughts."

He stood still—he was almost immobile. The thin beard and slightly pointed chin and receding hairline; the taut, precise, angled, and wired body; the eyes darting around the room; the penetrating voice that seemed to find students wherever they sat—he reminded me of someone physically, though I couldn't put my finger on it. At the moment, he was passionate—as angry as a biblical prophet in his scorn for straying tribes.

"I asked my seniors what their media totals were." He looked down at a sheet of paper in his hand. "The average is seventy hours a week. That's 3,640 hours a year. Over a period of seventy years, that's 254,800 hours or 10,616 days." More silence in the room. Was he serious? Yes, he was. He was assuming, I could see, that his seniors would live until they were eighty. Their media habits, in this calculation (and I checked his numbers later), took hold by the time they were ten. Then they would live with the same habits for the next seven decades. But could this be true? Lives vary, habits wear out, interests and needs shift. People become obsessed with new things, or withdraw into themselves. Still, Mr. Leon's numbers had their shock value. "We spend twenty years of that seventy years sleeping," he said, "and you're telling me you're going to spend another twenty years on this stuff. In the thirty years left over, will you ever wish you were somewhere else? How much time do you spend drunk or high? How much time do you spend *living*? It's a truism that it's not until we're near death that we begin wondering how we have spent our lives."

An *extremely* quiet room. I could hear my own breathing. He wanted to jolt the students out of easy acceptance of media habits that had become so much a part of life that most of them couldn't see they were *eating* life. Never mind the prophets. He was more severe than Hawthorne's veiled minister confronting his congregation. They had sinned against themselves. Facebook and texting were their way of wearing a veil. They substituted narcissism and a meaningless public persona for self-knowledge.

And now we heard it. "Starting at five today, I'm going to ask you to step away from all this for two days. No grades; we're going by the honor code. From five tonight until the end of school Thursday [this was said on Tuesday]. You really have to give it a shot. A digital fast—no cell phones, no TV, no iPod. If you need the computer for homework, okay, do homework but nothing else. Some students, when I've done this in the past, do nothing with the time. Try to do *something*."

They all went cold turkey. And the first day, a few did "something"— they sat down and did their homework right away. Then the troubles began.

Annabelle, talkative, with curly hair: "I had nothing to do, and I was really bored."

Jared Bennett, a darkly handsome boy who didn't speak much: "I was so restless I had to do push-ups and running in place."

"Good," said Mr. Leon. "You'll be in shape."

Maud: "I made my mother put on music. I couldn't do my homework without it."

Vanessa, who was often close to tears: "My TV is gone, so I had to read a book."

Jordan of the strong shoulders: "How can I make plans without cell phones?"

Fourteen students claimed that they had made it through the two days without giving in, fourteen out of thirty-two students, and Mr. Leon told me that two or three were probably fibbing. Only three of the holdouts—Vanessa, Jordan, and Hasan—filled the time by reading a book, and Vanessa sounded highly put upon when she said "I *had* to read a book." Later, a few of them wrote me letters about what happened to them.

John Gruen, the large blond kid, wrote, "I listen to music every morning and that is just something that can't be taken away from me. I gave up the digital fast in the morning because I need music during my travels or else it just won't be a good day."

And Latisha wrote, "I started off thinking that I could get through it. Since I don't do Facebook, I thought it would be easier for me than for other people. However, a few days in, maybe the second day, I started listening to music. I caught myself and stopped. But then I slowly started to text again. The fast didn't go very well for me."

And others wrote in the same way. Need overwhelmed the digital fast—need for texting their friends, need for music so they could work or get through the day. But, as Mr. Leon said, they might be using their chosen instrument to avoid direct contact. Marina, who could be sandpapery in class, wrote, "It was difficult to stay away from Facebook and I kept catching myself pulling my phone out in uncomfortable situations or while I was bored. After the fast, I definitely realized how I use my technology as a way to avoid uncomfortable situations, for example, sitting at the lunch table and feeling as though nobody wanted me there."

Even in her note to me, she had a wounded tone. She was very bright, a good, potentially great student, and she didn't have an easy life. I talked to her in the lunchroom. She lived with her father, who was Puerto Rican; he had a troubled past, and was now living in the back of a store that was rented out as a party space; he was a writer who had never been published. He was bitter, yet he was the one, she told me, who pushed her toward school achievement. Her mother was Dutch, a painter, a free spirit who didn't believe in education—"She thinks it indoctrinates us into a system that is bad." Marina had been shuttled back and forth between them, and had moved from one school to another. She had several brothers and sisters from her father's earlier relationships, and she had lost, she said, a half brother in a shootout and a sister who had been thrown down a stairway. She worked part-time at three jobs, at a hair salon, a grocery store, and a not-for-profit, and she managed to get through Beacon, but she didn't like the place, the first student I had heard say that. People made fun of her, she told me, because she was overweight, she was "different"; her direct, confrontational way was the opposite of cool. As we talked in the lunchroom, a few people sitting nearby smiled knowingly, but she plowed ahead, ignoring them, her words insistent, injured, but focused and brief.

Technology could provide a way of escaping depression, funk, a recourse against social rejection and failure, a way of coping. Jordan wrote, "It was hard for me because I have terrible insomnia. On most nights I will read for a while and then I will watch a movie, but during the digital fast I read more than usual and I did some drawing and painting. But I don't know if I could have done it for more than those two days, because drawing and reading are not as entertaining as watching TV and movies."

She was one of the three who filled up the electronic downtime by reading a book. She and her mom read every night. In the past, they had read Harry Potter books to each other, one chapter at a time, and on her own, she had read books from Mr. Leon's reading list— *Slaughterhouse-Five* was her favorite. Jordan was the student who had read Ian McEwan's *Atonement*. She was a genuine reader, one of the rare ones. And she also admitted that something outside electronic media exists. She rowed every day.

Nino also knew that life went on outside the digital circuits. In his letter, he told me he did not participate in social media (he was contemptuous of it), but after saying how much he needed the Internet for music and all sorts of information, he went on: "I felt desperate, as if I was deprived of valuable information, and that, if this continued for a long time, I might go crazy. But then it hit me that all the things I felt deprived from were all around me. I can make music on my own; I don't need iTunes to supply music to me. There are millions of books around me, and I can just go to the library, which is only a couple of blocks away, to find anything that seems of importance."

O marvelous boy! Perhaps he wrote what he imagined I wanted to hear. Still, I was impressed. The others, even Jordan and Latisha, sounded a little lost during the digital fast, decentered almost, grasping to find themselves—unstrung as well as unplugged. They didn't get along better without the Internet; some of them hardly got along at all. But Nino had an actual experience. He learned something about himself, and good luck to him. He's a little like John from the Savage Reservation, who arrives at civilization with his ideals of life acquired from *Romeo and Juliet* and *Hamlet* and hates the synthetic reality of the World State. In his own mild way, Nino was the individual fighting society.

They were stuffing their heads with images, sounds, texts; they were rarely alone when they were alone, rarely just thinking. Reading for them was associated with homework, not with enjoyment, and these were ambitious, college-bound kids, all of them blessed with at least one parent who, however unpleasantly, cared enough about their education to get them into a good school. Once there, they did a lot of work. They took history, science, math, maybe an elective in the arts. They joined clubs, some played sports, some had jobs. They did their written work on computers, and communicated with Mr. Leon through the school website. And they certainly read serious books for Mr. Leon's class. But even for these teenagers, with a few exceptions like Jordan, digits were a necessity and an obsession, and reading was a chore. *They didn't enjoy it.* Coming back to Mr. Leon's Huxley question—How had advances in technology affected the individual?—you might say, at least provisionally, that technology had killed teenagers' pleasure in reading books. I heard no expression of regret, saw no sign that they believed they were missing anything in particular. I left the digital fast in a sweat, depressed and worried, and I indulged the usual apocalyptic questions: Was advanced literacy coming to an end? What hope for a civilization that gave up on books?

Mr. Leon began the next class with some necessary straightening out: "The World State is actually the savage situation. The Soma group [the revival meeting that ends in orgy] is nothing more than a debauched party—getting high and having sex. Spiritually nil. In the Savage Reservation, the violence is at least human. The passion is organic, natural; the other passion is induced by a drug."

Cruelty, we agreed, was part of life in the Savage Reservation, but John Gruen responded to Mr. Leon's remark by saying, "The World State is also cruel, because it's depriving everyone of natural emotions." Marisa Lopez noted, "We see the destruction of the individual" in the World State. She had been mostly quiet up until now, and Mr. Leon congratulated her for "taking a risk." Suddenly, hands were raised, they were alive. Mr. Leon's bruising questions about how they spent their time may have awakened them. They seemed, at last, digging into what they had read. Mr. Leon wanted to give everyone a chance, and when a bunch of kids raised their hands at once, he wrote down the names on his palm with a ballpoint pen.

The discussion turned to happiness. The people in Huxley's new world are drugged and sated. But is it real? Can there be such a thing as *false* happiness? "Leonardo," Mr. Leon said, "would you rather be unhappy or falsely happy?"

Leonardo said, "I'd rather be happy. Do I get to live longer?"—which didn't quite answer the question. He was a boy who didn't laugh much, dark, very handsome, a Latino of Peruvian descent. Annabelle, who talked a mile a minute, and who did her homework early and was bored without media, followed up with, "I'd rather be falsely happy. It's just happiness." She smiled and shook her head, as if the rest of us were stiffs. How would you know you were *falsely* happy? Yet it was certainly Mr. Leon's belief that digital immersion, for one, was false happiness.

Digital happiness was narcissistic, feel-good happiness, as meaningless as the endless sex in the World State. What a comparison! Yet I thought he had something of a point about false happiness. I also acknowledged, with a pang of misery, that in some ways I was no different from the kids.

I was restless, hungry for information, and several times during the day I would rush from one site to another, from the *Times* website to the *Washington Post* website, from Talking Points Memo (liberal politics) to RealClearPolitics (conservative politics), from the *New Yorker* website to the online magazine *Slate*. I scanned Metsblog for news of my strong-armed, hitless team. I looked at pieces on music and movies; I constantly consulted Wikipedia and IMDb (Internet Movie Database) and sports sites. I read long articles on literature, politics, and economics, too, but if I really wanted to hold on to them, I would have to read them slowly, in hard copy. When I later thought back on what I had read online, the text was a sliding, unstable mass. I couldn't remember a lot of it. I read it too quickly and jumped ahead, and the experience, taking it as a whole, was a flirtation with everything and nothing at the same time. And yet, the activity satisfied in some way. My anxiety has been relieved. I had been *informed*.

The Internet informs, informs, informs; connects, connects, connects; but I could say from my own experience that it also dissolves deep concentration, maybe even dissolves the self, whereas reading something in depth patches it back together again. As you read in depth, you're in touch with the large movements of history, commerce, art. You listen to an artist who speaks to you intimately in her own voice and transfigures the street, the office, war, individual lives, common dreams, and outrageous fantasies, re-creating the language as she re-creates the world and mind. You move outward and inward at the same time, drilling into yourself, matching your own acts against those of men and women in fiction, in history, in sports, in science, anywhere. After that, the book settles into your unconscious; it affects you without your knowing exactly how.

Reading on the Internet—the new, jumpy, waterbug-on-the-pond style of reading—was beginning to interest neuroscientists. It was something we were doing to ourselves, a way of possibly messing with the neurons and synapses that made cognition work. Maryanne Wolf, professor of child development at Tufts University and author of *Proust and the Squid* (2007), a study of the evolution of "the reading brain," has done a lot of experimental work with children. In her book, Wolf has expressed her fears that "those children who have cut their teeth on relatively effortless Internet access may not yet know how to think for themselves. Their sights are narrowed to what they see and hear quickly and easily, and they have too little reason to think outside our newest, most sophisticated boxes." More recently, she speculated that small children who spend their time reading on screens may never be able to settle down into "deep reading"—the kind of sustained immersion in a text that yields the greatest pleasure and learning. "Reading is a bridge to thought," she told the *New Yorker* in 2014 (July 16). "And it's that process that I think is the real endangered aspect of reading. In the young, what happens to the formation of the complete reading circuitry? Will it be short-circuited and have less time to develop the deep-reading processes?" When they need to read seriously later, she fears, the circuits just won't be there. She needed, she admitted, to do "longitudinal" studies—to test children's reading over a long period of time. But her fear was alarming enough, since it raised the specter that incessant online reading in childhood could be a kind of lead-paint or asbestos poisoning.

Wolf was also troubled by the way adults were reading, and she gave her own experience as an example. After a day of scrolling through the Web and hundreds of emails, she told the *Washington Post* (April 6, 2014), she sat down one evening to read Herman Hesse's late novel *The Glass Bead Game.* "I'm not kidding: I couldn't do it," she said. "It was torture getting through the first page. I couldn't force myself to slow down so that I wasn't skimming, picking out key words, organizing my eye movement to generate the most movement at high speed. I was so disgusted with myself." She didn't give up, though. "I put everything aside. I said to myself, 'I have to do this.' It was really hard the second night. It was really hard the third night. It took me two weeks, but by the end of the second week I had pretty much recovered myself so I could enjoy and finish the book. I wanted to enjoy this form of reading again. . . . I found my ability to slow down, savor, and think."

Wolf sounds like someone recovering from illness or alcoholism. One wants to cheer her on as she retrains herself to read. But what about kids? "We can't turn back," she concluded. "We should be simultaneously reading to children from books, give them books, help them learn the slower mode, and at the same time increasing their immersion into the technological, digital age." In other words, we have to teach children to read books, but also teach them to read *on the screen*. We have to teach them how to monitor themselves and control their wandering impulses.

Well, good luck with that. My own experience is clear enough: In a chair, on an airplane, in bed late at night, I am alone with a book; I can read it, close it, think about it, toss it. When reading online, I'm constantly tempted to read email, check the stock market; I'm tempted to find out how much a used 2009 Accura or a new sponge-mop costs. An Italian red, a Barolo called Palás, which I drank once and loved, costs eighty dollars a bottle. Really, is it that much? Habitually, I jump. And kids are less patient than grown-ups. To get them to stop hurtling away as they read, you would have to confine them to computers without Internet access; or, more severely, mesmerize their attention, perhaps pin open their eyes and manacle their hands, doing to them what was done to Malcolm McDowell in *A Clockwork Orange*. Short of doing that, they will jump away and possibly, as the research suggests, retain little of what they consume. What they read online doesn't *imprint*.

Mr. Leon, I realized, was trying to plant new circuitry, though he certainly didn't put it that way. After the digital fast, and the question of false happiness, he made the students read a speech from Mustapha Mond, chief ideological spokesman for Huxley's World State. Mond forbids the publication of a brilliant scientific paper on the ground that it might lead people to think that "the purpose of life was not the maintenance of well-being but some intensification and refining of consciousness, some enlargement of knowledge." Well, here were the words of the Devil, absolute evil for Sean Leon. He was definitely in favor of "intensification and refining of consciousness." For the students, he was in effect posing the old question: Was it better to eat the apple or not? Even if knowledge makes us miserable, wasn't it better than blissful stupidity? After all, why would anyone want to live in any place as boring as Eden? Or in Huxley's mock Eden? Consciousness, something ruled out of the question by the controllers of the World State, was exactly what Sean Leon was trying to liberate in his students.

"Why does Huxley write this way?" Mr. Leon asked, referring to Mustapha Mond's prohibition of consciousness. "Identify four more passages that connect to this one."

They flipped open their copies of the novel, which by now were festooned, as Mr. Leon required, with yellow, purple, and aqua Post-its marking key pages. Again I thought that the books looked like some rare species of bird with too many feathers to get off the ground. But if the books remained stationary, the class took off. If they hadn't really gotten Huxley's novel at first, they had it now. One by one, they found passages in which the World State ideologues insist that every form of consciousness and knowledge threatens happiness, and they found scenes in which John, the *Othello*-quoting man from the Savage Reservation, speaks up for emotion, sensibility, intellect, even pain, and at a certain point Mr. Leon withdrew, sitting quietly in the back of the room as the conversation raged on.

At the end of class, everyone left, including Sean Leon, and I was alone in the sanctum, now quiet except for the half-muffled sound of shouts and greetings and the occasional squeal of rubber on linoleum as someone raced down the corridor. School music. What had Mr. Leon's digital fast established? I had given up my apocalyptic tremors. Still, many of the students, with their digital needs and satisfactions, were as much enfolded in pleasures as Huxley's sated citizens of the World State. Was that *bad*? Only a prig would deny students enjoyment, and Mr. Leon, however severe at times, was no prig. It was the amount of time they spent in social media and the rest that bothered him, and its mediocrity as an experience. As we saw in the poetry session, and as I was beginning to learn by talking to them, they had troubles, they could suffer, they had souls. Yet Mr. Leon implied that the students were in "chains," to use Rousseau's word that he placed on the board at the beginning of the year. He loved literature, he wanted students to love it, and he believed in the character-forming experience of reading difficult books. He wanted to strike the leg irons, open the links; he was out to make a new boy, a new girl. He wanted to get them to talk to one another, not to text one another. He demanded conversation rather than networking.

I roamed around the empty room and stood for a while at the front at Mr. Leon's place—where he stood before he began moving around. What was the soul, anyway? The question was an embarrassment for anyone but musicians, clergymen, and newspaper columnists. On social media, kids could develop a way of presenting themselves, even a way of branding themselves. They understood marketing, and they could become mini-celebrities in which every little thing that happened to them was of immense importance. But in this online world, the soul—dear God! The idea itself felt quaint, the term odd, outdated, vague. People now spoke of attentiveness, information, persona; they spoke of *skills*.

"Oh, but I have a strange and fugitive self shut out and howling like a wolf or a coyote under the ideal windows," D. H. Lawrence wrote. "Man has a soul, though you can't locate it either in his purse or his pocketbook or his heart or his stomach or in his head. The *wholeness* of man is his soul. . . . The soul of man is a dark vast forest, with wild life in it."

But no one talked that way anymore. No one talked like Lawrence. His insistence on the wholeness of experience was magnificent, but, worldly and practical as we are, we might put it this way: much of soulful life comes from parents, the culture and neighborhood in which you were raised, the friends and enemies you make, the work you care about, the God you worship; the soul emerges from the satisfactions you enjoy, the pains and losses you suffer, the hobbies you love, the music you listen to, the plays and movies and TV you watch, and—largely unknown to urban kids—the nature that makes you whole. You go through everything, match yourself against everything, and, after trying on many selves as a young person, something like an identity takes hold as a sum total of experience. The experienced self yields a soul. Education in the largest sense creates social beings, citizens, and also a soulful life, and reading has to be a big part of the slow-moving, slow-gathering process. At the end, reading something immersive and commanding, even losing yourself in it if you were lucky, falling into a book as if nothing else in life mattered, reading it at a lunch counter, in the subway, in bed, listening to it in the car—that was the time when you fell into happiness and reasserted your identity. If you don't read books, and if you don't get consumed by the physical and moral life of men and women in fiction and history, too many facets of yourself may never come into being.

Standing in the empty room, I knew that when the room was full, I wouldn't say any of this to the students. It wasn't my job. But it was Mr. Leon's job, and they were listening.

BEACON, DECEMBER
AND JANUARY: ORWELL

"This may be the most important essay you will ever read in school."

So Mr. Leon began. He had handed out to the class copies of "Politics and the English Language," the famous diatribe against vagueness, abstraction, and "humbug" that George Orwell published in 1946, just after the end of the greatest of all European wars. The piece was a response to a specific abuse of language—the clangorous propaganda that the adherents of fascism, communism, and democracy employed to marshal their fighting forces and citizenly morale. After the war, the piece survived its original impetus and was read as pungent general complaint against bad English prose. "Politics and the English Language" was familiar to thousands from freshman comp courses in college. But did it still make sense to teach it, and to teach it to a tenth-grade English class?

Thinking of the many political hacks he had heard in the thirties and forties, Orwell recalls "the curious feeling that one is not watching a live human being but some kind of dummy: a feeling which suddenly becomes stronger at moments when the light catches the speaker's spectacles and turns them into blank discs which seem to have no eyes behind them." But not just political hacks were given to the zombie style. Educated people in general were addicted to pretentious and lazy diction ("it is a not unjustifiable assumption that . . .") that served as a retreat from the difficulty of saying what they meant. "Prose consists less and less of *words* chosen for the sake of their meaning, and more and more of *phrases* tacked together like the sections of a prefabricated henhouse." And Orwell made a simple translation of good into terrible prose, a translation that the late David Foster Wallace, in a 1999 essay, "Authority and American Usage," justly called "famous." I would actually call the translation immortal, the single most devastating criticism of style ever composed. Familiar as it may be, I have to quote it. First Orwell summoned a magnificent passage from Ecclesiastes (9:11, King James Version):

I returned, and saw under the sun, that the race is not to the swift, nor the battle to the strong, neither yet bread to the wise, nor yet riches to men of understanding, nor yet favour to men of skill; but time and chance happeneth to them all.

And then he translated it into standard educated English:

Objective consideration of contemporary phenomena compels the conclusion that success or failure in competitive activities exhibits no tendency to be commensurate with innate capacity, but that a considerable element of the unpredictable must invariably be taken into account.

If any of us could understand—really understand—what that translation meant, we would hear a command in our heads—*"Don't be a fool"*—that would make it impossible to write a certain kind of terrible sentence. Along with Strunk & White's slim volume *The Elements of Style* (1959), and William K. Zinsser's *On Writing Well* (1976), Orwell's coruscating article was probably the most widely known of the many doomed efforts to get English-speaking people to blow the sawdust and stuffing out of their prose.

In recent years "Politics and the English Language" has been criticized as naïve and misleading. Orwell believed that if people made themselves write simply and clearly, they would find it harder to lie. But we could all think of liars and political nihilists who wrote and spoke plainly. As Louis Menand put it in a *New Yorker* piece (January 27, 2003), "Short words with Anglo-Saxon roots have no relation to truth or goodness." And, in his usage piece, David Foster Wallace pointed out that the title "Politics and the English Language" was redundant, since issues of usage and grammar are always enmeshed in politics. The powerful impose their usage on the less powerful. In his own account, Wallace once ran into angry protests from African American college students when he told them that they had to write standard English, not Black English, if they wanted to succeed in the world of "power and prestige." Standard Written English was what Martin Luther King Jr. used, and what Barack Obama and Henry Louis Gates now use, and it's the "dialect" in which black "judges and politicians and journalists and doctors and teachers" communicate. Wallace's own needs were clear. Despite the circus-car exhilaration of his prose—clauses popping out of sentences, line after exfoliated line of hyper-adumbration, elaboration, qualification—the hipster David Foster Wallace was as devoted to standard syntax as a mandarin writer like Gore Vidal.

Orwell's essay might be vulnerable, but it's still blunt and funny, and for Mr. Leon it was gospel. "This is important, folks. Not just in 1946. For people in totalitarian and Third World countries, language is very powerful. It's relevant to our country, too, because many of us sitting in front of TV have been hoodwinked." He went after Barack Obama's campaign speeches in the 2008 election. "What do 'hope' and 'change' really mean? How do we hold Obama accountable for hope? Many people voted for him because he said 'Yes we can.' Why? He made them feel good about the possibilities of the future."

Mr. Leon then challenged the students to find a published example of the crimes against language that Orwell wrote about, and, a few days later, they came back with slogans from Occupy Wall Street, the noisy street protest that was then roiling Lower Manhattan—"People Not Profits" and "Billionaires Your Time Is Up!" and "Wall Street Is Our Street." Not as bad as Orwell's hack political phrases from the thirties and forties—"bestial atrocities" and "stand shoulder to shoulder"— but bad enough. Mr. Leon was forcing the students to go beyond instinctive sympathies. Most of them, I guessed, came from liberal families, and they may well have agreed with the emotions expressed by the Wall Street protest, but he was asking them to find the dross and cant in sentiments they approved of. "You can get people riled up about one thing and it can be used for another issue," he said. "Obama is perpetuating the same trick as Republicans are. We fall into orthodoxy so quickly. When the times are bad, language suffers." And, inevitably, he turned Orwell's analysis against their own media habits. "If thought corrupts language, language can also corrupt thought," Orwell had written, and now Sean Leon said, "The way your generation is texting and instant-messaging, you could say your thoughts become degraded and that, in turn, makes it easier to have degraded thoughts." He was after them again.

When he gave the students copies of Orwell's essay, he asked them to annotate it with their questions and comments. After they had read it and discussed it, he collected the marked-up copies and graded the annotations. There were no passive elements in his class—not the texts, which were constantly being worked over, nor the students, who conferred in groups and revved or critiqued one another. Mr. Leon read their journals on a regular basis. He told them again and again that they would not get good marks for participation just by raising their hand a lot. They had to keep their notebooks open, take down what was happening in class. They were *busy*. So was he, and my mind and body quailed at the amount of work he did for this class, which was only one of four (two tenth grade, two twelfth grade) that he taught four times a week. After class, he occasionally munched on a power bar. "I'm going on faux energy," he told me once. Maybe, but I couldn't tell the difference.

He was driving them out of laziness and routine the way a coach challenges and drills a football team. Hating loose conversation, he made the students bring one set of ideas to bear on another, one quotation to bear on another. He required them to ask questions of each other along a common theme. "I'm interested in the psychology of who calls on whom," he said to me, and in that way he thought of the class as an organic being, forever redefining itself. In general, their contributions had to be connected, nailed, referenced, specific. Education in the humanities was all about intellectual charting—fitting and joining, marking and connecting, and, of course, those ever-useful high school exercises, comparing and contrasting.

But how do you compare one thing with another? By describing object A completely and then object B? Or by going point by point, back and forth, between the two objects? Every newspaper columnist, fitting his titanic argument into eight hundred words, has faced this awful problem. The latter—going back and forth—was the prescribed high school way. All through the discussion of *1984*, Mr. Leon was setting up the kids for a compare-and-contrast essay with *Brave New World*. At one point, just to get the comparative juices flowing, he asked two students to volunteer as objects to be compared and contrasted. Marco and Lena, grinning wildly, stood in the center of the room. The other students ran through Marco and Lena's shapes, bodies, hair color, clothes, attitudes. Slender and slender; curly and brown, curly and *very* brown; black and white sneakers, *pink* and white sneakers. Compared and contrasted, the two of them glowed like actors on the red carpet.

Sean Leon combined basic intellectual instruction with short, vibrant talks on the ethics of being a student. There was, forever, the sore topic of SparkNotes, the online "study aid" which no doubt obsessed half the English teachers in America. SparkNotes was a thorough and competent guide to classic works, including *1984*, so competent that it removed the necessity of reading books for students all over the country. When Mr. Leon made these remarks, another online aid, Shmoop, was just getting going. Shmoop's online site boasted, in a chorus of little kids, "WE SPEAK STUDENT," and it offered guides to the classics in short animated videos with pop-up graphics and nauseating colloquial language. On *1984*, Shmoop held forth as follows: "In the future, life kinda sucks." Shmoop dissolved literature into popular culture altogether.

"Know this," Mr. Leon said. "If you are relying on SparkNotes— and I know some of you are—it jumps out of your journals and your comments. If you read it in lieu of the text or take an interpretation from it, know that I know. I will never call you out in class. I don't mind if you use it to help you understand the text, a difficult stretch, but reading SparkNotes in place of the book is problematic."

He led the students up the mountain at times, but he also kept the tent pegged to the ground.

Mr. Leon's students still had the freedom to create themselves as individuals, if they would seize it. *1984*, published in 1949, was the book most powerfully devoted to the opposite condition—an absence of freedom so complete that its existence was rapidly becoming impossible to conceive of. As two generations knew, Orwell's bitterly satirical dystopian novel, along with his earlier satire, *Animal Farm*, in which pigs make a revolution that slips into dictatorship—"All animals are equal, but some animals are more equal than others"—the two Orwell books had, along with Arthur Koestler's *Darkness at Noon* (1940), done more to discredit

Soviet communism in the West than any other texts. (Solzhenitsyn's *The Gulag Archipelago* wasn't published in the West until 1973.) Reading *1984* again, I was eager to see if it seemed dated and overwrought— or merely lurid and masochistic.

To my surprise, I was more moved by it than I had been in high school. The hero, Winston Smith, an Outer Party member living in drab, dreary, cold, smelly London, capital of "Airstrip One," as Orwell calls it, works at the Ministry of Truth, where his job is to keep the past in sync with an ever-changing present—he rewrites and then files old newspaper articles. At home, he's assaulted by the TV screen, which is able to observe him while blaring party propaganda and exhortations from Big Brother, the ageless and probably nonexistent leader whose face and commands are everywhere. Winston Smith! With his physical debility, his varicose veins, his forlorn happy memories of childhood, his belief in the proletariat, whom the party ignores; his disgust, his hopes, his doomed "rebellious" love affair with a fellow worker at the Ministry, dark-haired, avid Clare—Winston was the sad intelligent Everyman of totalitarian society, a sputtering flame who suspects that he's the last conscious man alive.

Orwell published *Animal Farm* at the end of the Second World War; the book caused a sensation, and in the next few years he wrote dozens of articles and essays as well as *1984*. Yet the late forties was not a happy time for him. One totalitarian power was still in place, and it was rapidly taking over Eastern Europe. Orwell himself was falling apart from tuberculosis and other ills, which he intentionally aggravated by living much of the time in the damp and cold climate of Jura, in the Hebrides Islands. He was consciously heading toward death, a man tied, emotionally, to shabbiness and decay, as if these things had some truth in themselves that he needed to visit over and over. Yet, if he was familiar—too familiar—with pain, he had not relinquished his indignation over it. As a novelist, Orwell doesn't compare to D. H. Lawrence, James Joyce, Virginia Woolf, E. M. Forster, or the Ian McEwan of *Atonement*, but his grindingly earnest and passionately angry book has endured. There were far worse fates for a novel than becoming an ideology-destroying text and a high school classic.

Many of Mr. Leon's students, as far as I could see, knew little twentieth-century history, though Mr. Leon assumed that they were familiar with Nazism and the destruction of the European Jews. He told them briefly about Soviet purges in which "millions were killed for shadowy reasons," and asked them, as before, to do basic research on the Internet. They needed to read up. The ideological struggles of the twentieth century were a long way from them, and the struggle against Islamic fundamentalism was still in its early stages—not an emotional fact in their lives, though they had strong sentiments against unwinnable American fights in Afghanistan and Iraq. They wanted to get a good job, lead a good life, maybe do something useful, but they were not politically motivated—or even, as far as I could see, much *interested*—as my friends and I were as teenagers.

Mr. Leon, however, asked them to study Orwell's densely written invention, "Goldstein's book," a gift to Winston from the treacherous party intellectual O'Brien, who wants to ensnare Winston into subversion. The book, created by the party, is both a history of twentieth-century authoritarianism and a detailed tract explaining the necessity of single-party rule, a state of permanent war, unending surveillance, reduced consciousness leading to the destruction of the self—the entire panoply of totalitarian measures ruling Orwell's dystopia. It's a dangerous, truth-telling text. This was the students' education in the totalitarian temptation. They broke into groups, discussing how Goldstein's book crashed into contemporary politics. Justin mentioned China's restriction of Internet traffic, Jared Bennett the easiness of killing people with drones halfway around the world.

Mr. Leon moved away from history and took up his usual crosshatching of questions and responses. Ike, the round-faced boy who spoke little, asked Susanna, "Who accuses Winston of thoughtcrime?" and Susanna then asked Vanessa, "What is Winston writing in his journal?" and so on. The conversation moved to Winston's character, and

several students cited Winston's incoherent despair, early in the novel, as he sits before his diary, knowing that whatever he writes, or doesn't write, it will have no effect at all—*"down with big brother they always shoot you in the back of the neck i don't care down with big brother."* They traced his passage from that nullity to something like contentment and a more settled political purpose after meeting Clare. "She still expected something from life," Winston says of her. "She would not accept it as a law of nature that the individual is always defeated." A debate broke out over Clare's role—whether she had made him more determined to rebel or merely happy, and a few of the girls found him "selfish," which surprised me. Justin disagreed. "Relationships like this are so few and far between," he said mournfully. Winston, after all, is grabbing at the only moments of happiness he will ever know.

I had heard similar complaints before. A number of the girls—Maud, Marina, in particular—seemed irritated with the male characters who dominated these fictions. Marina even accused Winston of wanting personal power, of wanting "to replace Big Brother," which seemed way off. It was obvious enough what was behind the exasperation. Minister Hooper, Bernard Marx, now Winston. Mr. Leon's books were neither written by women nor featured women (except for crazy Miss Emily in Faulkner's story). The girls in the class did not challenge the reading list, but some sort of displeasure came through.

Sean Leon was drawn to writing that defined life in existential terms—Who are you? How will you live?—and, apart from Sylvia Plath, the writers he favored were all men. Which raised an old, very sore issue. Until recently, women had been discouraged from heroic composition in the arts, and, often enough, the crises that women wrote about in fiction were grounded in the material circumstances of life. Yet millions of readers knew that the issues were just as momentous. Jane Austen's marital comedies, which are devoted, among other things, to perception, ethics, risk, and self-knowledge, as well as manners, class, property—the novels certainly ask, amid the many delights they offer, how one should live one's life. (The evolutionary biologist Richard Dawkins made

a fool of himself in a *New York Times* interview, of September 12, 2013, by dismissing *Pride and Prejudice* as unworthy of his time. "I can't get excited about who is going to marry whom, and how rich they are." Not all philistines are as advanced in evolutionary terms as Professor Dawkins.) Mr. Leon might have assigned *Pride and Prejudice*. He might also have assigned Charlotte Bronte's tumultuous *Jane Eyre*. But both novels were written in the nineteenth century, and he wanted to keep the list modern. He assigned Hawthorne, whose sense of universal guilt anticipated Kafka, and Dostoevsky, who might be said to anticipate the future, but everything else was from the twentieth century. He might have assigned Edith Wharton's *The House of Mirth*, but Wharton is perhaps too worldly for fifteen-year-olds. He might have assigned Willa Cather's *Song of a Lark* or her story "Paul's Case." The class might have read stories by Charlotte Perkins Gilman or Katherine Anne Porter or Flannery O'Connor or Alice Munro.

When I mentioned the issue to him, he admitted it was a problem that he had never been able to solve. He said he had thought at various times of assigning Kate Chopin's *The Awakening*, written in 1899 and set in his home state, Louisiana, and also Simone De Beauvoir's 1967 novella, "The Woman Destroyed." De Beauvoir's tale features a woman who is married to a cheater but can't leave him. Sean Leon had taught it in twelfth grade, but "the women students were angry at the wife, not at the straying husband." That was the end of that, and he wound up rejecting both books for tenth grade. *The Awakening*, the story of a married woman's sexual and emotional arousal, would be awkward—intrusive, almost—as a subject for teenagers. Moral issues, yes; spiritual and existential issues, yes. Sex, no.

He taught Faulkner and Hawthorne, Plath, Huxley, and Orwell. Later in the year, he would teach Paulo Coelho and Herman Hesse, Kurt Vonnegut, Viktor Frankl, Dostoevsky, Sartre, and Beckett, which, all in all, was a formidable list for tenth-graders. He was introducing them to modernism, both as a literary movement and as a mood. He was passionate about those books, and he tried to get the students excited about

them, which was what counted most. Tenth grade, *his* class, was the beginning of their serious reading lives, a time of planting circuits. Intensity mattered more than inclusiveness.

In his happiest moments, Winston speaks of the proletarians—or "proles," as Orwell called them—as the hope of the future. But it became clear the students didn't know what the word meant. The Marxist rhetoric Orwell used satirically was foreign to them. Its time had passed. So Mr. Leon turned to a passage—both sorrowful and sympathetic—that describes the proles from Winston's point of view.

> They were born, they grew up in the gutters, they went to work at twelve, they passed through a brief blossoming period of beauty and sexual desire, they married at twenty, they were middle-aged at thirty, they died, for the most part, at sixty. Heavy physical work, the care of home and children, petty quarrels with neighbors, films, football, beer, and above all, gambling filled up the horizon of their minds. To keep them in control was not difficult.

"How is it possible," Mr. Leon said, "that a major part of the population would not take issue with Big Brother? Why are they not rising up?"

Unhappy Justin said, "They don't know any better," and Maud, whose remarks sometimes came off as haughty, said that "they are content." Outer Party members like Winston were monitored every second, but the proles were able to enjoy sex, have kids, lead a normal life. They had the elements of a working-class culture—newspapers, movies, old songs. In some ways, Maud was right.

"Think of the parallels with our world," Mr. Leon said. He mentioned a Hispanic student from two years earlier who brought up the situation of poor Latinos in the United States. "He railed against the bad publications on the newsstands, the lottery in the bodegas. He was very provocative," and suddenly Marco, as if picking up the torch from the earlier student, said, "They don't put anything in the newspapers, so they don't hear about anything real. They give them the sport, the crime." By "they," he meant the publishers of *El Diario la Prensa*, the big Spanish-language paper in New York. Marco had jumped in with such remarks before. His horsing around in class was a defense, I thought, against the earnest guy underneath.

The students latched onto a moving passage late in the book—Winston's admiration for a large, red-faced, working-class woman busy in the yard below the small room in which he and Clare meet. The woman has had many children, many sorrows, and never stops working. When Winston and Clare look at her, she is singing—the only active unpoliced culture in the book. "Her appearance shows how much experience of life she had," said plaintive Vanessa, who had a good bit of experience of life herself. Her mother was Chinese (born here), her father was Puerto Rican; they had split up recently, and she lived with her dad on Delancey Street, in a bad neighborhood. "My mom would scream a lot," she told me when I spoke to her. "I know she loved me, but I wanted to break free from her. I left my little sister behind, and I feel guilty about that. But when I'm with her, it's chaos. It's going sky-diving in my own head." She appreciated the hardihood of the woman in the yard; her own mother was failing her, refusing to support her plans to go to college, and it was tearing at her. Vanessa's life was almost unbearably freighted. Her tearful state, her sense of being oppressed in some way, grated on me at the beginning of the year, but she had more than earned her sadness. After I understood this, I rooted for her to triumph over it.

Jordan, also in appreciation of the woman in the yard, added, "She shows what is necessary to keep love alive," which was a key point in *1984*, in which the party does its best to destroy family love, sexual love—anything not directed at the party and Big Brother.

"Out of those mighty loins," Winston thinks, "a race of conscious beings must one day come. You were the dead; theirs was the future." And Orwell goes on as follows:

"We are the dead," [Winston] said.

"We are the dead," echoed Clare dutifully.

"You are the dead," said an iron voice behind them.

"What happens to Winston Smith at the end of the novel?" Mr. Leon asked, and together they went through the frightening scenes in which the sadistic O'Brien torments Winston, breaking down his resolve with electric current and brutal logic. Several of them returned to Goldstein's book: O'Brien had given it to Winston in order to fully enlighten him, and then to destroy him that much more thoroughly. Marina, coming around on Winston, said that Goldstein's book, which lays out the forms of totalitarianism, "shows that Winston isn't psychotic."

At the end, Winston, annihilated by pain and fear, betrays Clare. "Why does it matter that he loved—or didn't love Clare?" Mr. Leon asked. Marisa, who had seen, in *Brave New World*, the destruction of the individual, said, "If you love, you become a person," which was exactly the point. The person—the self—is what O'Brien destroys. Earlier, Winston had hoped to die loathing Big Brother and the party. But the last sentence of the book—"He loved Big Brother"—tells us his spiritual annihilation has been completed. In the end, they understood what had happened to Winston.

After reading the two books again with the class, I thought I was probably right decades earlier in my argument with my English teacher. As Nino put it, "In *1984*, it's the government power controlling you. In *Brave New World*, it's our fault, it's our nature." Huxley's predictions, based on the human desire for comfort and pleasure, were closer to our reality back then, and even more so now. By 2012, biologists had discovered methods of "editing" the genome of mice, rats, and monkeys, a technique that could be used on the human genome, to eliminate debilitating diseases—but also, just possibly, to enhance intelligence and beauty, the kind of engineering that Huxley was talking about. And

didn't we already have a society divided into castes? The castes were created by self-reinforcing patterns of wealth and poverty. And didn't we
have mood-altering drugs of every variety? A culture of spectacle and
sensation? Pornography universally available on the Internet? Some high
art (in museums) more loved than ever; other high arts (opera, symphonic
concerts) struggling to hold on to their audience? In 1932, Huxley had
anticipated quite a lot about postindustrial civilization eighty years later.

Yet Orwell's dystopian novel was a much more powerful reading experience, and it had its obvious sinister meaning for our time. In America
and Britain, we are constantly under surveillance, guarded for our own
good against terror. Our TVs don't watch us, as the screens do in *1984*,
although they may, sooner or later; meanwhile our telephones have turned
into involuntary tracking devices. As citizens of a hyper-wary state, we
were afraid of yielding to Big Brother, afraid of giving up any part of
liberty. Orwell was a stage—a rite of passage in language and political
consciousness—that high school students still needed to go through.

It's an amazingly grim book.

Is it good for fifteen-year-olds to read grim books? A novel in which
there is no escape? What is the point for them? The boys wore sweatshirts with college names on them (Cornell, North Carolina State) and
Nike Air Max; they fidgeted and slumped. The girls, with glinting pieces
of inexpensive jewelry in their hair or at their wrists, were better dressed,
more pulled together, more attentive. They were all perched between
childhood and adulthood. They knew full well that society could be
oppressive—that was the assumption behind a lot of their remarks
earlier in the year. But at first they didn't "identify" with the desolation
Winston felt, the elimination of memory, desire, and self. Located on the
far side of the awful twentieth century, they had trouble, at first, imagin-
ing a situation of total domination. Among other deprivations, Winston's
writing was always monitored, and some of the students—stupidly, I
thought—were giving away their privacy on Facebook. They caught up
to Winston's fate only at the end of their classes on the book.

Mr. Leon, treating them as grown-ups in the making, asked them to read texts produced by the fears and disasters of the last century. Modernity, in his teaching, was part of their moral education. Such catastrophes as totalitarianism, their elders told themselves wearily, remained a possibility for all time. Nazism and communism were gone; religious purity and racist fantasy were the latest totalitarian modes. The students would understand these things by comparing them to the older models. In effect, Mr. Leon said, "If you're fascinated by dystopia, let's read about the worst tendencies of our own society enlarged into literature." So they read grim books with curiosity, without protest. They didn't always understand the books fully, yet intimations of harder truths than those faced by most adolescents would become, I believed, part of their intellectual and moral armor forever.

MAMARONECK, ALL YEAR:
PERSONAL CHOICE

The physical plant of Mamaroneck High School was as splendid as Beacon's was mingy. The place is big—a quarter of a mile from one end of the school buildings to the other. The old Palmer Wing, with its red brick, its white columns, its general aura of Roman authority, was completed in 1928. The new Post Wing, an acceptably handsome mock-up of the original, was added in pieces in recent years, and the two sections of the school are now connected by a long concourse outfitted with pillars, benches, and a high wood-slatted ceiling, all it of rather in the style of an upscale shopping mall—but a mall without sushi, Ferragamo, and noise. In the concourse, students sat on the benches or slipped to the floor, talking about themselves, about friends, sometimes talking about books or even about physics. Among its other amenities, the school had a gazebo, a Japanese garden, a broadcast studio, and a large, very busy library. There were two sets of playing fields and lessons in golf. Also a Guidance Office, a Financial Aid Office, a Special Education Office, and a Teacher Institute.

Mamaroneck was the sole public secondary school in a wealthy Westchester County suburb eighteen miles north of New York (the school also serviced the adjacent town of Larchmont). Long Island Sound was close by, also a park, a country club, and a yacht basin. On the concourse, and in class, the girls were mostly groomed and alert, as if ready to step into jobs in finance or law or corporate business. Many of the boys were casual, even slovenly. Eventually, I supposed, they would clean up and step into those jobs, too. In all, 93 percent of Mamaroneck's graduates go to college (including two-year colleges), a wide selection of schools, though 61 percent of the acceptances were for private colleges or universities. Mamaroneck was a flourishing school in a mostly wealthy town. Yet it was also troubled.

In the academic year 2013–14, the administration and a part of the English teaching staff were engaged in an experiment. Mamaroneck wasn't the only school in the country performing the experiment, but, for them, the project was new. The English Department was trying to create something that didn't exist in many students, and their methods lay somewhere between pedagogy and conjuring. The thing that didn't exist was enjoyment of reading. Yet it wasn't too late, which was the necessary assumption behind what Mamaroneck was doing. The habits of ninth- and tenth-graders could be changed. The nonreaders, or grudging readers, could be gently but firmly pushed into becoming readers—real readers, not just functional readers. They could be pushed into enjoying themselves, which may sound obtuse and contradictory, though it doesn't have to be. The practical question was this: How do you awaken hunger amid indifference or disgust? Answer: With persistence, pressure, and subtlety.

At Beacon, I sat in three other English sections besides Mr. Leon's, and I never heard anyone raise such questions. The teachers there may have assumed that quizzing the students, watching them closely in class, and reading their papers and journals—all the usual grading mechanisms—were enough to keep them honest. The competitive atmosphere among New York kids would have the same effect. Among the students at Beacon, faking it, punting, just getting by were all infra dig—the place had a strenuous spirit. But who knew if the Beacon teachers were right? At every school, there were clever kids who survived without ever opening a book; they even boasted about it. At Mamaroneck, however, the administration and the English Department were talking about more than honesty or performance. The people I spoke to were book lovers, and, for them, nonreading was an offense against spirit. Just as much as Mr. Leon, they were out to save lives.

In the ninth grade at Mamaroneck, the students read *The Odyssey*, *Antigone*, and *Romeo and Juliet*; they read novels, stories, poems, and essays—all assigned "core texts." And in tenth grade, the students read *Macbeth* and Elie Wiesel's *Night*, the inevitable *1984*, John Steinbeck's Salinas Valley epic, *East of Eden*, and, again, stories, poems, and essays. (See appendix 1 for the complete list.) Just as at Beacon, the students took quizzes and wrote papers and prepared projects devoted to the core texts. But they also read a lot else, and that's what was new. At Mamaroneck, the drill went like this: *Get them reading. Let them choose their own books. But also monitor them and try to pressure them into choosing something better.* That was the tricky part—the something better. The school wanted the kids to surge past the simplest pleasures in reading and engage with more demanding work. The concept was called "laddering." If it worked, reading might become a lifetime habit. The experiment was modest in some ways, but it aimed at transformation. Free of their teachers, the students might—just possibly—climb rung after rung, as greater difficulty turned into greater enjoyment. Eventually they would settle: they would read easy books and hard, whatever they desired, whatever gave pleasure. That was the hope. But they had to begin somewhere, and Mamaroneck was committed to the beginnings.

In her ninth-grade class, Margaret Groninger, the head of the English Department, a tall, willowy woman with a light and easy way about her, held up a book: *No Easy Day*, Matt Bissonnette and Kevin Mauer's 2012 account of the Navy Seals' mission to kill Osama Bin Laden. Miss Groninger was giving a "book talk," which was really a scholastic version of a Hollywood pitch. A bit later, she would get to the play they were all reading together—*Romeo and Juliet*, with its blood-raising poetry of teenage love. For now, holding up *No Easy Day*, she said that the book was exciting, and she read a few passages: "The roar of the engine filled the cabin, and it was now impossible to hear anything other than the Black Hawk's rotors beating the air. The wind buffeted me as I leaned out, scanning the ground below, hoping to steal a glance of the city of Abbottabad." She had read the book and was enthusiastic about it. On another occasion, she held up *The Girl You Left Behind*, an ambitious historical novel (First World War, modern London) by Jo Jo Moyes. She gave a little of the plot—or at least the complicated premise—and read the first page aloud. "I was dreaming of food. Crisp baguettes, the flesh of the bread a virginal white, still steaming from the oven, and ripe cheese, its borders creeping toward the edge of the plate. Grapes and plums, stacked high in bowls, dusky and fragrant. . . ."

All right, then. Two books, neither of them close to literature. The first was written in hard "masculine" prose. Call it washboard-abs prose. The second was succulent indeed—too succulent by half—but the rhythms were appealing. Miss Groninger no doubt expected that the first book would interest boys more than girls, and the second the reverse, though she didn't say that explicitly. There was no need, in advance, to limit interest by gender. Anybody could read anything—that was implicit in the experiment.

Every week, almost all year long, Miss Groninger gave a couple of

book talks, which meant, in practice, that she and the others in the
experiment had to do a lot more reading than most high school English
teachers. As well as prepping for *Romeo and Juliet* and *The Odyssey*, Margaret Groninger had to keep track of what was coming out, what the
recent good books for teenagers were. There was no way of way of looking at *everything*, so she read reviews and the flap copy of new books;
she took recommendations from other teachers, and sometimes invited
one of those teachers into the classroom to stand in her place and make
a presentation. In the end, she often chose books from the commercial
world of publishing, including some young adult novels. Miss Groninger
was forty-two, married, with three kids. She ran the English Department
and taught "only" (her word) sixteen hours a week; she also had to do an
hour of prep for every fifty-two-minute class. Again, I was astonished
by how hard a successful teacher had to work.

At first blush, the book talks might seem a capitulation to undevel-
oped tastes. A few of the traditionalist English teachers at Mamaroneck
felt that way, and they initially chose not to participate in the experiment.
They complained that the school was giving up the battle, abandoning
the canon. Their belief, roughly stated, was that they taught classic
books, and that, in any generation, only a minority of students was likely
to read them well. But Mamaroneck was not abandoning the canon.
The ninth- and tenth-grade core readings were solid. In eleventh grade,
for the record, the students were assigned *The Great Gatsby*, *Hamlet*, Fred-
erick Douglass's first autobiography, Jumpa Lahiri's *The Namesake*, and
either *Huckleberry Finn* or Twain's other masterpiece, *Pudd'nhead Wilson*.
Eleventh-grade honors students read *The Scarlet Letter*, Whitman, Emerson, Thoreau, Emily Dickinson, and Allen Ginsberg.

Mamaroneck's get-them-reading strategy was initially created by
necessity and a certain exasperation, even anger. The grudging readers
and the fakers were cheating themselves and in some way insulting their
parents and the school. And how were they going to do college work?
In freshman year, depending on the college, students might be asked to

read two or three hundred pages a week, or even more. They had to get over their resistance to reading. But remonstrating with teenagers in high school—threatening, warning, exhorting—was an obvious way to fail. Teen habits aren't changed by exhortation.

I met with administrators and teachers in a conference room attached to the office of the school's principal, Elizabeth Clain. "English teachers want to talk about Melville," Miss Clain said. "But we have to teach reading as well as literature." Annie Ward, the assistant superintendent for curriculum and instruction in Mamaroneck, building on Clain's remarks, said, "We were stuck." Ward, a woman about fifty with short blond hair, laid out the ground of the school's discontent. "We were constipated in these roles—the teacher as tour guide. 'Okay, now read chapter three by Monday.' But we knew a lot of the kids were not reading. They were getting the content of the book in class and through SparkNotes. So we sought to change an English teacher's role from that of book warden/tour guide to that of outfitter: 'We're going to equip you for a wide and wild reading adventure.' The *kid* was the journey. We were the outfitters."

Mamaroneck was not a charter or a magnet like Beacon. "We take every kid who walks in the door," Miss Clain said. Later, I accompanied her around the school. An elegant, driven woman, she rushed through the enormous spaces with her glasses perched high in her hair, nodding and waving to individual students. "Did you get your paper in?"—"Yes!"— "Good!" Clain was born in Zimbabwe, and came to the United States in 1976. She taught here for twenty-five years (mainly social studies), including sixteen years at Mamaroneck. She became principal in 2011. As kids went past us, she said to me, "I can never get enough names and faces. They drop out of my head."

There were 1,460 students in all. Seventy-six percent of the student body was white, many from prosperous families. Eighteen percent of the students were Hispanic, and many of them spoke English as a second language—their parents were often immigrants. Three percent were African American, 4 percent Asian. Even in this wealthy town, 14 percent of the students received free lunch, which means that their families lived below the poverty line. "I have kids with mansions along the shore," Miss Clain said, meaning the coast of Long Island Sound, "and kids whose parents work as servants in those mansions."

The low-income students were not scoring well on standardized tests. But it wasn't just those students that Mamaroneck was worried about. In 2010, in the name of "college and career readiness," New York State abruptly changed the scoring of its tests in math and English. They raised the passing marks in grades three through eight. Overnight, kids who would have been "proficient" in English by earlier measures (gaining a score of 3 or 4) suddenly were deemed "not proficient." In 2013, the Common Core standards went into effect, and actually raised the *difficulty* of the tests, rather than just the way they were scored. Compared to other schools in New York State, Mamaroneck was doing decently, but by its own standards that wasn't good enough. The school district, led by superintendent Robert Shaps, was determined both to close the gap between rich and poor students and to get more kids reading.

In the past, faced with a reading crisis, Mamaroneck and other schools like it would have invested a great deal of time and money in remedial work. Not this time. "Rather than layer on remedial intervention services," Shaps told me, "we decided to double down on the single most powerful thing known to develop students' reading: high volume of high success reading. We needed to get kids reading a LOT. We built classroom libraries at our middle school in 2010 and began to provide time during the school day for kids to read books of their choosing." In that summer (2010), the district created what Annie Ward called a "book flood" at Hommocks Middle School, which was a feeder for the high school. "We set an ambitious, public goal that each Hommocks student would read 25 or more books over the year," Ward told me. "We built time into the school day for all kids to read." They also set up little book clubs for groups of kids to talk to one another about what they were reading. By the time the Hommocks students came to Mamaroneck High they had developed new habits. "When they read more, their skills go up," Miss Clain said. "You have to find the passion, create a social culture of reading."

Miss Clain had an action plan, with money and support from the district supervisor. But a social culture of reading? At first, I wasn't sure what she meant. Wasn't reading one of the great solitary pleasures?

Everyone I spoke to at Mamaroneck was quick to disclaim originality for the experiment. They mentioned the research of Richard Allington, professor of education at the University of Tennessee, who insisted that if students read a lot at their own level, they built up fluency and capability, a happy experience that eventually leads them to take on more difficult texts. The pedagogic rubric for this, as Robert Shaps said, was "high volume, high success" reading. A student finished a book because she actually enjoyed it, and then went on and read another from beginning to end, in an endless chain. High volume, high success, an experience charged by pleasure. Allington had been publishing the results of his research for years. Mamaroneck was ready to act on it.

And then there was Penny Kittle's *Book Love* (2013), which, judging by the multicolored cover—happy teens with stacks of books—looked like a standard illustrated teaching manual. But the Mamaroneck teachers and administrators loved the book, and, after reading a few pages, I saw why. A teacher and reading specialist in Conway, New Hampshire, Penny Kittle was the real thing, a candid and funny writer—impassioned, penetrating, and affectionate in her description of students, and highly critical of teachers who failed to get their kids reading. In my experience, no American high school teacher ever wrote better prose. In her own high school English days, Kittle remembered, she had been bored and unresponsive. In college, she came alive as a reader—Jane Austen, the Brontës, Tolstoy, Henry James, one revelation after another. Eventually, she returned to high school as an English teacher. Then reality set in:

> Suddenly it was all too familiar: the slouching students, the yellowed pages of novels they weren't reading, the "doing time" feel to the curriculum assigned to me. Surely my ineptitude contributed to the lack of engagement I faced, but my classes were also filled with students I didn't recognize from high school: students who could barely read, who had no memories of book love to carry them through the dull parts in a play or a line that confused them in a poem. Students who had never been read to. Students who told me reading just wasn't for them. Nice students, not defiant, just not interested.

If they ran into trouble somewhere in a novel, they quit and never got back into gear. They listened in class, read SparkNotes, faked their way through the course, but essentially they were apathetic. The problem, according to Kittle, was widespread. "I've asked groups of teachers in nearly every state and almost all the Canadian provinces," she writes. "I get similar answers. Teachers tell me they think about twenty percent or fewer of their students read the literature assigned."

Twenty percent! It would be nice to think that the teachers were exaggerating. But even thirty or forty percent would be sad. In any case, Kittle had a solution: get them started as readers by giving them books they could easily enjoy, including young adult novels; get them caught up in narrative, stories, outcomes.

> We can't give up and accept so few readers. We also can't have every student start with Austen, no matter what the Common Core or your department chair says. A book isn't rigorous if students aren't reading it. Every student must become a reader who *can* read Jane Austen. How? We start where they are. We start with an entry to a reading life

and engagement with whole books, even if we feel they are less worthy than the classics. Yes, even *Twilight*, if that's the book that will get a student reading.

Kittle proposed that teachers set up a kind of parallel structure in which the teacher would work with the students on their personal reading and also on the book the class was reading together. The project was anathema, as she admitted, to some English teachers in her New Hampshire school. "They say teachers like me, who believe in young adult literature, just don't have the guts or the talent to make *The Great Gatsby* work for everyone. We can't let them bully us. They're wrong. Independent reading allows students to build stamina so they can read *Gatsby*. Pretending to read it is far more damaging." Kittle quoted the novelist Ann Patchett, who wrote in the *Wall Street Journal* (January 17, 2009): "I'm all for reading bad books because I consider them to be a gateway drug. People who read bad books now may or may not read better books in the future. People who read nothing now will read nothing in the future."

No one in Miss Groninger's ninth-grade class was required to read either of the books she pitched—not then, not on any day. The book talk was meant only as a prompt and a show of enthusiasm. But the students *did* have to have a book of their own going, and going at all times—an Independent Reading Book, in the school's language. They could choose a book from anywhere—from the teacher's recommendations, from home, from the town library, the school library. They could also take advantage of attending school in a wealthy suburb: each ninth-grade classroom and some tenth-grade classrooms had recently been outfitted with a small library of its own—maybe 300 books divided into such categories as history, romantic fiction, classics, dystopian, funny reads, graphic novels, sports, and adventure. A few classics, some current affairs, thrilling young adult titles, but no outright junk.

When I saw the library in Miss Groninger's classroom, modest as it was, I remembered the recurring fantasy of a twelve-year-old boy. A stairway led to a labyrinth at the top of the stairs, a labyrinth with row after row of books and shelves that turned into odd corners. The library at the top of the stairs was entirely his. It was a dream of endless happiness, but also a dream of power: proprietorship.

And what was it that this dreaming boy was reading? What created love? As a child, at the recommendation of a school librarian, he had read book after book in Walter R. Brooks's immortal series devoted to Freddy the Pig—Freddy, a poetry-writing porker, gentle, inquiring, bold (Freddy went into outer space among other places). Later—no surprise—there were the Hardy Boys, respectful teenagers with neatly parted hair who took on gangsters, swindlers, international villains, their adventures chronicled by a variety of newspaper hacks who were paid $75 or $85 a volume, all working under the formidable collective pseudonym Franklin W. Dixon. And still later, about the time the library fantasy floated into his mind, the boy read the wonderful Landmark books (Random House) devoted to adventurers and explorers. Lewis and Clark killing a buffalo and drinking the hot, filthy water from its stomach remained his favorite emblem of survival. Yes, there were also the magnificently illustrated classics, *The Adventures of Tom Sawyer* and *The Swiss Family Robinson*, and many others, in sturdy hardcover volumes, the reading centerpiece of many bourgeois American households—you can still find them somewhere on the Internet or at the library. Shy and often lonely, with loving, hardworking, newspaper-reading parents, he needed adventure, bravery, death defiance to nourish a faltering ego. In school, he was pronounced "jumpy," and at home, he read slowly, with many pauses—concentration was hard-won and blissful when it arrived. Later he discovered the all-encompassing art form of darkened theaters, the screen commanding, enfolding, even overwhelming.

As time went on, the boy's actual proprietorship of books—*my* proprietorship—became more complicated: the neatly ordered volumes in an Upper West Side apartment were both a flattering mirror—I *am* these books—and a constant reproof, since it was a good chance that many of them were unread, or half read, or merely consulted. Still, I appreciated their presence as I appreciated sunshine; they provided reassurance and also an opening to endless possibility. Mamaroneck's classroom libraries were hardly labyrinthine, but they would do well enough as a place in which a nonreader might emerge from reading poverty into wealth by owning something—a part of himself, perhaps.

Some chose "hard" books, some easy; some switched in midbook because they were bored. One girl, defeated by Elizabeth Gilbert's *Eat, Pray, Love*, said, "Can I give this back?" and Miss Groninger turned her toward *Wild*, Cheryl Strayed's memoir of trekking up the Pacific Coast Trail. Their reading skills and curiosity and endurance varied a great deal. In Miss Groninger's ninth-grade class, the students chose such books as *Orr: My Story*, an autobiography by the great hockey player Bobby Orr; Tolkien's *The Hobbit*; Veronica Roth's *Divergent* ("one choice can transform you") and its sequel, *Insurgent* ("one choice can destroy you"); Eric Schlosser's *Fast Food Nation*, a dissection of the commercial food industry and what it is doing to us; *Perfect Storm*, Sebastian Junger's sea story; and Audrey Niffenegger's *The Time Traveler's Wife* (he travels, she doesn't; they mate when they can). The choices were all over the place, which was exactly the point. Many of the titles may have been familiar as movie titles, but they were good books, better than the movies made from them. Except for Eric Schlosser's *Fast Food Nation*, they were all books with a strong narrative drive.

After Miss Groninger's pitch for *No Easy Day*, the class, with only a quick word from her, pulled their personal choices out of backpacks and fell silent. Discussion of *Romeo and Juliet* would have to wait. Virtually every day, usually at the beginning of the class, ninth- and tenth-grade students had a ten-minute reading period. In Miss Groninger's class, the girls laid the books out flat on their desks; they were as still as monks in a thirteenth-century monastery examining old manuscripts. The boys scratched and shifted and tucked one leg under their butts or knocked their knees together rhythmically, but they hung in there and kept read-

ing. Meanwhile Miss Groninger walked around with an iPad. She had
everyone's books listed on it, and she quietly intervened with kids who
appeared to be idle, or who needed a difficult passage explained. She
talked to two students about their books in some depth during the period;
eventually, she got around to everyone. One side effect of the independent-
choice strategy, as Miss Groninger told me, was that teachers got to know
their students better. A few of the students read on an iPad themselves.
Another privilege of going to a wealthy school: In 2013–14, every ninth-
grader at Mamaroneck was given an iPad as a loaner for the year. In the
next year, tenth as well as ninth-graders would have iPads, and eventually
the entire student body would have them.

In Miss Groninger's class, the students entered the title of the book
they had chosen in a classroom log—"the clipboard," literally a clipboard,
now unseen outside of doctor's offices. They signed in every week, noting what page they were on. When they finished, they had to choose
another book, and then another, all through the year. They also had to
keep a journal about their reading, and they held forth about their chosen books on Goodreads, the website on which millions of users become
critics. Sometimes students talked to each other before or after class,
exchanging opinions, hectoring each other about a book—or warning
off their friends. One girl fell in love with Margaret Atwood's *The Handmaid's Tale*, from 1985, a literary dystopian fiction about a theocratic
revolution in the United States that leaves women completely subservi-
ent and ignorant, valuable only as concubines and breeders. She came
to class one day saying "If you guys think *The Hunger Games* was good,
wait until you read this book," and eventually, even though she hadn't
finished the novel, Miss Groninger persuaded her to give a book talk to
the class. When she finished reading *The Handmaid's Tale*, however, she
flew into a rage and threw it across the room. She was disappointed in
the ending. Which meant she was definitely a reader. People who don't
give a damn drop books on a table. People who are excited and then disappointed throw them across the room.

Restlessly innovative, Margaret Groninger would sit the students down, once or twice a year, for what was known as a speed-dating event. The idea was stolen from the New York and Los Angeles hook-up scene. Each student would have two minutes to talk over what he or she was reading and would then move on to the next student. The person who received the pitch would write down the title of the book she had just heard about and mark the title with a heart, which meant "I think I'm in love and want to read the book sometime soon!" Or perhaps, she would mark it with an open book, which signified "I'm intrigued, but need a second date to make up my mind." And so on, down to the cold-shoulder "Not my type." In two minutes, the students had to work hard to close the sale.

After a while, I saw what Elizabeth Clain meant by a "culture of reading" at the school. The changed culture included teachers as well as kids. The teachers—all the school's teachers—had to put up a little laminated poster in the hall just outside their classroom. With dry-erase markers they wrote down what they were reading at that moment. Mary Beth Jordan, an English teacher, was reading *Suspended Sentences* by Patrick Modiano. A social studies teacher opposite Mary Beth Jordan's classroom was reading *The New Jim Crow* by Michelle Alexander. This public display of honor was part of Elizabeth Clain's attempt to shake the place up. No shirkers or hypocrites. Miss Clain told me she planned to send a memo to social studies and science teachers asking them to request books for new libraries in *their* classroom. A "book flood" was the term of art at Mamaroneck. Surround them with books. Connect teachers and students to books and to one another.

Independent reading programs were notoriously risky. In other schools, students, when they weren't monitored, might read less and less, sometimes stopping altogether. But Mamaroneck's ninth- and tenth-graders weren't allowed to stop or even pause, and a few of the students got excited; their competitive instincts kicked in, and they became heroes of reading, including one girl I heard about who consumed twenty-four books on her own (mostly romance and fantasy fiction, but some historical fiction, too) by May of the school year. She was a special case. What about everyone else? According to Mary Beth Jordan's calculation, a tenth-grader who did all the assigned texts for English at Mamaroneck read about 1,500 pages. A student who read a full load of independently chosen books read perhaps another 1,500 pages. So the amount of pages doubled.

In all, Mamaroneck's approach in its independent reading project couldn't have been further from Sean Leon's stern syllabus at Beacon. His students were given no choices, and they were pressed, challenged, even overwhelmed, at least at first. Leaving aside the core readings, which remained mostly intact, Mamaroneck gave in, initially, to the students' desire for ease and companionability. But then the pressures began. High volume, high success was just the beginning.

Annie Ward, the assistant superintendent for curriculum and instruction, told me a few happy stories. There was the student who went from reading nothing at all to reading four "independent" books a semester. And there was the tale of another nonreader, a boy named Jack—"I don't read. I just don't." So Ward suggested that he read Tucker Max's jocular and boastful *I Hope They Serve Beer in Hell* ("My name is Tucker Max, and I am an asshole"). His mother bought the book for him, so the school didn't anticipate a parental complaint. But Jack, it turned out, didn't much care for *Beer in Hell.* "Every chapter was pretty much the same," he told Ward. "He gets drunk and hooks up with different girls, but it's pretty much the same." Well, Jack was right about that; he was not a reader but somehow he was a critic. Annie Ward then tried something else. "Staying in the profanity-in-the-title genre," she told me, "I gave him my copy of Justin Halpern's *Sh*t My Dad Says*, which I'll admit I'd read and thought was funny, and he read it. It was definitely a notch above *Beer in Hell* in that it is a memoir with a narrative arc. After that, I moved him to David Sedaris, beginning with 'Turbulence' [funny *New Yorker* story about a socially disastrous plane ride]. I thought the shortness of a single story would be palatable to offset the increase in literary quality. The last time I conferred with Jack, I left him with Sedaris's collection, *Holidays on Ice.*"

Well, that's a pretty good reading ladder; in fact, it's a terrific ladder. From "I just don't read" to David Sedaris. If this kid was ambitious and lucky, he might get to read funny essayists Nora Ephron, Paul Rudnick, or Andy Borowitz. Or even funny critics Clive James, Anthony Lane, and James Wolcott. Why not? Jack obviously had a taste for outrageous wit and satire. All right, I'm running wild—the kid did nothing more than read a few stories by David Sedaris. But the possibilities were exciting. Everything was open to the newborn reader, not just my own choices; he would be free. But even if none of this happens, and he remains a lifelong fan of David Sedaris, he has already jumped from the Dark Ages to the Renaissance.

I heard stories from other English teachers at school. Mary Beth Jordan, whose tenth-grade class I was visiting, had a few good ones. Miss Jordan was fifty-two and, like Miss Groninger, a mother of three. She had worked in magazine journalism most of her life; this was only her second year of teaching, her first at Mamaroneck, and she was gung ho for the independent reading experiment. She had large blue eyes that widened as she told me about pushing kids up a ladder.

There were three working-class Hispanic friends in her tenth-grade class. They were generally not good students, absent a lot, their lives in turmoil. She interested them in Coe Booth's 2007 young adult novel *Tyrell*, which was about a fifteen-year-old African American boy up to his ears in trouble, sex, and drugs, but a good guy in many ways who tries to take care of his mother and little brother. The book was written in a literary version of street talk: "When I pick Novisha up from school, she actin' all weird and shit," it begins. The three students were astonished by the details of the book; they were "amazingly articulate," said Miss Jordan, "about what they liked and didn't like." Some of it was very close to their own lives. "I ghetto when I read that book," said one girl, whispering the voices to herself as she read. The three girls, Camila, Valentina, Valeria, called themselves "the Gangstas," and they kept on reading. Next the Gangstas read Cupcake Brown's *A Piece of Cake*, from 2006, a memoir of Brown's teen life as a foster child and then as a high-living and quickly low-living teen prostitute (Brown eventually became a lawyer). They had become an on-the-fly reading group: they met outside of class with a campus supervisor, a kind of mentor and guard at the school—"She runs the school," Elizabeth Clain told me— who kept them going as much as she could. They had plenty of troubles of their own, they cut school often, but, meeting with the supervisor, they continued to read, moving on to Adrian Nicole LeBlanc's brilliant nonfiction work, *Random Family* (the subtitle was: *Love, Drugs, Trouble, and Coming of Age in the Bronx*).

Miss Jordan had a student, a boy, who liked thrillers, and she moved him from A. Conan Doyle (*The Hound of the Baskervilles*) to Dennis Lahane (*Mystic River*); she had another male student who began with a novel about a troubled wealthy family, *We Were Liars*, by E. Lockhart, and wound up reading about the Zodiac killer and the Columbine murderers. I don't know if this is a ladder up; it could be a ladder to hell. But perhaps *Crime and Punishment* is at the end of it.

"So what?" might be a response to all of this. That was the mocking question Mr. Leon insisted students apply to their own writing. *So what? Some suburban kids took up easy books, and some of them went on to better books. It's hardly a revolution.* No, it's not, and that's the point. The grudging readers and nonreaders had made a start, and they were likely to succeed only by degrees and only when propelled by enjoyment and perhaps by self-approval as well. Mamaroneck wanted to build a kind of reading ego: having chosen a book on their own, the students took control of it and enjoyed pride of ownership, a very American idea. They would become proud of what they were doing, just as they would be proud of mastering calculus or figuring out the best way to reduce turbidity in water. Awakened by pride as well as interest, they might be roused from electronic stupor. They might make a preliminary movement toward the compulsive habits of adults who couldn't put a book down.

"High volume, high success reading" was what some people called happiness.

Of course, they didn't always climb the ladder. Some of them chose the same kind of book over and over again. What then? The teacher would propose a friendly conference. "Why do you find horror stories so fascinating?" If the student responded, "I like being creeped out by weird stuff," the teacher might say, "If you liked *Asylum*, maybe you'd like *Frankenstein* or *The Strange Case of Dr. Jekyll and Mr. Hyde*." The teacher had to feel the student out and stick with it. It was marathon work.

Miss Groninger wrote me about a ninth-grader named Lanier, who read the *Pretty Little Liars* series for months:

> I mean, who knew there were dozens of them? I was after her in every conference—we had to try something different. Her response was always that when she finished the latest installment, she would move on. Like any soap opera, there was always a next installment. According to my notes, she read *Prep* by Curtis Sittenfeld in the late winter [adventures of a South Bend, Indiana, girl among jaded kids in a New England school]. She loved it. She then started to read Ransom Riggs's *Mrs. Peregrine's Home for Peculiar Children* [horror fantasy-adventure built from strange old photos]. She struggled with it and gave up after about 50 pages. She had a hard time with the characters, and the narrative was not as straightforward as she was used to. It's really not a difficult book, but she didn't respond to it.

Even so, not a bad ladder. Certainly a few rungs up from *Pretty Little Liars*. Anyway, Lanier was right: Ransom Riggs's book is strange. She made a critical judgment, not a simple rejection, just as Jack had made a critical judgment on Tucker Max's rancid effusions. In the end, Lanier, after passing through John Green novels, did a paper on the work of Howard Gardner, the Harvard developmental psychologist, which is more like leaping into the sky than climbing a ladder.

"My biggest failure this year," Miss Groninger went on,

is with Jose. I can honestly say he read less than one book all year,
despite the dozens of hours he had in my class. My notes on him are
full of my own frustration. Jose told me in October that he hated
English class, that he never had seen the point. "Everyone knows how
to read and write. Why do we need a whole class for it? That's just
stupid," he said. Anyway, I threw books at him all year. He is the only
one who never took the bait, yet one day I did find him reading *The
Fault in Our Stars* under his desk. So I played it cool and didn't ask
too much. But the book disappeared.

 Flash forward: Jose almost failed my class—he actually did, but
we worked out some overtime in June and he passed with a 65. He
sent me an email apologizing for messing up my year. I asked him if
he still had the book. He said yes, but didn't offer to return it. I told
him I dared him to read it and not cry. He did try *Bodega Dreams*
[Ernesto Quiñonez's Spanish Harlem noir] at the end of the year, but he
didn't finish it. I mention that, because I think part of my failure with
Jose is the fact that I didn't match him with the Right Book. Annie Ward
and many other smart literacy experts argue vehemently that there are
books for every kid. Annie moves mountains to make reading a reality
for the most struggling students. I should have worked harder for Jose.

But Miss Groninger didn't fail, and neither did he. She got him reading, and she cared so much for his stubborn soul—Jose was her *work*—
that he was embarrassed and apologetic. He felt he hadn't come up
to what she expected. My guess is that Jose will remember Margaret
Groninger's interest in him, and, out of guilt or affection or ambition,
he'll wander someday into the last bookstore in the United States, buy a
book, and read it.

BEACON, JANUARY: SATIRE

Some of the Beacon students read on their own, of course; I got an idea of the class's reading habits with my questionnaire in the middle of the digital fast. Choosing their own books, however, was not part of school-work. Mr. Leon had other ways of giving students something of their own—explicitly, something they could kick around and have fun with. God knows they deserved it.

Both *Brave New World* and *1984* were satires, one jaunty, even glee-ful, the other embittered and fatalistic. Mr. Leon asked the little groups that he had set up at the beginning of the year (four or five students each) to create their own satire of something. Not a strange idea for them; the media are full of josh and play, mockery and snark, travesty and ridicule of all kinds, and some genuine wit. Stephen Colbert and Jon Stewart are smarter than anyone I can remember on TV from years ago. Together, those two had changed the tone of public discourse.

Still, this was school, so there had to be lessons, definitions, an orga-
nization. Mr. Leon came in for the satire classes wearing a striped dress
shirt, rolled up at the sleeves, a vest, and loosely knotted tie. Some sort
of key chain on a lanyard was hanging from his right pocket. He was a
little jauntier than usual. He led the class through the different meanings of satire, parody, spoof, and then the conversation turned to irony.
What is irony? There is the literary kind in which you say one thing
and mean the opposite; the dramatic kind, in which the audience
understands something that someone on stage or in a movie does not
understand; and the "situational" kind, harder to isolate and define, in
which you expect one thing out of life and get upended by a completely
different result. That was the kind Alanis Morissette was talking about in
her hit song from 1996, "Ironic." Mr. Leon played it for the class, project-
ing the Alanis video onto a screen (every Beacon classroom had a similar setup). There she was, driving though a snowy highway, larking with
different versions of herself in the backseat, hanging out of the window,
and singing such lyrics as:

> *A traffic jam when you're already late*
> *A no-smoking sign on your cigarette break*
> *It's like ten thousand spoons when all you need is a knife . . .*
> *And isn't it ironic . . . don't you think*
> *A little too ironic . . .*

But how much of Morissette's lyric was ironic? Mr. Leon then played
another video. It was a stand-up routine—the beanpole Irish comic Ed
Byrne tearing the song apart. "She's a moaning *cow*," was how Byrne
began. Jumpy, pale, and narrow-faced, with stringy hair hanging down
the sides of his pale puss like damp curtains, Byrne attacked relentlessly:
"She kept naming all these things in the song that were supposed to
be ironic. And none of them were. They were just unfortunate." He
slated in particular the "ten thousand spoons" line—"That's not ironic.
That's just stupid."

What, then, is irony? The students came up with examples of situational irony. Lauren, whose name no one could remember on opening day, now spoke up, and said, "People asked if they could give blood to a children's hospital and they didn't realize their blood was infected with AIDs." That was a kick in the gut. *1984* may have gotten to the students more than I had thought. And was it irony? Nino said, "It reverses the expected outcome," and Mr. Leon, wincing a bit, agreed, saying, "I like it. It's kind of awkward saying I like it, but it's irony."

Nino took a shot: "A sword-swallower chokes on a chicken bone." Okay, *next!* Marina said, "It's from *Hamlet*, actually. Hamlet kills Polonius when he means to kill Claudius." But that's not ironic; it's a mistake. John Gruen came up with the moment when Yankee first baseman Wally Pipp sat down with a headache, in 1925, and Lou Gehrig took over and played the next 2,130 games. "I don't see irony there at all," Mr. Leon said, and he offered one of his own: "A water vendor dies of thirst." Mr. Leon bombed with that one, but he meant to bomb. "See, it's irony, but it's so obvious. We want to craft an irony that has more levels."

He asked the groups to come up with what he now called the Alanis Project—it could be satire, parody, or spoof. They would create scripts, songs, videos, posters, whatever they wanted. "You need to choose your form and your target," he said. "You may not be original, but you must be fresh. Satirizing political candidates or what it's like to be a Beacon student—those things have been done again and again." Alanis herself, after getting swatted by Ed Byrne for "Ironic," had parodied the sexy-sleazy 2005 Black Eyed Peas video, "My Humps," in a video of her own. Slowing the number down, Alanis took over Fergie's role as a jewelry-loving vamp. Mr. Leon showed the kids the video, and they then proceeded to have a Very Correct conversation about women degrading themselves by complying with stupid stereotypes. Most of the girls in the class hated the Black Eyed Peas number and appreciated Alanis's mockery of it. John said, "Fergie is hot," but no one paid him any mind.

Mr. Leon showed us a couple of videos put together by tenth-grade students in earlier years. There was a spoof of an Internet-dimmed family, with zombie kids, unhitched from their computers, walking into walls. There was a joint parody of *1984* and Sean Leon. A bunch of students gathered in Central Park. "LEON IS WATCHING YOU," said a sign. "His English class has become a place of terror!" screamed a malcontent. "We must move past English and attain freedom in history!" A mash-up video of Hitler and Stalin haranguing their followers came next. "English class must be eradicated altogether!" shouted a Radical Girl. The point of view was a little confusing, both totalitarian and revolutionary at once, but the spirit was willing, and Mr. Leon was greatly amused.

After the troubled *1984* conversations, he was getting them into the mood. "We need a barbaric yawp to get us going," he said. The reference was to Whitman: "I too am not a bit tamed, I too am untranslatable, / I sound my barbaric YAWP over the roofs of the world."

"Yawp," they said.

"Louder!"

"Yawp! *Yawp!*"

How, I wondered, did Sean Leon summon the energy and emotional resources to do what he had to do day after day? You could ask the same, I suppose, of any dedicated teacher. As I heard, Margaret Groninger ran the English Department at Mamaroneck; she taught "only" sixteen hours a week, prepped for each class, did all that extra reading for the book talks while raising three kids with her husband. In class, like Sean Leon, she seemed to be in touch with everyone in the room, checking them out, revving them up. Many Americans worked exhausting hours while raising kids, but teachers had to be responsible, at the same time, for the educational, moral, and spiritual progress of perhaps ninety students in different sections—well, it surpassed ordinary understanding.

Sean Leon, a bachelor with no children, lived in Harlem, at 152nd Street and Amsterdam Avenue, in an apartment he shared with a roommate. By Friday afternoons, he was dead, and he tried not to do any schoolwork on Saturday. He would shop, hang out with friends, maybe play basketball in playground pickup games. He liked to sit in Riverside Park, along the Hudson River, reading near the water and perhaps writing a little. On Sunday, he was back at work again, prepping, reading journals, reading drafts of papers and then the papers themselves. He had started as a teacher ten years ago at a salary of $39,000 a year. He now made $80,000 a year, which would be good money in many places other than New York.

Talking to him at length in school was impossible, since students always wanted to grab him for conferences or just to chat, so we met for lunch on a Sunday at PD O'Hurley's, an Irish pub on West 72nd Street. O'Hurley's was like many such traditional places in New York: a narrow, deep room, with a long bar on one side; above the bar, an endless row of dark bottles and TVs playing soccer and rugby; high oak tables along the opposite wall; and a surprisingly substantial menu. We sat midway through the pub, and I ate an enormous platter of smoked salmon while Sean ate much less. He had arrived with a gym bag and was obviously on his way to a workout. We talked for about ninety minutes on that day, and met again later in the semester, and then again a year later, and Sean also wrote to me, answering further questions.

He was always a bit of an outsider, a man born Catholic in largely Protestant Northern Ireland. I knew that his mother was Irish, his father an American navy man of Italian descent stationed at the U.S. base at Derry (the base is now closed). Lamont Leon was his name. He told me in O'Hurley's that he was the couple's second child (he has an older brother), but that soon after he was born, in 1972, his father took off. "I've never met my father, but I've heard that he was charming and funny," he said.

"As I never knew my father and his family," he wrote to me later, "I never came to understand my Italian heritage. Growing up, I came to know myself as Irish. I came to self-identify with being solely Irish due to my mother, of course, but also because of my continued relationship with my family in Ireland. To this day, I still visit Ireland and spend my time with my family there."

After his father left, his mother remarried in Ireland—another American navy man. His stepfather, Maynard, eventually had three girls with Sean's mother. When Sean was four, Maynard moved the family to Opelousas, a Louisiana city of roughly 20,000 about two hours west of New Orleans. Opelousas calls itself "the spice capital," but it's also known as the yam capital, celebrated annually with the Yambilee Festival. Outside of town, there's a large Walmart distribution center where Sean's older brother once worked. But Maynard took off, too. Sean's mother and stepfather have been divorced since 1996. His mother was now alone; all five children have left. Sean talked frequently of her loneliness.

In class, his voice was normally so lively and penetrating that it seemed to dominate every corner of the room, his eyes darting and flashing as he kept track of thirty-two students. I was a little startled by how softly he spoke now. Teaching, among other things, is a performance; a teacher must construct a classroom version of himself as much as an actor creates a character. The voice was still clear, distinct, and expressive, even in quiet, but he spoke intimately, with a steady gaze.

"We had a public school, a parochial school, and two private schools," he said. He went to the public high school, which was 75 percent African American. Most of his friends were black or Hispanic. "During the day, I heard one sound, southern, another at night, Irish. So I wound up with a neutral accent," which ended my puzzlement over his untraceable tones. But I still couldn't figure out who he reminded me of, even then, sitting across a high table from him in O'Hurley's.

He majored in English at Louisiana State University, and graduated in 1995. After school, all through his twenties, he went back and forth between Northern Ireland and Louisiana, where he was getting a master's degree in mass communications at LSU. The Irish Troubles was part of what drew him back to Ireland. In Derry, in 1996, his eleven-year-old cousin, Stephen McConomy, was shot in the back of his head with a plastic bullet by the British and died three days later. Other relatives died or were imprisoned fighting the British military and police. "I did a lot of writing about that," he told me at O'Hurley's.

Back in the States, in the summer of 2002, he participated in a summer program with a New York City Teaching Fellowship. "That summer before we entered the classroom was spent taking three theory-based courses. Frankly, I don't remember the course titles, nor do I remember what I learned in those classes. I only remember a developing anxiety as the summer wore on. I, and my peers, did not know what to do in the classroom in those first few weeks of school. The basic logistics of classroom prep and management were not covered. We were assigned to Jordan L. Mott Middle School in the Bronx. Within days of assignment, the *New York Post* ran a story on the city's "Dirty Dozen Schools"— the twelve schools with the highest rates of criminal reports. Jordan L. Mott was the only middle school on the list. The rest were high schools.

"I didn't sleep at all the night before my first day. I remember being overwhelmed with a feeling of inadequacy before I even started! How was I going to help these kids?" Once Sean got to school, the principal turned out to be furious that he had been assigned to Mott without her approval. The room for his sixth-grade class was dirty, filled with stacked desks, broken chairs, and rodent feces. He and the children cleaned the place up, reordered the desks, and turned it into a classroom. "The principal who gave me such a hard time lasted the first couple of months of school before she was replaced."

Caught in hostile circumstances, he was thrown back on his own resources at the very beginning of his career as a teacher. Jordan L. Mott was split into two schools, and, in his second year, Sean became a seventh- and eighth-grade English and social studies teacher. His new boss gave him some freedom in choosing what to teach and how to teach it, which turned out to be the moment of salvation. He was neutral in tone in describing his early years as a teacher, but now, in the pub, his voice rose in contempt. "Every year the teachers were presented with a new solution to raising text scores. A huge box of instructional materials would arrive in September. Everything shiny and glossy, but dumbed down and uninteresting. So I ignored it, and we read the likes of Poe, Shakespeare, Emerson, Hawthorne, Maya Angelou, Neruda, etc. My students felt ready for the seventh-grade state test. They knew those were the scores used for high school admission. Long story short: twenty-four of the thirty students scored 3s and 4s, in the upper half of test scores."

In 2006, he took some of his eighth-graders for a school visit to Beacon, and he met Ruth Lacey, who quickly hired him.

" 'You have to challenge them.' That's what Ruth said to me." She also gave him, in keeping with Beacon traditions, and drawing on his own practice, it turned out, freedom in shaping the reading lists and teaching methods in his classes. Within a few years, he became a revered teacher at the school.

In the following days, the Alanis Projects rolled in. One group did a *Twilight Zone* spoof—a black-and-white mini-episode in which the women go to work, and the men stay home as house husbands: "I'm so tired of cleaning every day," said Adam Steinberg, a studious, thoughtful boy from Park Slope, in Brooklyn; he was wearing an apron. When the women come home, they read the newspapers, while the men cook. "Things would be different," says one of the boys, "if men were in charge." He was doleful, angry. All of which was a neat spoof of gender roles that managed, at the same time, to suggest that the boys knew what feminist women had been talking about.

Another group, led by Nino, produced what they called a satire on religion. Yet this project wasn't really a satire at all. It was more of an exposure of what the group took to be self-delusions—"religion as an addiction," as Nino called it. The group went to a mosque, and made video interviews on the street; they also interviewed some students at Beacon. An atheist boy, with a mocking smile, said, "You wanna think there's something better, a higher power, a better life." The clear implication was that there wasn't any such thing. A Muslim on the street, an intense young man in a skullcap, said to the crew, "I depend on God for everything. What I save, I save for him. I am nothing; he brought me to something. He keeps my heart beating in the hospital, not the doctor." Parody had been left behind. He was dead serious.

As Mr. Leon remained quiet, the rest of the students talked it over. Maud—slender, expensively dressed, looking older than the other girls—replied to the Muslim young man, "I'm not dependent on God. I believe in being independent, dependent on yourself. Are you being the best person you can be if you're dependent on *God* for what you can be? What comes out of religion is war—people are sacrificing themselves before God, killing others at the same time." Marina, not in the project group but joining the conversation, complained scornfully of "people's dependence on religion even if they don't really believe it."

This was atheism with a vengeance. Mr. Leon, critiquing the project, said, "The Muslim was the most authentic. In contrast with the young atheist who was laughing." He told them that in Louisiana most of the students believed in God. He had been raised a strict Irish Catholic himself, and had lost his faith, as he admitted several times during the year, but he disliked impiety, and he sounded angry at the glib remarks he had heard. "In my senior class, when we talk of belief, the believers find it hard to speak, the non-believers talk a lot." He looked them over. There were certainly religious students in the class, but at that moment they were not about to say so. "How many people here will articulate belief?" he asked, and nobody answered.

John, Susanna, and Annabelle offered a video parodying MTV's reality shows, *16 and Pregnant* and *Teen Mom*. A teen actress (no one in the group, a friend) turned up to play a girl named Rhea. "I live to party!" she said. "I live to shop! I'm a girl. I have fun!" Rhea has two tiny baby dolls—her children—on her computer. Suddenly John and another boy, James Richards, show up as female producers, both pregnant themselves. They are interested. "I'm pregnant. I want to get on the show," she says to them.

"It was satire and parody combined," said Marco, impressed. Yes, and

with burlesque and cross-dressing thrown in. The students' point was
that *Teen Mom* was hypocritical right from the beginning. The show pur-
portedly demonstrated how hard it was to be a teen mother: the teen
moms were always talking in interviews about how they wanted to *warn*
girls. Oh yes, warn them! But, inevitably, the show made the teen moms
celebrities who suddenly had a way to make money. One teen-mom show
spawned another, yet some day the celebrity teen moms would be just
single moms. The students said the shows were providing incentives to
get pregnant—they were a sick American media racket covered in sanctimony, and they were onto it.

One group parodied paranormal activity movies, with ghosts in huge,
ill-fitting sheets led by Latisha to a ghost-family therapy session. Another
created a video in which Paris Hilton interviews people to find out
who her best friend forever was—a spoof of an actual show. Marina
appeared, saying: "I want to name my baby after Paris." In the cross-
dressing buffoonery and mockery of the Alanis Project—a kind of mild
saturnalia—the students were liberated from grim books, from Hawthorne, Faulkner, Plath, Orwell. They were back in touch with their
own lives as amused consumers of the media, but with a new critical
awareness of what they were watching and listening to every day. Was it
a "barbaric YAWP over the roofs of the world"? Barbaric, no; but it was a
bit of a yawp nonetheless.

CHAPTER NINE

BEACON, FEBRUARY:
COELHO AND HESSE

- Wingspan
- Journeys
- *The Alchemist*
- The Eightfold Path
- Be There
- *Siddhartha*
- The River
- No Special Key

John the big kid was standing at the front of the class. He held his arms out straight to the sides—for a fifteen-year-old, he had quite a wingspan. Mr. Leon gestured toward him. "From the end of one arm to the end of the other. That captures the entire existence of the universe—animals, nature, people, everything else. If you are going to locate *us*, you would have to shave off one little bit of his fingernail," and here he touched the edge of John's fourth finger. "That's *you*. We just have a moment to live." And he read something aloud:

We are travelers on a cosmic journey, stardust, swirling and dancing in
the eddies and whirlpools of infinity. Life is eternal. We have stopped
for a moment to encounter each other, to meet, to love, to share. This
is a precious moment. It is a little parenthesis in eternity.

It was a passage from Paulo Coelho's *The Alchemist*, a fable about a
young man's search for his personal destiny.

"What are your dreams?" Mr. Leon said. "What do you want to do
with your lives? At your age, I wanted to be an astronaut, an archaeolo-
gist uncovering great treasures in the sand. And before that . . . I could
go on about my own life as a Catholic boy from Northern Ireland. I
was told every day, 'Your dreams are nothing.' I moved to this country—
to Louisiana—and met an African American family that faced impos-
sibility every day. They were *shredded*, every day. The Washingtons.
Mr. Washington and his wife had nothing. He worked at odd jobs
and refused to go on welfare. But what are your dreams? Do you have the
courage to confront your own dreams? The reality is—*snap!*—you're here
this long. Then why not pursue your passions? Now you're fifteen, sixteen.
Soon you'll be eighty"—he clapped—"*that* quick. What did you *do*?"

Dear God. What did we do with our lives? What did we *want* to do?
The only dream I can recall having at fifteen was hitting forty home runs
for the Brooklyn Dodgers. My hero was Duke Snider, the Dodgers' center
fielder. There was a moment's silence, and then a great many hands
went up.

Lena, who talked a mile a minute: "I want to be a marine biologist,
and have my own reality show, so I can be a help to others. And I want
to live on a desert island, but not alone—with a family."

Marco, the class clown now retired from clowning: "I want to be a
lawyer, an architect, something to do with sneakers, maybe design them."

John: "A vet. I love animals."

Marina: "I'd like to go into the wilds, into Alaska."

My mind stalled for a moment at the thought of brilliant, needy
Marina in Alaska, among the caribou. But I may have been unfair.

Cheryl Strayed's *Wild* had just been published, and if Strayed, who was willful and prickly, flourished in the wilderness, Marina probably could, too. Anyway, many more students spoke in the same vein, offering multiple careers in some cases, some of them entirely contradictory.

The question was this: Could you set goals for yourself and then spend your life trying to reach them? Was life a journey, with triumphs, disappointments, detours, evasions, but a journey nonetheless that had the shape of an epic poem or a novel? Or was it more like a day-to-day scramble whose shape became apparent only afterward, the pattern emerging from the semiunconscious daily muddle—going to school, passing tests, going to work, falling in and out of love, parking the car, feeding the kids, losing some battles, winning others? These were questions that fifteen-year-olds couldn't possibly settle for themselves at that moment, but they needed to know that the questions existed. Fall had given way to winter, and English section 10G, at the Beacon School, on a dreary street behind Lincoln Center, debated these issues unrelentingly. It was the time in Mr. Leon's reading list of *The Alchemist* and *Siddhartha*—"quest" books filled with "wisdom," and perhaps a little literary pleasure, too.

The young hero of *The Alchemist*, Santiago, an Andalusian shepherd, leaves home and wanders about. He meets gypsies, wise men, an Englishman who wants to be an alchemist. At last, he meets the greatest of all alchemists, who adopts him as a protégé. Santiago stays in towns, travels across the Sahara, attains magical powers. He falls in love with a beautiful girl, Fatima, but he never gives up his search for his "Personal Legend"—a treasure buried near the Pyramids. Coelho's little book, which feels at times like a young adult novel crossed with a self-help volume, was composed in two weeks, in 1987. Coelho, living in Brazil, and writing in Portuguese, had trouble getting it published, but he persevered, and *The Alchemist* eventually became an international bestseller of enormous proportions—allegedly, 65 million copies have been sold. The book had caught the fancy of dreamers everywhere.

Set in some vague, premodern period, *The Alchemist* has a slightly cloying ingenuousness and a tendency to smooth banality. An old king tells Santiago, "When you really want something to happen, the whole universe conspires so that your wish comes true." Oh, yes, right. I had trouble getting through the book, short as it was, but the students liked *The Alchemist*, and Mr. Leon took Coelho's ideas seriously. He led the class through a discussion of some key passages, asking them to interpret Coelho's fables and incidents. He did a literary reading with them, but his real interest lay in pushing them hard on the idea of a goal, a journey. Earlier they had announced their far-flung dreams. But now they had trouble with the idea of just jumping off. They had trouble locating a horse that they could mount as "destiny."

Marina, leaning over her desk, said, "It was scary to me. I didn't see much connection to my own life." Mr. Leon asked, "Why is that scary?" Marina came back: "I know I lack understanding of the world, but I feel Coelho simplifies so much. And I don't think anyone can drop their whole life and go in search of their destiny." She was scared, I thought, because she felt more weighted and anchored by her responsibilities than she wanted to be. I remembered her situation: worked at three jobs, constantly needed money, her family life a rolling disaster, unhappy at school. She was too hampered by the circumstances of her life to think of taking off.

Grave Leonardo agreed with her: "We're connected," he said, "to where we are by technology. We can't run; and we live with our parents." Leonardo's dad was a Peruvian who had come to New York when he was twenty-five; he had graduated from City College and become a city project manager on construction sites. His mother was Puerto Rican; they met in Brooklyn and never married. Math came easily to Leonardo, but "reading, not really. Reading just puts me to sleep." At the beginning of the year, Mr. Leon told me, "you looked into Leonardo's eyes, and you saw the question 'What is this English literature?'" But Leonardo was becoming more active in class as the year went on, and he insisted now that we were too caught in our lives to pick up and run. He liked *The Alchemist*, but he didn't buy what it was saying, and neither did Ike Pressman, who said, "I have a hard time thinking I wanted to just drop everything. But maybe we could go on a journey within ourselves."

A journey *within* was, for once, not what Mr. Leon meant. He meant a tumbling out of habit, a big risk, travel somewhere, young men and women putting themselves in peril. He seemed a little abashed by their pullback. For my part, I was sorry that starting a business—one of the great American adventures throughout our history, and always perilous—was not part of his thinking. No, he meant jumping off the college-job-marriage track that most Beacon students (if they thought about it) wanted to be on. As always, he wanted to transform his students, but this time they balked. After saying earlier what they dreamed of doing, the students now acknowledged what most adults acknowledge: our life is conditioned and we are never more than partly free. We are encumbered by family, by culture, by society, by expectations, by fear, by the need to earn a living. "*My* journey," Hasan told me later, repeating what he said earlier, "is to live without a father in a female-dominated household. I feel responsible for the family": his mother and his three sisters.

None of the students said that freedom was an illusion, but they were realists nonetheless. They may have seen society as oppressive, but, it turned out, they weren't that eager to give up its protections. In other words, they were caught, pretty much like the rest of us, between longing and fear. The conversation produced by *The Alchemist* satisfied no one; it had gone stale, even become depressing.

As a way of supplementing the two short novels, Mr. Leon had asked the students to study the elements of Buddhism; in particular "The Noble Eightfold Path," from later Buddhist teachings, a set of aspirations or steps that an individual might take to rid himself of what plagued him and everyone else—dissatisfaction and suffering. Some of the steps: Viewing reality as it really is, renouncing harmful actions and idle chatter, speaking truthfully, and so on, all of it reinforced by meditation.

The goal was the renunciation of egotism. Suffering would end when one ceases to *want* things; one could then, just possibly, after much meditation and discipline, enter a state of enlightenment, in which illusion dies and truth begins. Mr. Leon was dead set on pulling the students out of themselves. This time he was trying to offer an alternative to purely Western modes of thinking. Also, without understanding a few things about Buddhism, Hesse's *Siddhartha* wouldn't make much sense.

"To what extent can we really live our lives this way?" Mr. Leon asked, and he divided the class into three large groups and asked them to discuss the "eightfold path." The students, it turned out, admired the call to virtue, but found the day-by-day practice of it hard to imagine. "Western society is always moving forward," melancholy Justin said, and Mr. Leon smiled and said, "Progress is great, but what have we lost along the way? Why are we angry all the time? Is it jealousy, because you don't have something that other people have? Why do we say one thing and mean another, bad-mouth people behind their back?" In response, the students, one after another, traced malice and bad-mouthing to technological improvement. They were embedded in capitalism and the Internet, Facebook and texting, and they knew it. They said they could not renounce envy, desire, trivial and malicious thoughts, and all the other things that Buddhists wanted to renounce. Under Mr. Leon's tutelage, they were hard on themselves, but I wondered whether fifteen-year-olds in the nineteenth century were any more virtuous—or whether the old virtues were covered in sanctimony that made them blind. These kids were not blind—a little unhappy and self-serious maybe, but not blind.

Mr. Leon himself must have had mixed feelings about Buddhist ideals, because the day after discussing the eightfold path, the following words, unexplained, were written on the whiteboard as we came in:

You can hold yourself back from the sufferings of the world, that is something you are free to do and it accords with your nature, but perhaps this very holding back is the one suffering you could avoid.

"How many have heard of Franz Kafka?" he asked. Only three or four hands went up. "That's him back there, that odd-looking man," and he pointed to the poster-sized photograph, in the back of the room, of the very young Kafka, eyes wide open, thick rug of dark hair extending down over his forehead. Kafka had been casting his liquid doleful gaze upon the class all year long. "Of all the modern writers, he most understood the human condition in the alienated industrial world," Mr. Leon said. The extraordinary sentence on the board, like so many of Kafka's remarks (it's one of his aphorisms), looped back on itself before breaking into clarity. The students took a crack at it:

Marco, in serious mode: "No pain, no gain. If you don't suffer, you won't grow, learn anything."

Vanessa: "You can't experience happiness unless you experience pain."

They didn't quite have it. Here was Kafka, in his incomparable way, telling us that the attempt to avoid suffering was damaging—it only added to your suffering by cutting you off from the heart of things. His remark was (no doubt unintentionally) a devastating rejoinder to Buddhism's insistence that the attempt to *escape* suffering was central to the spiritual life. Kafka's remark suggested you could try, but you would diminish yourself by trying. Mr. Leon didn't explain this drastic dialectical opposition. I wondered again: Where was he going?

"How many of you have experienced suffering?" Mr. Leon demanded. "How many of us indulge ourselves with video games and drugs to *avoid* it?"

He was on their case again. Their "journey," he was telling them, would not be trouble free. Trouble would come find them, he wanted them to be sure of that, and the attempt to avoid it was a mistake. He enjoyed a great many things, but, philosophically, you could not call him a hedonist. "I've led a life," he said, "in which I've seen a lot of people die—six or seven family and friends who have been snatched away."

Silence.

"For many of us it comes down to love, to being touched by love. You're in the position of seeing Mom and Dad every day. You don't realize how lucky you are to see them. You forget that as you go through life, they are getting old."

How many high school teachers spoke this way? Mr. Leon preached no doctrine, but it was clear by now that he had intense spiritual and moral preoccupations—responsibility to others, a love of family, the search for some purpose, a desire to take off into adventure, and what seems inescapably a part of adventure, the active life linked to disgust for the digital morass he saw the students falling into. After a pause, he said, "What does it mean to be *present in the moment*?" So much for Coelho's talk of goals, dreams, and personal destiny. What of the present moment?

"When you read," Mr. Leon said, "*be* there."

Born in Germany, in 1877, Herman Hesse, after some early success as a novelist and poet, traveled to the East just before the First World War. He studied Eastern philosophy and religion and then returned to Europe, living for most of the rest of his life in Switzerland. *Siddhartha*, published in 1922, distilled his understanding of Buddhism—and also his partial resistance to it. The novel (for some reason) was not translated into English until 1951, but it quickly became famous, reaching a pinnacle of popularity in the sixties, when it was one of the books carried by undergraduates on Telegraph Avenue in Berkeley and many other campuses. I should know, I was there—not at Berkeley, except as a visitor, but very close by, at Stanford, in Palo Alto, where I drank Jack Daniels and read the *New York Review of Books* as a way of fighting off the fumes of pot and Eastern philosophy that settled over parties and conversations. I had never read *Siddhartha*, and I can't say that I was now looking forward to it.

Hesse set his novel at the time of the Gautama Buddha—*the* Buddha—which places the story around 520 BCE (the Buddha's dates are in dispute). He doesn't give dates; he ignores geography, pays scant attention to money, property, food, the ordinary material life. The book is a swift-moving fable of discovery. Siddhartha, a handsome, well-born young man, a Brahmin dissatisfied with the spiritual exercises that his father teaches him, leaves home (without ever saying good-bye to his parents). He makes common cause with a friend, Govinda, loyal but not too smart, and the two of them join the Samana, the ascetics who pray, fast, sleep outdoors, and go from village to village begging for food. They lead a life of extreme simplicity and forbidding austerity. "Siddhartha had one single goal—to become empty, to become empty of thirst, desire, dreams, pleasure and sorrow—to let the Self die."

He actually meets the Buddha. He admires the leader's beauty, his serenity, and his wisdom. But it's contrary to his nature to become a follower:

> If I were one of your followers, I fear that it would only be on the surface, that I would deceive myself that I was at peace and had attained salvation, while in truth the Self would continue to live and grow, for it would have been transformed into your teachings, into my allegiance and love for you and for the community of the monks.

After this rather haughty remark, Siddhartha takes himself off, leaving Govinda among the Buddha's cohort. He travels about, and, after additional years of self-denial, falls into the hands of "the beautiful Kamala," a courtesan who, among other things, teaches him that

> one cannot have pleasure without giving it, and that every gesture, every caress, every touch, every glance, every single part of the body has its secret which can give pleasure to one who can understand. She taught him that lovers should not separate from each other after making love without admiring each other, without being conquered as well as conquering, so that no feeling of satiation or desolation arrives nor the horrid feeling of misusing or having been misused.

Which, all in all, is a lot of advice to hear from anyone. The students never talked about sex in class, but this was no doubt good stuff for fifteen-year-old American boys to absorb.

Siddhartha, happy with Kamala, and restored to his youthful good looks, goes to work for a successful merchant, and soon masters every element of the merchant's business without caring about any of it. He becomes rich and takes up gambling—and becomes the greatest of gamblers, making and losing fortunes. By this time, the reader begins to wonder if Hesse, whose style is both swift and solemn (an unusual combination, I admit), could possibly be unaware of a comic element in his book—namely that Siddhartha, who talks of losing the self, is incomparably the best at whatever he does. He's the most distinguished faster, the best ascetic, the most arrogant of nondisciples, the best lover, the best businessman, the most dissipated of gamblers. To our eyes, he's a consummate egotist, and his journey to empty the self has been nothing greater than search for ego gratification.

Just when we're about to get exasperated, Siddhartha realizes this, too. So this had been Hesse's plan all along: to pull the rug out from under a narcissist. Nauseated, Siddhartha gives up his past life—his past lives—and almost throws himself into a river to make an end of it. At the last minute, he holds back, and falls into a long sleep. When he wakes up, refreshed, and listening to the river, he is ready to begin a new life.

For Mr. Leon's students, the question, as before, was this: Was life conceived as a journey even possible? They feared the constraints of "society" yet had trouble thinking of leaving it. Society, however, is what's missing from *Siddhartha*, just as it's missing from the placid pages of *The Alchemist*. It's as if Siddhartha passed through a nearly empty corridor in which his body and soul were the only elements that mattered. I wondered if these "journey" books didn't border on nonsense. Nothing in ancient India—no village, no trade, no family, no young, marriageable woman— pulls at Siddhartha, hampers him, limits him. Nothing ennobles him, either, or makes him care about someone else. Is the journey purely a literary idea—a fantasy that could exist precisely because it detaches itself from the splendid and miserable world that everyone lives in?

Siddhartha falls in with the ferryman at the river, who tells him to listen to the river and he will hear what he needs to know there. And he does; he hears all the voices of humanity in the river. And, for the first time, he suffers failure and loss: he tries to raise the son that he and Kamala had together, and the boy, refusing to acknowledge him, and nasty as well, runs away. Siddhartha's grief over the boy is his finest moment, certainly his most humanly appealing moment, and it suggests that Hesse and Kafka, two of the giants of German-language literature in the twentieth century, were in agreement after all: to run away from suffering was to lessen oneself. After a while, Siddhartha is at peace: he surrenders to "the unity of all things." He reunites with clueless Govinda, still a follower of Buddha, and sets him straight on life:

> The world, Govinda, is not imperfect or slowly evolving along a long path to perfection. No, it is perfect at every moment; every sin already carries grace within it, all small children are potentially old men, all sucklings have death within them, all dying people—eternal life. . . . Everything is necessary, everything needs only my assent, my loving understanding; then all is well with me and nothing can harm me.

Which certainly helps all of us a great deal. I nearly gagged when I read it. No doubt about it: I would always be an unenlightened Westerner. My kind of meditation is called *anxiety*.

"Can we connect as city kids to what the river has to teach?" Mr. Leon asked, and several students said that the river was nothing less than Siddhartha's past, and that's why he heard things in it, which was certainly a very shrewd observation. Listening to the river, Siddhartha arrives at an understanding that he had to go through everything in life—asceticism, sensuality, greed, self-disgust—to arrive at the moment of tranquility, and the class broke into a debate over this approach to experience. "Is it important to experience everything yourself?" Mr. Leon asked.

The self-assured Nino said, "I live like that. It can be dangerous, but good can come out of it," and Latisha insisted "I believe it myself. I know if I'm told it's bad, I'll want to do it," and several students agreed that Siddhartha should not look with disgust at any aspect of his past. The idea of a single "goal" or "destiny," unifying all the appetites and ambitions and ends of life—that idea, never strong among these students, had faded. The "journey" conceived as a long arc was fading, too. "You have to learn not just from the past or the future," said Ike, "but from the present if you want to know yourself," which put the entire idea of "a journey" in a different light. A journey was not some grand quest but the experience of each moment joined together. Other students agreed. And then, with Mr. Leon's encouragement, the students raised their hands one after another and enumerated special times when they had felt the happiness of *the present moment*—with friends, or while dancing, or just doing what they love. "I guess it's impossible to jump into a plane and go home to Louisiana," Mr. Leon said, "so I would say that I'd rather be here than anywhere."

"There *is* no special key," said Jared Bennett, who spoke rarely but was suddenly excited. "You learn from everything. It's a matter of living life and experiencing all of life."

Coelho's and Hesse's notion of the long arc was now officially dissolved: Jared Bennett had said so. As he spoke and others agreed, I realized why Mr. Leon had begun talking about suffering and then "the present moment." He was trying to tell them that yes, the totality of their experience did matter, and that the only way to achieve that totality was to be fully engaged, all the time, in pain and happiness. *That* was the journey, the long arc—the wholeness of experience that constituted the soul, as D. H. Lawrence put it. For students enveloped by the media, Mr. Leon implied, the unlived life was a constant temptation. No, they had to *be there*. No lapsing out, no avoidance. Especially when reading a book for his class. High school reading had a new mission: Be there.

But was he right in his exhortations? Was he right as a prescription for living all the time? As the class talked about Siddhartha hearing truth in the gurgling water, I wondered what Mr. Leon would say to Huck Finn lolling by *his* river. *Snap out of it?* No, you couldn't say that to Huck Finn, and I thought, Do I really want to *be* there every instant of the day or night? I don't think such a life would be sufferable. A life without daydreaming, without lapsing out now and then, wandering, dreaming, just letting thought arrive and depart? Better to drift on the river once in a while. Mr. Leon woke students up from sloth, and he woke me up from sloth, too. But I saw some virtue in fading out, now and then.

At the end of the Hesse classes, John spoke up—John, the student whose wingspan was all of eternity, and whose fingernail on his fourth finger was the life of Mr. Leon's students. John had a reputation for being disruptive in other classes—but there was no sign of it in English 10G. He now pointed to one of Siddhartha's lessons for Govinda. In Siddhartha's words: "When someone is seeking, it happens quite easily that he only sees the thing that he is seeking; that he is only thinking of the thing he is seeking, because he has a goal, because he is obsessed with the goal." This was a good moment for Herman Hesse and thunderously relevant in the twenty-first century. Among other things, Siddhartha's remark is a shrewd rebuke of fanaticism, especially religious fanaticism. Seeking a single goal was madness. And other students seized on this passage, too. As Jared Bennett had said, there was no single key to life. They would seek many things. Whether or not they wanted Mr. Leon's never-ending alertness and engagement, they had no use for fanaticism, no use for it at all.

CHAPTER TEN

BEACON, FEBRUARY: VONNEGUT

- Vocab
- *Slaughterhouse-Five*
- Who Goes Off to War?
- Serenity
- A Moment of Memory
- Film Running Backward
- Comedy and Tragedy Together

As we walked into class, the following words were on the board:

> sordid
> tepid
> encroach
> conspicuous
> obstinacy

It was a vocab exercise. "Use each word in a separate sentence," Sean Leon said.

They put their heads down. Silence, except for the vague noises I always heard from somewhere within the building: a locker slamming, a laughing fit that trailed off, someone shouting "All right! ALL RIGHT!" For the students, using unfamiliar—or half-familiar—words in a sentence wasn't all that easy. Some of the students just stared at the paper in front of them. I spent some time staring at the words myself. What else was there to do? I was in school, for God's sake.

Tepid, I decided, was a good word. Sordid, too. A large part of life was either tepid or sordid. But what about encroach? Encroach? I liked the sound of it—the second syllable was emphatic and crunchy. But was "encroach," I wondered, a word that fifteen-year-olds needed to know— I mean, needed to know more than any other semiobscure word? I tried to remember if I had ever used it in a sentence. In the room, the silence continued, and my mind, like the mind of Kurt Vonnegut's hero Billy Pilgrim in *Slaughterhouse-Five*, began to shred. I had to stay in focus.

How about this: How about using all the words in a single sentence? A single sentence! In my notebook, with some effort and many crossings-out, I wrote the following:

> The apartment, with its sordid furnishings, its tepid water from the tap, encroached on Herbert's sense of well-being, but his conspicuous obstinacy kept him from despair.

Which has to be one of the worst sentences I have ever written. The students were still silent, heads bent over papers. A second try:

> Obstinacy as a personality trait is conspicuous among the people of Switzerland, a country in which sordid   or even tepid—reality never encroaches upon the enjoyment of natural splendor.

Lousy, and meaningless. Natural splendor is just as much "reality"— no more, no less—as Herbert's sordid flat. And what do I know about the Swiss, anyway? They may spend all their time looking at mountains *and* contemplating sordid reality. Give it up.

By now, the students were finishing, for better or worse, and I looked at my own two contributions without satisfaction. But I also thanked God for something. Words were like integers; you could move them into almost any pattern you wanted. My tepid little adventure made me feel free, even if the sentences were terrible. Waiting for the conversation to begin, I thought that this freedom to move things around, to invent, to reshuffle the elements of life (dream and experience), and most of all to be silly while being tragical—that was what *Slaughterhouse-Five* was all about. The book, published in 1969, was widely read, but after more than forty years it still feels strange and fresh—both madly playful and grief-struck, a fantasia devoted to the absurd contingency of life.

The full title of the novel is *Slaughterhouse-Five or The Children's Crusade, a Duty-Dance with Death*. People are always dying in this book—in accidents, in all manner of freak occurrences, in plane crashes, and in the massacre of German citizens and soldiers in the Anglo-American bombing of Dresden, in early February 1945. Vonnegut, a captured American soldier, survived the bombing while being guarded by German soldiers in the basement locker of a swine abattoir. "So it goes," Vonnegut comments after each tiny or grand bit of mayhem. *So it goes?* Was he making a protest against meaningless fatality? Or telling us, "Get used to it. This is the way life is—full of crazy insult and death"? Or both? It's a very funny book, and the comedy comes out of the general havoc, but the point of view is elusive.

The winter break had come and gone, and Sean Leon, suffering through family problems—his older brother in Louisiana was gravely ill—had missed five classes at the beginning of the spring term. (When he was away, I stayed away, too.) A substitute had filled in, and now that Mr. Leon was back, the students said they were unhappy with their classes so far on *Slaughterhouse-Five*. "We spent a lot of time on characterization," several said. They'd figured out that talking about characters was an inadequate way of dealing with Vonnegut's novel. His hero, Billy Pilgrim, flimsy, weightless, hapless, with wispy blond hair and spectacles—Billy exists less as a person than as a medium on which dreams and fantasies play. Billy was a touching figure, but if you tried to assign any substance to him, he would dissolve in your fingers, which was Vonnegut's intention. Most of the people in this novel are caught up in enormous events. "One of the main effects of war, after all," he tells us, "is that people are discouraged from being characters."

"I don't know what it's about," said Maud, which was candid; and mild, round-faced Ike said, "It's not linear. It's about everything," which is almost true. They were all a little dismayed. The book's fragmented structure left them unmoored, and Vonnegut's seemingly casual way with death hurt and puzzled them.

"How many of you are confused?" Mr. Leon asked, and I remembered that on opening day he had virtually promised them they would have trouble with Vonnegut. Almost all of them raised their hands. "Okay, that's good," he said.

As Vonnegut says in his first chapter, *Slaughterhouse-Five* is the book he couldn't write for years—the unachievable book about his experiences in the Dresden bombing. "There's nothing intelligent to say about a massacre," he insists, a sentiment that caused him to throw out thousands of pages. Or so he says: You can never tell when Vonnegut is being straight with you, which is part of the puzzle and fun of reading him. Does he mean it? The judgment that nothing intelligent can be said about a massacre can't be true. Dozens of good nonfiction books have been written about such things. But it's believably true for a novelist. The scale of the carnage deadens emotion and renders ordinary representation trivial, individual character immaterial—literally bodiless in Dresden, in which the burned corpses had shrunk to the size of tiny mummies. A fictional narrative built around the death of thousands might seem pathetically beside the point, an attempt to lend aesthetic order to slaughter.

Vonnegut's solution was to write a mock-novel that at the same time is a genuine novel. If realism doesn't make sense after a massacre, then throw out linear plotting (as Ike said), jump from one place to another, one kind of representation to another. Vonnegut turns to a goofy invention from earlier books, *The Sirens of Titan*, in particular—the Tralfamadorians, benevolent creatures who look like "plumber's friends," and who can see past, present, and future. They are gods who resemble toilet plungers. The Tralfamadorians kidnap Billy Pilgrim, and instruct him in their belief that linear time is meaningless. For them, everything that happened in the past, and everything that will happen in the future is happening now. They have entered another dimension, and they take him along. Once he's theirs, Billy can remember the future. He may be the strangest protagonist in American literature, feeble and visionary at the same time.

Structuring his book, Vonnegut enters a Tralfamadorian universe. Billy, helplessly moving forward and backward in his life, has become "unstuck in time." The Battle of the Bulge, his captivity in Dresden, his domestic life after the war as a successful optometrist and family man in Ilium (i.e., Troy), New York—all of that is always present, in fragments, the pieces commenting on one another. The fragments make up his being, in which everything is present at once. The rhythms of *Slaughterhouse-Five* can be frustrating, even baffling, since Vonnegut intentionally avoids most kinds of momentum. Near the end, he does offer, in fragments, a kind of climactic moment, which he builds very carefully and then savagely throws away. The actual attack on Dresden occupies no more than a few pages. It's an extraordinarily mischievous book, glancingly cruel and funny.

"A lot of people read the 'so it goes' as 'let it be,'" Mr. Leon said. "But this is an antiwar novel. Who goes off to war?" he asked abruptly.

He meant who goes off to war in the present, not in 1945, when almost any man might have gone off to war. "They recruit people from the lower class," Nino responded, "because they know they can control them." The students were moralists, or at least moralizers—that much had been clear all along—and they dealt with Vonnegut's puzzling novel by talking about soldiering and injustice. The United States was still engaged in two endless and largely pointless wars—Iraq and Afghanistan—and the students were angry about the way the armed forces glorified service.

Mr. Leon talked sympathetically about poor kids in his Louisiana high school. Military recruiters, he said, preyed on low income teenage boys who suffered from a sense of worthlessness. Maud, as if putting a final stamp on the issue, said, "The homeless are largely veterans," which is not true (about 10 percent are veterans). Perhaps she meant the statement the other way around: "The veterans are mainly homeless." But that wasn't true, either. A minute later, she added, "The war"—by which she meant the Iraq War—"gives people a purpose. They get attention they might not get at home," which was a remark meant in a kindly way but came out sounding patronizing. The students, cued by Mr. Leon, perhaps, made recruitment sound intrinsically evil—a form of seduction.

The class was veering into liberal condescension. There were the Beacon students, who were presumably okay, and then there were "the poor," who needed the armed services. It was a parochial Manhattan and Brooklyn view. In the South or the Midwest, and in the Bronx or Queens or Staten Island, too, many families—and not just poor families—would be happy if their sons and daughters entered the army or the navy. The children of middle-class Manhattan and Brooklyn didn't know many such families; they might not know a single person who had served in Iraq or Afghanistan or even on an army base in the States. I knew only two myself, both college-educated officers who had served in Iraq.

Of course, there was another possibility: Were the students unwittingly expressing not so much condescension as fear? They may have been from middle-class families, most of them, but poverty was something they were afraid they might fall into, and one of the aspects of poverty for them was that you became fodder for bad wars. It was hard to make out exactly what lay underneath their attitudes except extreme distaste for war.

"Is war ever justified?" Mr. Leon asked, moving things along. In this context, it was a potent question. Most older people would say, "In the case of the Second World War, absolutely." And yet Vonnegut writes about that war as a bedraggled ridiculous theater of mishaps, folly, and cowardice, with only occasional acts of valor—and those most likely to be punished by death. "War is never necessary," said good-hearted Vanessa. "We should have arrested Hitler, put him in an insane asylum, taken away his power." These wonderful suggestions were received with stunning politeness (Mr. Leon had forbidden derision under any circumstance). Both boys and girls in the class suppressed smiles and stoutly said that Hitler was implacable and had to be destroyed.

The structure of *Slaughterhouse-Five* was much harder to talk about than these gummy ethical issues. Vonnegut's playful and wounding tone wasn't easy to handle, either. The students understood the horror of the book, but the humor of it escaped them. As was clear from the Alanis Project, they were at home with parody, spoof, satire, *SNL*, *The Daily Show*, mash-ups, and media shenanigans of every kind. But black comedy and absurdism were new. They were not experienced enough as readers to know what awful things they could laugh at. They were, I supposed, too young for *Slaughterhouse-Five*. But how do you advance in understanding if you don't experience things that you're too young for?

Clare, an earnest girl who was another of the students reticent early in the year but speaking more now; Clare, a warm presence in the room, her voice soft and low, came closest to the book's strategy. "Vonnegut uses sarcasm so he doesn't have to express his emotions fully," she said. Clare may have used the wrong word. "Irony"—pitch-black irony—rather than "sarcasm" was the essence of Vonnegut's deadpan wit. The book was actually exploding with rage. But Clare understood that *Slaughterhouse* was an act of displacement, in which Vonnegut expresses powerful feelings of disgust as casual jokes, deadly jokes. Here was a true alchemist! He turned rage into comic fiction. Vanessa, recovering from her noodling remarks about Hitler in an asylum, followed Clare by

turning to the Tralfamadorians: "Billy invents them to escape the horror of his reality," and she cited Billy's epochal meeting, in a psychiatric
ward, with Eliot Rosewater, an intelligent man who killed a fourteen-
year-old fireman, mistaking him for a German soldier. "They were trying
to reinvent themselves and their universe," Vonnegut comments. "Science fiction was a big help."

"Is religion portrayed positively or negatively?" Mr. Leon asked.
"Negatively," said Vanessa. "Definitely negatively," said Ike. Marina had
been silent, but now she burst out. "Christianity versus science fiction is
a big element in the novel," she said, and she made it clear that science
fiction, with its childlike made-up world, its arbitrariness and whimsy,
had won out in Vonnegut's mind over organized religion, whose insistence on a morally accountable universe was rudely and persistently
violated by the arbitrary disasters of life, the *casualness* of death.

"How could God allow the killing of thousands of people in Dresden?" asked Mr. Leon, with some heat. He had set out in that class to
tie together the book's structure, but the students noticed Vonnegut's
many needling jokes about Christianity, so he suddenly plunged back
into ethics and the most troublesome of all ethical inquiries: How can
a perfect God allow evil? The name in theology and philosophy for such
an inquiry is "theodicy," and people had been debating its leading question for two thousand years at least. No answer, putting it mildly, has
been satisfactory. But Marco and Jose rejected the others' acceptance of
Vonnegut's blasphemies. "I have to disagree with you," Marco said, very
politely, when the students expounded on Vonnegut's jokes. He cited the
small touches of belief in Vonnegut's desolating landscape, the mentions
of Jesus Christ and the Bible. The Latino students Marco and Jose could
not—or at least would not—live in a world in which there was no dis-
cernible moral order.

Mr. Leon brought up Vonnegut's use of the Serenity Prayer, which
would seem to offer a daily method of coping with life's outrages. Billy
keeps it on his office wall. The Protestant theologian Reinhold Niebuhr

had devised the prayer—in 1943, probably, though Niebuhr wasn't entirely sure of the date. If that year is correct, he wrote it right in the middle of the war. By the seventies and eighties, the Serenity Prayer was turning up everywhere. Alcoholics Anonymous and many other thera-peutic groups cited it; you could find it in car-repair shops, replacing naked Marilyn.

GOD GRANT ME

THE SERENITY TO ACCEPT

THE THINGS I CANNOT CHANGE,

COURAGE

TO CHANGE THE THINGS I CAN,

AND WISDOM ALWAYS

TO TELL THE

DIFFERENCE.

"Courage to change the things I can" suggests power to make a dif-ference in the world. But Vonnegut immediately follows the prayer with these words: "Among the things Billy Pilgrim could not change were the past, the present, and the future," a chilling remark that Mr. Leon pointed out was a direct contradiction of the prayer itself.

Yet even if Billy can't change anything, he does experience a moment of real connection to his own life, a single moment of consciousness that redeems his entire blank, wiped-out passivity. It's the closest thing to a climax that Vonnegut offers. At a party of optometrists in Ilium, a group of friends in a barbershop quartet sings "That Old Gang of Mine," and Billy, mysteriously, "was pulled apart inside." His face collapses, and some of his friends notice it. Later that night he realizes what moved him so much: In Dresden, in 1945, when he and a few other Americans were put in the meat locker under the pig slaughterhouse, the four Germans guard-ing them would climb to the surface now and then. They would look at Dresden burning, and then return, their eyes rolling. "They looked like a silent film of a barbershop quartet," Billy remembers, and that's why the barbershop quartet in Ilium wipes him out. Vonnegut tells us: "He did not travel in time to the experience." At that moment, he's not unstuck; he *remembers*.

For an instant, Billy seems sound, even whole. But can Billy survive without his usual madness? Marina didn't think so. "His relations to the Tralfamordians is the only thing he has," Marina said, with some alarm. "He might really go insane without them." A terrific remark, but Billy's actual memory kicking in suggests that all is not lost—no perception *completely* fades into blankness. You may not be able to change anything, but, as Nino, summing up, said, "Your *perceptions* of the past can change." That may have been no more than a minimal bit of hope to gather from *Slaughterhouse-Five*, but it was hope nevertheless. After their initial bafflement, the students understood Vonnegut's pessimism, and his tiny movements away from it.

Vonnegut's greatest moment, however, was not something the students could possibly grasp. At least not fully, since they hadn't grown up, as I had, with documentary footage from the Second World War constantly playing on television. In chapter 4, Billy, at home in Ilium, comes unstuck in time. He sees a movie on television, a movie about "American bombers in the Second World War and the gallant men who flew them." Billy's mind, well, *encroaches* upon the film. Unstuck, he sees the movie backwards, which Vonnegut renders as follows. I quote it at length because it's one of the most moving things ever written about the Second World War:

> American planes, full of holes and wounded men and corpses, took off backwards from an airfield in England. Over France, a few German fighter planes flew at them backwards, sucked bullets and shell fragments from some of the planes and crewmen. They did the same for wrecked American bombers on the ground, and those planes flew up backwards to join the formation.
>
> The formation flew backwards over a German city that was in flames. The bombers opened their bomb bay doors, exerted a miraculous

magnetism which shrunk the fires, gathered them into cylindrical steel containers, and lifted the containers into the bellies of the planes. The containers were stored neatly in racks. . . .

The American fliers turned in their uniforms, became high school kids. And Hitler turned into a baby, Billy Pilgrim supposed. This wasn't in the movie. Billy was extrapolating. Everybody turned into a baby, and all humanity, without exception, conspired biologically to produce two perfect people named Adam and Eve, he supposed.

From the Dresden bombing to the innocence of creation—the passage is a reverse dramatization of the fall of man. What it expresses, of course, is a wish that the bombing run had never happened, a wish rendered in tragicomic form that reinforces the truth that it did happen. The students may not have understood the passage when they read it—we never mentioned it in class—but after a month or so of discussing *Slaughterhouse-Five*, they appreciated the aggressive humor of Vonnegut's toilet-plunger gods and the value of his bizarro science fiction as a way of dealing with everything that was inexplicably awful in life. Without understanding that comedy and tragedy were mixed together, you had little chance of a reaching a halfway sane attitude toward existence. Vonnegut, the grief-struck joker, makes us face the seeming contraries. Billy may have come unstuck in time, unstuck in his life, but we were stuck in ours, and Vonnegut wanted us to know it.

CHAPTER ELEVEN

BEACON, MARCH:
VIKTOR E. FRANKL

- Where Was Joy?
- Rebellion (If That's What It Was)
- Viktor E. Frankl and the Meaning of Life
- *Hier ist kein Warum*
- A Death in the Family
- Sophomoric

Okay, this was enough. *Enough.*

The students needed a break from grim books. *I* needed a break from grim books. *Slaughterhouse-Five* was black comedy, and funny in its morbid-whimsical-fantastical way, but death ran right through it, and I wondered, Where was the exhilaration of the body in movement, the triumph of heroes and heroines, the happiness of youth as well as the strivings of youth? Mr. Leon's moral intensity was powerful, but where was the rest of life? Joy? Exhilaration? Art as delight? The pleasures of story? I agreed that middle-class students in a privileged atmosphere needed some shaking up, but they needed happiness, too. Along about this time, the students could have used, well, some Shakespeare. *Much Ado*

About Nothing, say, with its dueling Beatrice and Benedick, its play of ridicule and intrigue, and its ruling notion—the ruling notion of all romantic comedy—that "the world must be peopled." Yes, the notion that banter and flirting and quarreling between men and women leads to romance and bed and the perpetuation of the race. But never mind the perpetuation of the race. Exuberance, play, nature, sex, life in the world, narrative—where were they?

Somehow, Mr. Leon did not respond to my desires. He did not hear my silent complaint. Instead, he pressed ahead. Earlier in the year, he had written a sentence of Nietzsche's on the board: "He who has a *why* to live for can bear almost any *how*." Now he brought it up again: if you have a purpose in your life, you can put up with almost anything. Nietzsche's sentiment was central to the next book on the reading list, Viktor E. Frankl's *The Search for Meaning*, an account of Frankl's time in several Nazi concentration camps. With a sigh, I read the book, which was new to me.

Frankl was a Viennese psychiatrist and neurologist with general medical training, and therefore of some value to the Nazis, who kept him alive despite his Jewish identity. Arrested with his wife in 1942, he survived and even flourished in Theresienstadt, the "model" camp near Prague that the Nazis used as a propaganda tool to demonstrate their "benevolent" treatment of the Jews. In 1944, he was transported to Auschwitz; he survived there, too, but got moved again, to a Dachau subsidiary camp, and was finally liberated by the American Army in April 1945. His brother, parents, and pregnant wife, Tilly, all perished in the camps.

Later that year, he wrote a short memoir (allegedly in nine days). The original title (in translation) was *Say "Yes" to Life: A Psychologist Experiences the Concentration Camp*. When Frankl published the book in America, in 1959, he added a new section, and the title became *From Death-Camp to Existentialism*. Sometime later the title morphed into *Man's Search for Meaning*. In the 2006 paperback edition, the book had acquired a foreword by Rabbi Harold S. Kushner, author of *When Bad Things Happen to Good People*. The "message" of the book (it may seem vulgar to use that word in relation to the camps, but this book does have a message) is that even in the most extreme situations, life has meaning, and it's precisely that search for meaning—the "why" in Nietzsche's formulation—that helps people stay alive.

Frankl's book posed the most essential questions about identity. How do you react to extreme experience? How do you make a self when you have been stripped of everything—work, family, home, possessions, clothes—and just reduced to a number and likely death? What do you live for? *Why* do you live? That last question was Mr. Leon's, and once again he wanted the kids to challenge their own lives. He turned to Luisa, a girl who had not contributed much up to that point, and said, "No one has ever lived that life before [meaning *her* life], and it will never be lived again—that's a wild idea." Luisa looked a little startled. And then, to the class: "Do you have a purpose to live, a *why*?"

Vanessa raised her hand. "We don't have a purpose, but we enjoy many things. We're *fifteen*, we don't have a concrete purpose." As she had told me earlier, she was breaking away from her family, defining herself, and she couldn't yet say what she lived for. "I want to revolve around thoughts," she told me. "Being so obsessed with actions can lead to decay in yourself"—a remarkable sentence, a little puzzling, but remarkable. "I don't read enough," she admitted. "I see the value of literature, but I need to think apart from a book." Vanessa, who no longer wept in class, wanted to be a therapist. "Thoughts" were active agents for her. In her own way, she was reacting against Sean Leon's insistent vitalism.

"My purpose in life," Vanessa said in class now, "is to find a purpose, if that makes any sense."

It made a great deal of sense. A ripple of amusement greeted Vanessa's remark. Mr. Leon smiled, and other students raised their hands. Clare said, "I don't think we know yet. You grow—you're not born with a purpose."

Was it just my own restlessness? Or was I hearing the smallest out-
break of rebellion? The students of English 10G admired their teacher—
that was obvious from the first few weeks. But they may have been
groaning internally over the job of reading a concentration camp
memoir—reading it after studying first a whimsical then a morbid fantasy of totalitarian rule, followed by an outraged, absurdist fiction of the
Second World War and its aftermath. They didn't say as much; none of
them would have challenged the reading list. But they resisted saying, at
that moment, *why they lived*. They didn't know yet. It was, after all, a
bullying question.

In class, the rebellion (if that's what it was) spread a little further. A
pale, skinny boy, Adam Steinberg—the boy in the apron in the Alanis
Project video—took up the *why* question. Adam, as I was learning, had
a stubborn streak, even a streak of intellectual pride. "Sylvia Plath had a
why," he said, "but she still killed herself. She chose to kill herself because
she couldn't bear the *how*." In other words, Nietzsche's remark, which
Frankl quoted, was inadequate: There were people who had a *why* but
still couldn't bear to live. Poetry was the *why*; the difficulties of living,
the difficulty of being Sylvia Plath, was the "how" that she couldn't put
up with. I admired Adam's formulation, but then Jordan of the strong
shoulders and candid gaze, topping Adam, said, "Her purpose in writing *was* to kill herself, so that became her *why*." Not exactly a joyous
exchange, but the two statements taken together made one of the nifti-
est, most spontaneously generated bits of conversation of the year.
Mr. Leon looked pleased. If this was rebellion, he liked it.

I knew this stuff. That was part of the problem for me. I had been reading about it my entire life. "The Holocaust" was not a phrase current
when I was a teenager, but the fifties and early sixties produced a conse-
quential amount of journalism, nonfiction, and fiction about the Nazis'
war on the Jews. There were extraordinary historical and theoretical
works like Hannah Arendt's *The Origins of Totalitarianism* (1951), which

I read in college; Raoul Hilberg's *The Destruction of the European Jews*
(1961); later, Arendt's *Eichmann in Jerusalem*, which drew heavily on Hilberg's work; and many other studies, including Martin Gilbert's numerous volumes. Anne Frank's *Diary of a Young Girl*, published in English
in 1952, became an enormous international success. Elie Wiesel's memoir
Night, published here in 1960, had, in its emotionally devastating way,
commanded a huge readership; *Night* has been widely read in American
schools for decades. There were many, many other histories and fictions
and also critical studies of Holocaust literature itself by Terrence Des
Pres (1976) and still later by Ruth Franklin (2010). And, of course,
television shows and many movies including Claude Lanzmann's epic
documentary film *Shoah* (1985) and Steven Spielberg's *Schindler's List*
(1993), and, finally, the development of an academic discipline devoted
to the Holocaust, which produced fresh material and controversies every
year.

Now, as I began Frankl's book, I felt a wave of revulsion. Not at the
book; at least, not at first. But at myself. I had read a great deal about
the Holocaust. Had I become addicted to the catastrophe? Hooked on
the self-importance that reading about it conveyed to me, the reader?
What was the point of reading another death-camp memoir?

The students, of course, were not addicted, and, if pressed, I would
say that they should know in detail what happened to the European Jews
in the middle of the last century. So, calming myself down, I focused on
the obvious question: Was the book any good? Writing just after the
war, in 1945, Frankl no doubt wanted to tell Germans and Austrians
what had been done in their names. When he describes the rituals of
dehumanization in the camps, and when he sticks to the physical degradations, he's powerful and convincing. At the point of initiation, the
SS guards give orders. And then:

> With unthinkable haste, people tore off their clothes. As the time grew
> shorter, they became increasingly nervous and pulled clumsily at
> their underwear, belt and shoelaces. Then we heard the first sounds of

whipping; leather straps beating down on naked bodies. Next we were
herded into another room to be shaved: not only our heads were shorn,
but not a hair was left on our entire bodies.

Mr. Leon read the passage very slowly and distinctly, and then he
asked the students to break up into their groups and talk over what such
an experience might mean. The students conferred in hushed tones for a
while, and then Mr. Leon called them to order. "Stripped of everything,"
he said, "what do you have?" When he said that, I remembered the first
class of the year, and his insistence on every student's identity. The
students had to acknowledge one another, look at each other when they
spoke. Identity was the center of human life for him.

"They are all the same," said Marco. "They felt empty because we
always put such an emphasis on material things, and they were shaved,
left with nothing." Vanessa, reading a slightly later passage from Frankl
aloud, insisted that they still had their shoes. "They had possessions and
might have them again some day," which was a hopeful thought about
a place with very little hope. (I remembered again her telling me how
important the space inside her head was.) Susanna added, "Your *memory*
is there," at which moment Marina, building on Susanna's point, said,
"They can choose, go inside themselves for meaning rather than allow
the Nazis to define their meaning in their possessions. The Nazis, their
intention was to dehumanize, to eradicate. But if you choose to use
that stripping to go within yourself, that leads to empowerment."

Which certainly was the essence of what Frankl believed: you could
triumph *inside* by insisting on a purpose, a goal, a justification for your
life. But then Clare, who had been shrewd about Vonnegut and was
beginning to capture the emotional meaning of the books we were
reading, raised her hand and said, "We will never understand what was
there," which was a remark that moved me in itself and crystallized my
gathering irritation with *Man's Search for Meaning*. Viktor Frankl was
clearly a strong man, and very likely a good man as well. His specialty
before the war was treating suicidal patients in Vienna and convincing

them that they had reasons to live. He did the same in the camp, arguing with people who wanted to quit, even lecturing them. A noble pursuit. But Frankl had the unpleasant habit—it was both a moral fault and a compositional fault—of setting up shop as a psychiatrist in the middle of a concentration camp memoir. And then drawing banal lessons out of what he had experienced and observed.

Love, it turned out, was what you had to live for—the *why* that could help people bear the "how." The vanity of Frankl's professional lessons and easy moralism enraged me, since, of course, those who lost hope and those who didn't lose hope, those who loved and those who hated, those who were virtuous and those who were evil pretty nearly all perished together. That group included Viktor Frankl's family. It may be impossibly arrogant for me, as a mere reader, to say so, but Viktor Frankl seems only to have half understood what he and his fellow inmates were subjected to. We can all agree that it's better to be strong and life-loving at any time. But what the Nazis intended—and largely succeeded in doing—was to destroy heroism and martyrdom and sacrifice alike in the endless silence that descended on millions of people. That's why Clare's remark—that we couldn't know what was inside the mind and spirit of the victims—was powerful. Clare respected the silence.

Viktor Frankl little realized what another camp survivor, the great Italian writer Primo Levi, insisted on, that the true witnesses to the camps were dead, and that anyone who survived, including himself, had to be an exception, even an anomaly. Levi spent eleven months at the end of the war in Auschwitz. In his extraordinary book *If This Is a Man* (original American title: *Survival in Auschwitz*), published in 1947, and later in *The Drowned and the Saved* (1988), Levi speaks of "the drowned"— those obviously sick or weak or guileless. When such people arrived at the camp, the inmates marked them as unable to survive more than a few weeks. And then there were "the saved"—those who had some special skill or charm or knew how to make themselves useful to the camp administration and therefore improve their chances of survival. Levi distinguishes between those who possessed hardihood and cunning, and those who did not. It's not a moral distinction—in fact some of the saved, he says, were morally reprehensible. So having a *why* was beside the point. The *how* was the only thing. Not only that, Levi's many works disprove Vonnegut's insistence that nothing intelligent could be said about a massacre.

What was happening to me? I was competing with the teacher. And not just any teacher, either. Mr. Leon led the students through an emotional discussion devoted to a single passage. In the section of the book set in Theresienstadt, Frankl reports his happiness at meeting a young woman who knows that she is going to die yet finds consolation in looking at a barely blossoming tree outside her hut. With Mr. Leon's prompting, the students, one after another, spoke of what it meant to know that life goes on after individual death—along with Frankl, they believed that clinging to the natural world was a way of holding off despair.

The conversation was detailed and fine; they were serious kids. Yet I wanted to tell the students about Primo Levi. He was the person to read on these matters, not Viktor Frankl. I kept my mouth shut, but what I would have told the students about Levi is this: He survived because he was useful to the Nazis as a chemist, and was given some extra food by another inmate, an Italian. Then he got lucky. In January 1945, as Soviet forces approached from the East, the SS evacuated the camp, taking most of the remaining inmates (some 60,000) with them. But Levi was sick with scarlet fever and, along with about 7,000 others, got left behind. The Soviets liberated the camp, and Primo Levi, after a long, bizarre journey (described in a subsequent book, *The Truce*) got home to Italy.

The "meaning" that Levi found when he wrote *If This Is a Man* lay in confronting, as a writer, the reality of what he had been part of, not moralizing about it. In the most famous moment in the book, Levi, a new prisoner at Auschwitz, and suffering from thirst, noticed an icicle through an open window and tried to grab it. A Nazi guard knocked it out of his hand. *"Warum?"* (Why?), asked Levi. *"Hier ist kein Warum"* (Here there is no why), answered the guard. In recent years, *"Hier ist kein Warum"* has become one of the most quoted lines to emerge from the war, indeed from the twentieth century. There is no why, no justification, only power.

"Hier ist kein Warum" becomes an unintended rebuke to Viktor Frankl's use of Nietzsche and the notion that as long as you had a *why* to live you could figure out a *how.* Yes, the meanings of *why* are quite different. Frankl was talking about a purpose that keeps someone alive; the guard was telling Levi that he doesn't have to give a purpose—reasons—for anything he does. The guard's assertion of power negated the *inmates'* purpose. They might have a purpose, they might not, but in that place it didn't matter; the guard's power obliterated theirs, whether he had a "why" or not.

So went my thoughts, in class and later that week, as the students chewed over Frankl's text—pointing, under Mr. Leon's guidance, to one passage or another, pulling the parts together, doing their work as readers and interpreters. In between these discussions, in an exercise that struck me as strange (in this context), they worked on sentences—active voice, passive voice, dependent clauses, misplaced modifiers. Mr. Leon now told them that the passive voice was the right voice when the subject of the sentence is being acted on: "Baby Annabelle was delivered yesterday by Dr. John Gruen," which made both John and Annabelle glow. Mr. Leon, as always, injected a little grammar into soul-making and a little soul-making into grammar. Punctuation, too. Could you use contractions in formal writing? He said no. School writing was formal writing. Okay, you had to know the rules before you broke them. Myself, I can't and wouldn't refuse to use contractions, which brought speed and informality into prose.

Obviously, I had to stop competing with the teacher. Sean Leon was not a Puritan divine; he was not a Catholic missionary (though he certainly had the temperament of both); he was definitely not a sixties-style countercultural guru. He was an English teacher, and he would get them writing in good sentences while asking them what their purpose in living was.

But that was not the end of the matter. Arriving one day in March to hear the end of the Frankl discussion, I saw students standing in the halls in clumps. Some were in tears. Others just looked grim or disbelieving. It seems that a teacher many of them knew, Jon Goldman—Mr. Goldman— had died the day before, alone in his apartment. His mother entered his place and found him on the floor. He was fifty years old. He had a son, not living with him, who was eleven.

Coming as it did, right then, in the middle of the existential discussions and the camp discussions, the death was something that Vonnegut might have turned into an insolent little scene. It was almost a sick joke. The question of "Who are you, and what do you live for?" became exactly the point, right there at the Beacon School in the course of an ordinary school day. What Mr. Leon was always trying to get the students of 10G to recognize—that life was too short to waste—had suddenly become inescapable. But I didn't have the heart to say, "So it goes."

Mr. Leon came into the room and stood silently in front of the class for a long time. He held his hand up to his face—a gesture I had never seen before—and he was very still.

"How many of you had Mr. Goldman last year," he asked, finally. A few hands went up, and there was another long silence, and the two silences together, I thought, amounted to a kind of memorial service. Mr. Leon walked around the front of the classroom, his palm still pressed against the side of his face. "I'm really trying to think where to go with today's class," he said at last. "Do we talk about it on its own, talk about Viktor Frankl? What do you want to talk about?"

The fearless Marina, her hair flying wildly to the side, got things going: "I had a lot of trouble with my English teacher last year. I used to go to Mr. Goldman and talk about writing. I had a conversation with him, and now I can't."

Mr. Leon nodded. "I'm not a very good business-as-usual kind of guy. When something happens, I can't just go right ahead. So we'll talk about what happened. I'm not going to pretend that Mr. Goldman and I were friends. We weren't close like that. But if you think of your life as a narrative, Jon Goldman was a narrator of my life. Never again will he be a narrator, I'll never shake his hand again, and that's strange." And he began talking about Jon Goldman, his teaching at Beacon, his love for his eleven-year-old son. "What's left behind? Life is very tough sometimes. What's left behind? All your thoughts are extinguished. What's left behind is that his son will remember the rest of his life that his father loved him. That's one hell of a legacy, to leave that mark."

I slightly knew Jon Goldman myself. Earlier in the year, I had talked to him in the "faculty lounge" at the school—a drab room with computers, copy machines, and a couple of round white tables. Between classes, teachers ate a sandwich on the plastic tables and graded papers. The room couldn't really be called a lounge at all, but at cramped Beacon, except for an empty classroom, it was the only place for teachers to go. Several times, when I wandered in, Jon Goldman was planted there. I never went to one of his classes, but he told me about the unorthodox reading lists he had favored recently—science fiction and noir fiction, which he loved, and probably got students to love. He wanted to break down the distinction between core literary texts and genre work. He was enormously friendly, and he spoke passionately about Beacon and about teaching. But he was also clearly unwell. He sweated heavily, and he rambled in a way that unnerved me. In the spring semester, he was on forced leave. At home, suddenly not teaching, he had died of a heart attack.

I thought I understood why Mr. Leon, standing in front of the class, had been silent for so long. He was not close to Jon Goldman, but a fellow soldier had fallen. Teaching had been Mr. Goldman's identity. When his job was extinguished—when he was stripped of his identity, in Viktor Frankl's terms—his life came to an end. And Mr. Leon was troubled himself. Some weeks earlier, he had ruminated aloud in class. His older brother, though only in his forties, was very sick—dying of cancer—and he spoke of quitting and going home. His mother had raised all five children and was now alone, and she was "lost, utterly lost." He was distressed about being away from Louisiana. Then he stopped and said, "Being a teacher—is that my entire life? What else is out there? If I stop being a teacher, what will become of me?"

The students went silent on that day. *They* couldn't answer his question. At least not aloud. He hectored them about their lives, and it couldn't have been clearer to them that he had a calling. They put up with his hectoring because he took his job—and them—so seriously. *They* were his purpose.

As he talked about Mr. Goldman, I remembered what he had told me in PD O'Hurley's—that he had never met his father, Lamont Leon. "I heard he was charming and funny," he said. Now I remembered what else he said—that his father, after abandoning the family in Ireland, became a popular English teacher and poet in Tampa, Florida. And that he, Sean, found out about him only in 1998 when someone sent him a newspaper clipping. Lamont Leon had died in school of a heart attack. "He looks animated in the photo; it's scary how much he looked like me," he said.

Mr. Goldman's death had made him silent, and no wonder. He had recently been asking himself what else he might be doing with his life, and here was a teacher whose life ended the minute he stopped teaching. Yet Sean Leon's vocation, his vocation as an English teacher had been set all along, an inheritance from the father he had never known. It was a mixed blessing. Jon Goldman's eleven-year-old son, as Sean Leon told the class, had the great benefit of knowing that his father loved him. But Sean Leon would never know whether his father loved him.

The students talked about friends and relatives who had died, and gloomy Justin spoke about a friend of his mother's who committed suicide—"the liveliest person I've ever known"—and how everyone danced after the funeral. Several of the girls said that Mr. Goldman wasn't teaching well the previous year. They had resented that—some of the kids had made a joke out of it at the time. But now they wished they had reached out to him. "Mr. Goldman was sweating bourbon in the hallway," said Marina, who knew what trouble looked like. "I asked him, 'Is there more than what we see?' But I didn't push it. He was a grown man." And the others made similar remarks. They had nothing to be guilty about, but they felt a vague sense of responsibility for a teacher who had gone off the rails. At least the girls did.

As the conversation wound mournfully toward the end of the hour, I felt an easing in myself: Viktor Frankl, whatever his vanities, had known what "naked existence" felt like and had gotten some of it down on paper. That was an achievement no one could take away from him. And I felt sure that Mr. Leon's habit of reading ominous books with his students and asking them why they lived and other such questions was just what they needed. The death of a teacher may have been tough for students to handle, an unwarranted and unwanted intrusion, but they handled it, and I admired their strength. Mr. Leon treated them as adolescents uniquely qualified to talk about things that, later in life, too burdened or sophisticated, they might try to avoid. They were sophomores—high school rather than college sophomores, and their conversations were sophomoric, thank God.

In a further twist—this was the beauty of Mr. Leon's way of teaching—his furrowed-brow reading list, his obsessive insistence on self-definition, *did* give pleasure. Mr. Leon flattered his students, and, whatever their occasional resistance, they knew it and benefited from his flattery. They did not—putting it mildly—read joyous texts, but literature provoked and licensed the conversations they had, and the result for the students of English 10G, in the end, was a lot closer to happiness than misery.

CHAPTER TWELVE

HILLHOUSE: THE YEAR

- ✤ Read Around Day
- ✤ Jessica Zelenski
- ✤ *To Kill a Mockingbird*
- ✤ Fathers and Children
- ✤ Information
- ✤ Harrison Bergeron and Francis Macomber
- ✤ Shakespeare
- ✤ Presentations
- ✤ Ishmael Beah

Absolute silence. Hardly a sigh or a shift in position. Twenty-three students were reading in silence, and I thought to myself, "You can't fake attentiveness—there's always some giveaway." If you weren't reading, your eyes would be elsewhere or veiled, looking inward. These teenagers were lost in books.

Two weeks earlier, in late April, it wasn't clear that anything like this would happen. On that day, the students, tenth-graders at the James

Hillhouse High School, in New Haven, Connecticut, were taking part in a classroom ritual called a "Read Around." The students sat in four groups, pressing chairs with tablet arms together and making a kind of stable common ground for each group. Of the twenty-three students in Period 3 English, thirteen were girls, ten were boys; eighteen were African American, four were Hispanic, and one was white. Their teacher, Jessica Zelenski, placed multiple copies of a single book before each group, and asked them to read some pages that she assigned—a sample, not very much, but enough to get the feel of the thing. After a while, she moved the books from one group to another until everyone had sampled all four. Three of the books were memoirs, one was a novel. The memoirs were *A Long Way Gone: Memoirs of a Boy Soldier* (2007), Ishmael Beah's account of his time in Sierra Leone as a teenage warrior in the nineties; *Reading Lolita in Tehran* (2003), Azar Nafisi's best seller about teaching English and American literature to Iranian young women after the Ayatollah's revolution, the same book that was so important to Sean Leon; and Elie Wiesel's harrowing concentration-camp narrative, *Night* (1958). Miss Zelenski also offered the students Amy Tan's *The Joy Luck Club*, a popular novel from 1989 about Chinese immigrant moms and their daughters in San Francisco.

Initially, on Read Around day, the students looked at the books without much interest. They turned them over, reading the back-jacket copy, flipped them around again, putting them down, picking them up and putting them down. "Books smell like old people" said Denzel Jefferson. A boy with thick dark hair and a long, sorrowful face, Denzel fell in and out of focus in class, and occasionally made devastating remarks. One girl, a redhead who could be tough, took a look at Ishmael Beah's volume and said, "I won't read this. This doesn't interest me." Amy Tan had a couple of takers, but Azar Nafisi, I could see, was not doing well—the book was too grown-up, a mistaken choice, as Miss Zelenski later admitted.

I had been visiting Hillhouse all through the academic year 2013–14, the year after I attended classes at Beacon. New Haven was proud of its magnet schools, and it also had a variety of ambitious charter high schools. Hillhouse was one of two comprehensive—i.e., regular neighborhood—high schools in the city (the other was Wilbur Cross High School). Seventy-six percent of the students at Hillhouse were African American, 20 percent Hispanic, 2 percent white. A little over three-quarters of the students' families lived below the poverty line. A Hillhouse internal audit, done in the spring of 2014, revealed that for every ten students who entered the school, fewer than six finished in four years, and that 42 percent of the 960 students were chronically absent (missing over 10 percent of school days). If one judged by standardized state tests in math and English, and by SAT scores, Hillhouse was the worst-performing public school in New Haven and one of the worst in the state. "There is a dynamic of not wanting to demand too much from students for fear of upsetting them," the report said. But Miss Zelenski, a white, forty-two-year-old veteran teacher, believed that inner-city kids needed literature. "Maybe they'll enjoy life more, if I can get them reading," she told me. "I would like to nurture in them the idea that there are other worlds. You don't have to experience things the way you do now."

On Read Around day, Miss Zelenski moved from group to group, clopping around quickly in boots. She told the students about the background of the books—the situation of women in China in the 1940s and in Tehran after 1979, and so on. At each table, if the sampling wasn't going well, she would read a few paragraphs aloud and then hand off the book to a volunteer, who continued reading aloud to the others. "Don't worry about mispronouncing words," she said. The other students at the table, eyes on the text, grudgingly followed along or just listened. Things had settled down.

Miss Zelenski's chosen texts were her way of interpreting an academic unit called "Social Injustice." Like the teenagers at Beacon, these students were fascinated by disaster. And like such books as *Slaughterhouse-Five* and Viktor Frankl's memoir, the books she chose were devoted to experience embedded in history. Neither Sean Leon nor Jessica Zelenski assigned feel-good narratives or pop fiction. At Hillhouse, Miss Zelenski's students had to commit to reading their choice and writing a paper on it; finally, they had to make a class presentation on related issues of social injustice suggested by what they had read. That was the commitment. But on April 24, on Read Around day, I wasn't sure the students would actually read the books they had chosen.

Hillhouse is located on Sherman Parkway about a mile northwest of Ezra Stiles College and the rest of Yale. The redbrick building, constructed in the fifties, is grand and spacious, with long and wide halls; the athletic facilities, which the school shares with the city, are superb (Hillhouse has a history of good teams). Standing on the front steps and looking out, I saw neat small houses, lots of small cars, and a big playground across the street. My provincial Manhattan eyes didn't see a city, but New Haven, with a population of around 130,000, is actually the second-largest urban center in Connecticut (after Bridgeport). Yale and a raft of good hospitals dominate the local economy—it's an "eds and meds" economy, as people said. Yet it was still a poor city, one of the many urban victims of deindustrialization in the fifties and sixties. The median family income, averaged for 2009 to 2013, was $37,000, a little more than half the median family income for the state; the murder rate in New Haven in 2013 (per hundred thousand people) was six times that of the entire state, the rate of rape two and a half times that of the state. The awful days of the crack wars—at a peak in the eighties and nineties—were long over, but, still, only 4 percent of American cities were rated more dangerous than New Haven. During the school year 2013–14, three young men, former Hillhouse students, were shot and killed in gang violence near the school. Some of Miss Zelenski's students knew one or more of the men. They were stoic about it when I asked. "It's life; it happens," said Denzel Jefferson, who had lost a friend. His long face was set in a mask; he averted his eyes and wouldn't say more than that. At

Beacon, when a teacher dies, the school comes to a halt. At Hillhouse, when former students of the school are murdered or a current student loses a friend to gang violence, life simply goes on.

"We get the dropouts from the magnet schools," Miss Zelenski told me. "The magnets also purge low-performing kids before state tests, and they come here. We get kids with learning problems, behavior problems. We can't turn them away, and we can't kick them out." Kermit Carolina, the school principal, a large man with a strong voice, confirmed what she said. "We take everybody," he told me in his office. "Kids with no credits, kids who have been incarcerated. A lot of these students have been distracted by the social environment they grew up in—absent parents, brothers in jail, crime in their neighborhoods. Many of them come to us with low skills. We also have kids from foreign lands, lots of English-language learners. Then there's the transient population. People move round." According to a PowerPoint presentation prepared by Mr. Carolina's office, only 25 percent of Hillhouse students are ready for high school work when they enter in the ninth grade.

Kermit Carolina himself grew up in a single-parent family a few blocks from the school. "Hillhouse is surrounded by very poor neighborhoods, and the school is a kind of oasis for these families. The most important thing," he said, "is to keep the kids in the building."

On Sherman Parkway, a police car was permanently parked in front of the school, sometimes two cars; two armed policemen, big guys, lounged just inside the building. The walls were surprisingly bare of the drawings, collages, photographs, and constructions that covered other high school walls—some mistaken notion of cleanliness made the halls look prisonlike. Yet there was nothing dangerous or threatening about the halls. Between classes students gossiped and laughed, they hugged and high-fived and mock-punched one another. Some had ear buds connected to MP3 players, the wires dangling across their chests like skinny necklaces. Once the class bell rang, the halls were virtually deserted; staff members occasionally patrolled, and a formidable-looking woman with heavy keys, catching a student in the wrong place, said, "Commit to your

education! You're not engaging with school!" The lunchroom was noisy
and happy, with students jumping from table to table; the large, well-
stocked library, with many displays featuring African-American writing
and biography, was quiet and mostly empty. Physically, Hillhouse was
well equipped. But I thought of Mamaroneck High School with its
extraordinary student services, its crowded library, its teacher-training
programs. Hillhouse did not have a college office—no one person to
guide the students through the maze of applications, tests, financial aid.
The gap between rich and poor America couldn't have been any clearer.

The Read Around, after its stuttering start, was going well. The group
that was reading the assigned passage from Elie Wiesel's *Night* was a
little shocked, and a girl named Anika Roberts, pretty, very dark, with
a round face and large eyes, said she couldn't believe what she read in
the book about massacres, she would have to see them for herself. As it
turned out, this was exactly the reaction of Wiesel's town, Sighet, in
Romania, and Wiesel himself, when a survivor returned in 1944 and
told everyone of mass executions of Jews not far away. No one believed
him. Anika had caught the mood of disbelief that, in the beginning,
pervades Wiesel's tragic narrative.

The girl who said "This doesn't interest me" when she was presented
with Ishmael Beah's book heard some of Beah's hair-raising experiences
and good prose, and now she was interested. In 1993, Beah fled the
marauding Revolutionary United Front in Sierra Leone, joining other
boys in the swamps and forests. In his description of his early days on
the run, the prose breathes with fear:

> I was scared when the wind blew, shaking the thatched roofs, and I
> felt as if I were out of my body wandering somewhere. There weren't
> footprints of any kind. Not even a lizard dared to crawl through the
> village. The birds and crickets didn't sing. I could hear my footsteps
> louder than my heartbeat. During these visits, we brought with us

brooms so that we could sweep away our footprints as we went back to our hiding place to avoid being followed.

His parents, as he found out, had been killed by the rebels. The government armed forces corralled him; they gave him weapons, amphetamines, and cocaine. According to Beah's account, at the age of thirteen, and for two years after, he killed dozens of people in Sierra Leone's civil war in a state of amoral exhilaration. He survived and settled in the States in 1998 when he was adopted by an American woman, Laura Simms, who worked for the UN. He studied at Oberlin, where he had a great writing teacher, novelist Dan Chaon. When *A Long Way Gone* was published, in 2007, he was only twenty-six.

After they sampled the four books, and talked them over a bit, most wanted to read *A Long Way Gone*. Miss Zelenski was eager for the kids to read it, but the school didn't have additional copies, so she went to the Yale Book Store and bought all they had with her own money. In the end, after some changed minds and swapping around (Anika switched to Beah), nine students read Wiesel, six read Beah, four read Amy Tan, and two read books not included in the original quartet, Khaled Hosseini's *The Kite Runner* (2003) and *A Thousand Splendid Suns* (2007).

On May 9, two weeks after the Read Around, Miss Zelenski tried to start a class discussion of the books' common themes. But Anika, the girl with the quickest responses in class, suddenly burst out, "I want to read!" A little startled, Miss Zelenski asked how many students would rather read than talk; most of them raised their hands. That's when the silent reading period began, and it lasted for twenty minutes; it would have lasted longer, but Miss Zelenski finally broke it off and began a discussion. The silent reading of a book they had chosen was the students' victory, and it was hard-won. School had started in September. It was now May. It had taken eight months, five classes a week with Miss Zelenski, eighty minutes a class, for the students to get to this point. At the beginning of the year, most of the class had been unwilling to read at all.

They came into class with elaborate handshakes, hilarity, mimicry, hugs, studied rebuffs, then mock-accusations, quarrels over small things. Lost pencils, lost assignment sheets, who sits where. Meeting at 10:40 in Miss Zelenski's room, the students, back in September, took a considerable time to get ready. "Miss, I almost got arrested yesterday," said one boy to Miss Zelenski as he came in. A girl who had received a good grade on a class essay, asked, "Are you proud of me, a little proud?" "Yes, I'm very proud," Miss Zelenski said. A few were prepared for class, but many others were entertaining the room, and some were lost in their cell phones and MP3 players, texting or listening to music. A few sat dead-eyed, half-asleep, and then laid their heads down on the desk and dozed. Some ate candy or cookies, and I wondered if they had eaten much for breakfast. Or if they had gotten up early to get younger brothers and sisters off to school.

Jessica Zelenski started shouting over the noise; she shouted through it, *into* it, until the students quieted down or woke up. If she were a singer, Zelenski would be called a belter. She was brass-lunged, and she mixed it up with the students, demanding answers, chaffing, taunting, and then offering praise, her voice changing from strident to almost caressing as she welcomed something a student said. She was five five, but her boots, her high heels, her big voice, and her way of striding around the room made her seem taller. When students didn't show up, cutting school, or hanging out in some corner of the vast building, she was angry. They had to be there, in her room.

Her operating method was less about maintaining order than about grabbing the students' attention and making them engage— "engagement" was a repeated word around Hillhouse—with whatever the class was reading. She rode the wave of noise, and then exercised her powerful voice on it and turned it in the direction she wanted. She asked the students to raise their hands, but at the beginning of the year they mainly burst out with what they wanted to say, often speaking at the same time. She responded to some of the blurters, pulling a single sentence out of the noisy cross talk. If she hadn't done that, many of the comments would have been lost forever.

The girls wore tight tops and faded jeans and hoop earrings. Some could be combative, as if they had to be that way in order to survive. "I don't care about your class; I don't care about *you*," one girl told Miss Zelenski. A few minutes later she was happily reading aloud in class. The boys, in hoodies and jeans mostly, were a little abashed. They acted as if they didn't know what they were doing in English class; it seemed like a joke to them, and many of them clowned around, interrupting whatever was going on.

Miss Zelenski roused the sleepers, razzed the inattentive and the rebellious. "Sweetheart," she said to one girl, a repeated no-show who was rude when she did show, "I miss you when you're gone, and sometimes I want to strangle you when you're here. Leonardo [a boy who slumped and drifted], I'm disappointed. You're doing that laziness thing again. Honey [to another boy], 'douche bag' is the wrong thing to call your teacher. It's not school-appropriate language. But yes, being a douche bag is bad." They would take the rebuke with an outraged look, and then a few seconds later, they would grin. They liked the roughhouse style, and they would come back at her ("You're mean today") and sometimes flirt ("Take the bun out, Miss, we like you with your hair long"). As often as not, she would praise the kid she had scorched a few minutes earlier.

Jessica Zelenski was born in Connecticut—in Wallingford, about fourteen miles from New Haven, where she still lived. A Catholic single mother of Italian and Polish descent, she had a beautiful three-year-old daughter named Amia whose picture was prominently displayed on the wall behind her desk. (The girl's father was Jamaican, a special-education teacher in town.) She had light brown hair, parted in the middle and falling down on her shoulders, hazel eyes, a radiant smile. In September's warm weather, she wore a short red skirt, brown fishnet stockings, and high boots. She was excitable and gregarious; she taught from all over the room, and was contemptuous of teachers who remained behind desks. She wanted to force the issue, whatever it was. She was a little like Julia Roberts in *Erin Brockovich*. Her attitude was, "Deal with it."

She taught three sections of tenth-grade English. Each class was eighty minutes, and the classes met five times a week. She was also one of three union representatives in the school. She made a salary of $60,000 a year.

"I'm asking for some compassion for the girl; I didn't say you had to like her," Miss Zelenski said.

After the preliminary readings in September, including a famously provocative story by Ursula Le Guin, "The Ones Who Walk Away from Omelas," the class had launched into the first major reading of the year, Harper Lee's *To Kill a Mockingbird*. The girl in question was of course Mayella Ewell, the nineteen-year-old who insists that she was raped by a black farm hand, Tom Robinson. When she takes the witness stand, Tom's defense counsel, Atticus Finch, gently but persistently works her over. As much as two greater novels, *Huckleberry Finn* and *The Great Gatsby*, Harper Lee's *To Kill a Mockingbird*, published in 1960, had become American scripture, read in countless high school courses. Set in Maycomb, Alabama (Harper Lee's Monroeville), in 1932, the story is told through the eyes of Scout Finch, six when the novel begins, eight when it ends, brave and irrepressibly curious Scout, who flourishes as the much-loved daughter of the stalwart, sublimely calm Atticus Finch, the role Gregory Peck was born to play.

Read again as an adult, *To Kill a Mockingbird* feels a little smug in its gently patriarchal view of the African Americans in Maycomb. But Miss Zelenski's students were reading it for the first time, and, in any reading, *Mockingbird* offers the enchantment of childhood, the mild thrills of gothic fable, the pleasures of indignation over obvious

injustice.* Many Americans remember it fondly for its humor, its sensu-
ous and lyrical realization of small-town southern life in the early thirties.

At the climax of the trial in *To Kill a Mockingbird*, as Atticus persists
in his questions, it becomes obvious that Tom Robinson, who has a with-
ered arm, couldn't have raped Mayella—that she had in fact asked him
into the family house and had thrown her arms around him, only to be
discovered by Bob Ewell, her alcoholic father, who called her a whore,
beat her, and then brought charges against Tom. Mayella, who found
the robust Tom attractive, and maybe even loved him, was easily intim-
idated. She was a victim—not as much as Tom, who doesn't survive the
trial and its aftermath, but an oppressed, abused, beaten creature.

The class began talking about Mayella after spending several weeks
on the book. In the beginning, the discussion had stalled. Most of the
students did not read *To Kill a Mockingbird* at home. They simply
wouldn't do it. They came in looking blank, as if the assigned pages were
some kind of mistake, a strange imposition on them. Miss Zelenski had
been teaching at Hillhouse for thirteen years, and she had seen this
refusal in other classes, and rather than making a big deal out of it, she
began reading aloud: "MAYCOMB WAS AN OLD TOWN, BUT IT
WAS A TIRED OLD TOWN WHEN I FIRST KNEW IT," she
shouted. "IN RAINY WEATHER THE STREETS TURNED TO

---

* These classes took place in the fall of 2013, almost thirty months before the publication
of Harper Lee's *Go Set a Watchman*, which was widely described as a new book but was actually an old book—a discarded first draft. The book's publication set off an enormous contro-
versy. In *Go Set a Watchman*, Scout, a grown-up living in New York, recalls the Atticus of her
childhood as a bigot. Much of the public and private conversation that followed about race
and representation was fascinating and touching, but it was also, as a discussion of literature,
willfully naïve. Atticus Finch is not a real person; he did not "evolve," as some people absurdly
said, into a bigot; the bigoted version came *first*. If anything, the character of Atticus, after the
editor Tay Hohoff worked for years with Harper Lee, "evolved" into the benevolent version of
the character in *To Kill a Mockingbird*. But even putting it that way is misleading. There's
something simple that an amazing number of people could not get through their heads: Atticus is two fictional inventions serving different purposes in two separate narratives. Since the
issue is unlikely to go away, the question is this: What should teachers like Jessica Zelenski do
in the future if they want to teach Harper Lee? Well, one thing they could do is teach both
texts together—not just to further a discussion of race, history, and racism but to demonstrate in the most material way how fiction works.

RED SLOP; GRASS GREW ON THE SIDEWALK, THE COURT-
HOUSE SAGGED IN THE SQUARE."

She had their attention, and after a while she asked for volunteers.
"Reading aloud—how many afraid?" she said. A few raised their hands. "I
don't want to force you to be uncomfortable. Don't you find it obnoxious
when people giggle and groan when you don't know a word?" General
assent, and then as people began reading and someone got stuck, one of
the other kids would help out. On this occasion and many others, Miss
Zelenski's students did not put each other down. Just the opposite. They
supported each other whenever they could. When the class stopped
reading and talked the book over, the boys, who earlier seemed unwilling
to let the conversation go forward—they joked nervously through
class—got up out of their chairs now and then and congratulated a guy
who said something funny or interesting.

After much reading aloud in class, the students finished *Mockingbird*
on their own. They were alive to the emotionally plangent moments in
the book, and when the conversation caught fire, the students talking
back and forth to one another, Miss Zelenski let the ragged class move
along without interruption. She wanted to get them going, but, at the
end of one conversation, she got tough. "Don't use Sunday school lessons
about kindness," she said. "You're almost adults. And some of what you
hear about life isn't good."

Then she turned the discussion in their direction. The class was
talking about Scout's aunt and uncle, who disapprove of her tomboy
behavior, and Miss Zelenski asked, "How many of you have a mean
relative?" The girl who was initially uninterested in Ishmael Beah, and
then changed her mind, cried out, "*All* my relatives are mean!"

That was a conversation-stopper. Miss Zelenski moved the issue to
fathers. What kind of father was Atticus Finch? He could be a little
remote, but he had extraordinary judgment about many things, and he
gave Scout and her brother Jem the freedom to find things out on their
own. To sharpen the question, she set up a contrast. Late in the month-
long span of classes on *Mockingbird,* she showed the kids Benh Zeitlin's

lyrical and brutal independent movie, *Beasts of the Southern Wild*, from
2012. In *Beasts*, an indomitable little African American girl, Hushpuppy
(Quvenzhané Wallis), who is roughly the same age as Scout, and her
alcoholic father, Wink (Dwight Henry), live in the bayous south of New
Orleans in the Bathtub, a sloshy, ramshackle but happy community. The
off-the-grid poor families in the Bathtub hold to a powerful and defining code: you don't let anyone down who's in trouble. Wink, speaking
in his coarse, strong voice, leaves Hushpuppy for periods, but he's there
when she needs him. The students loved the movie, although one girl, in
tears at the end, said furiously to Miss Zelenski, "I'm a G [gangsta]. How
can you make me cry in front of these people?"

Most said they would prefer Wink as a father. He was wasted and
harsh, but, as Denzel said, others agreeing, "He taught his daughter
how to survive." This led to a full-scale conversation about fathers. What
was a good father? Should fathers lay down the law? Or should they let
kids do what they want to do? "He wouldn't know if I was dead or alive,"
one girl said. "For how many of you is your father your hero?" Miss Zelenski asked. Five raised their hands. "How many live with your father?"
The same five raised their hands. There were twenty-three students in
the class.

"He keeps a roof over my head," said Denzel. "He stops by. He provides some money to the household. But he's not close." In class, Denzel
would be lost in music playing into his ears; suddenly, he would raise
his palms, do a kind of Egyptian shimmy, moving from the back corner where he sat into the center of the room even as people were talking.
Yet he encouraged other students to speak, and he took Miss Zelenski's
side in arguments. He was the principle of order and disorder at the same
time. As a child, he had been diagnosed with ADHD and Oppositional
Defiance Disorder. At 10:40, he was supposed to be attending a study-
hall class for special-education kids, but Miss Zelenski figured he would
learn more by sitting in her class. All through the year, he wandered in
and out of the discussions, saying smart things, poetic things, outrageous
things.

"What do we know about Mayella when the trial begins?" Miss Zelenski asked. "We know someone beat the crap out of her. But we don't know what happened to her. She doesn't speak well, does she?" Everyone said no. "What societies are there in Maycomb?" Students shouted out: "White people. Poor farmers. Niggers." "The Ewells are in a society of their own," Miss Zelenski said. "What is it?" "They dirty, they lie." And Denzel said, "The nigger don't lie."

"Guys, he has a name. It's Tom. Why do you keep saying that?" She paused. "What's the Ewell home like?" and they called out, "Cold, dirty, everyone sick." They knew what Mayella was—white trash. Some thought she was worthless—at least at first they did. But Miss Zelenski wanted some sympathy; she wanted to engage their sense of what a tough life was like and, at the same time, push them out of themselves and make them realize that other people also had troubles. Later she told me, "They have heard about slavery, racism, Martin Luther King Jr. and the civil rights movement since grade school. They need to hear something else." She now said to the students, "Imagine if you had to do what Mayella does, get up in the cold every morning to haul up a bucket of water." A girl named Malia raised her hand, and said, "She may have been raped by her father, she's poor, she's one of seven children."

"Okay," said Miss Zelenski, "why don't you write about that?" And she asked them all to write a short paper in defense of Mayella. The request produced some dismay. Why do it? They were being asked to write about someone worse off than they were, a white farm girl who had been beaten and likely abused by her father. In class, Malia read aloud what she had written: "In Mayella Ewell's defense, she is a lonely nineteen-year-old girl. She was never treated properly with respect. . . . Tom was the only person who showed her respect so she became excited and wanted him." A womanly girl with a soft voice and intimate manner, Malia didn't speak much in class, but she was one of the best readers Miss Zelenski had. Her mother and father, she told me, had never married, separating as a couple before she was born, and her mom had two other kids, each with a different father. She remembered her father "around" when she was a child. "He doesn't work now," she said. But her grandmother had motivated her. "She was my mom. She read to me, pushed me through school."

Some of the other girls wrote in the same vein as Malia, but most of the boys balked. Leonardo, the boy who lazed and slumped, a fifteen-year-old of mixed Latino and Italian background, fished around in his notes, and read, "The life of being an outcast is intimidating," and much more of the same, eloquent but vague. "It stinks," said Raymond, an African American boy sitting near him, and he read from what he had written: "You can't blame Mayella for lying about Tom. If she had told the truth, her father would have been arrested, and so no one would be there to take care of them in that shit-ass house. You can't blame Mayella because she hasn't been brought up right. She's one of seven. She stays away from society so she doesn't know right from wrong."

These were the most sustained remarks that Raymond had made so far. I talked to him after class. He was slender, handsome, with a thin mustache, an earring in his left ear, and an engaging, furtive smile. His mother worked as a Certified Nursing Assistant. His father, at the age of five, arrived in the States from Trinidad. He was now in prison in the Corrigon-Radgowski Correctional Institution in northern Connecticut. Raymond hadn't asked him what he was convicted for. "I'll wait till he comes home to ask him," he said. He has three brothers, three sisters, all his mother's children except for his older brother.

After school one day, I met him in his own neighborhood, the Tre (pronounced "Tray"), about a mile from Hillhouse. In the early nineties, during the wild crack wars, gang violence ruled the Tre, and, according to a veteran reporter in New Haven, Paul Bass, now editor of the *New Haven Independent*, every streetlight was shot out, grown-ups stayed away from windows, and kids were known to sleep in bathtubs to protect themselves from stray bullets. Those days were over, but the Tre was still a ravaged piece of the city. Walking around, we passed a boarded-up Chinese takeout, a boarded-up pizza joint. It was a New Haven–style bad neighborhood—nothing like such deserted war-zone wrecks as the South Bronx in the seventies and eighties. There were trees and hundred-year-old wood houses on separate lots, but many of the houses were fenced, chain-locked, worn-looking. At New Haven's industrial peak in the years immediately after the Second World War, relatively prosperous families lived in these buildings. But the industrial plants had closed down, including Scovill Industries, in nearby Waterbury and, in 2006, the Winchester Repeating Arms Company in the New Haven neighborhood of Newhallville. The life was sucked out of the Tre. During the day, the streets were not so much menacing as forlorn, like a small town in the middle of the Depression. We walked into Dunkin' Donuts, the only commercial enterprise flourishing in Raymond's part of the Tre, and the site, over the years, of gang violence, and he ordered a strawberry Coolatta.

He has an eleven-year-old brother at home. "I keep him out of trouble," he said. He spoke very softly, barely above a whisper, as he pointed to a spot a few blocks from his house where he and his brother play basketball. "I try not to make friends in the neighborhood. I don't want to be with people when I don't know what they do."

Denzel lived in a still worse neighborhood, Dixwell, and said the same thing. You went out at night, got caught up with strange kids, you didn't know what they were into, and suddenly there was a fight—not a gang thing always, maybe a quarrel over a Facebook insult or a girl, but someone might get stabbed or shot. Anika said virtually the same. And so did a tall, very dark, extremely gentle boy in Miss Zelenski's class, Philip Todd. These were not kids in gangs, kids in trouble with the law. They were not, in current sociological terms, "disconnected"—teens who were both out of school and unemployed. They wanted to go to college, find their way, maybe get out of New Haven, join the middle class or better. At the very least, they were trying to get through their teenage years without being hurt. But they were already hurt: all four were essentially imprisoned in their homes at night.

⋙——⋘

As they read through *Mockingbird* together, Miss Zelenski talked about the Deep South in the thirties. She gave the students a sense of the technology and transportation, the food different people were likely to eat. She seemed determined to teach them not just the book but everything that could be suggested by the book, and everything that was needed to understand it. "Frontloading" was the pedagogic term for what she was doing, except that she loaded in the front, in the middle, and in the rear. She used whatever they were reading to create knowledge of how the world worked, even a small corner of it. If they could understand one corner, they might be able to understand many corners. After discussing how Maycomb was structured socially, the students grappled with a complicated situation: Mayella, a white woman in the South, was nominally superior in class and status to Tom, but when she exercised her freedom, breaking a racial code, she got a beating.

The students I talked to knew a lot about families, about love and the absence of love, about loyalty and betrayal, and a great many other things. They knew how to take care of younger children, and they were perceptive about the character of the people around them. They knew whom to trust, they knew about their neighborhoods, how to stay safe. They demanded fairness; they had a very active sense of justice—not in the legal sense, necessarily, but in all the relations of life.

But many of the Hillhouse students lacked necessary information—*facts*, for want of a better word. When wars took place, how American politics worked, who were the country's great men and women, how a bank did its business, what, exactly, they had to do to get into the professions or get any kind of good job—general information about how the world worked. What they experienced every day was shaped, in part, by political and economic forces that they were barely curious about. They also lacked the rich vocabulary of students who had been frequently read to when they were children, and had then developed reading habits of their own. Except for Philip Todd, who, it turned out, was passionate about movies, they didn't cultivate curiosity, at least not openly, and at times they seemed defensive and irritated, as if they felt that learning some new words or specific things about politics, business, science, and art would somehow make them responsible for learning everything. But of course no one is responsible for learning everything.

Some kids from poor families do brilliantly in school; some rich kids barely make it through or drop out (and get second, third, and fourth chances). Some poor parents invest time and imagination in raising their kids; some rich parents are negligent and distant. Family wealth is not the necessary *cause* of good or bad school performance, but, in general, as many studies have shown, it's the surest predictor of it, with performance highly correlated to family income.

A famous experiment in the 1990s by University of Kansas researchers Betty Hart and Todd R. Risley established that children from professional families heard more than three times as many words per hour as children in families on welfare. By the age of three, wealthy children had heard millions more words than poor children. Later research, completed at Stanford in 2013, established that a gap opened as early as eighteen months: children from prosperous families were already several months ahead of children from poor families in language proficiency. Follow-up studies indicated that differences in language and interaction experiences have lasting effects on a child's performance later in life.

The thematic rubric for tenth-grade English at Hillhouse, it turned out, was the same as at Beacon: "The Individual and Society." At Beacon the students had an abstract notion of society as an oppressor, but they sensed that they would flourish as individuals. They could even talk, in their *Siddhartha* classes, of life as a journey composed of special moments in which existence was at its most intense. But at Hillhouse, the African American students didn't openly claim the privilege of being individuals. Mere survival came first, before selfhood and "journeys." And for Hillhouse students "society" was not so much a hostile abstraction as a blank, something so little known that it was hardly mentioned.

The knowledge gap that many of the Hillhouse students suffered from was created by poverty. Most of the students lived in large, mixed, even chaotic families, with fathers and stepfathers and their mother's boyfriends coming and going, and sometimes with fathers or brothers in prison. Of the students I spoke to, only one, Malia, said she had been read to much as a child (by her grandmother). I talked to several of the students' mothers, and they said they had been sorely tried just to get food on the table for two, three, four children while holding a job. They spoke of the difficulties of getting by, and said nothing when I mentioned childhood reading. How could they find time, I wondered, to get to the library and take out books for their kids? A lot of the parents may not have read much themselves, and if you don't enjoy reading, why would you read to your children? The complicated tangles and sorrows in these teenagers' lives, making them strong and weak at the same time, spiraled back a generation or two.

The troubles for Hillhouse kids started when they were born in poor families, but Hillhouse had let them down, too. There were dozens of computers at the school, but computer education was intermittent, and the absence of a college office was a grievous failure. The school constantly spoke of prepping the students for college, but no one actually helped them get *in*. When I asked the principal, Kermit Carolina, about it, he mournfully said that the New Haven School District would not support such an office. In eleventh-grade English classes, some of the teachers would devote time to writing a college-application essay, some would not. Most of the students' parents could not assist them. They were on their own.

Yet there was a promise of aid. Yale University and the Community Foundation for Greater New Haven had joined in developing a program called New Haven Promise. If you graduated from public school in New Haven with a 3.0 grade point average and were accepted at a public college or university in Connecticut, Promise would pay your tuition, up to $10,000 a year. When I asked students about college plans, they were generally vague, but several mentioned the program. The Yale initiative, it turned out, both helped them and trapped them in town. Many went to local colleges and universities—Southern Connecticut University, the University of New Haven, or Gateway Community College, a two-year school with vocational training. But if current patterns held, about 70 percent would leave four-year colleges by the end of sophomore year. They might run out of money, or find the work too difficult, the college life too hard to adjust to. Miss Zelenski knew all this, but she said that a larger issue than college entrance was at stake. They needed literature to live.

The curriculum Miss Zelenski was using in tenth grade was designed to be aligned with the Common Core standards, a set of guidelines commissioned in 2009 by the National Governors Association—a set of *standards*, not an imposed federal curriculum as some conservatives believe, or pretend to believe. The states and the local school districts make up the specific curriculum. The Common Core standards call for a partial shift from fiction to "informational" readings, but the absence of general knowledge—concepts, forces, words—frustrated the students when Miss Zelenski, late in the fall, asked them to read essays and journalism. Many had trouble following what they were reading. If they came to words they didn't know, they quickly gave up. "Miss, why are we reading this?" said Anika when Miss Zelenski gave them an essay from Stephen Kern's *The Culture of Time and Space* about technological change in the premodern period, the 1890s. ("Too hard, too hard," Miss Zelenski moaned later.) She dropped the essay and discussed technology in the 1890s without any further reference to it. The unit was devoted to learning how to cull and synthesize information; the students had to answer a set of questions about the social and personal effects of technology, but it was a challenge to get them to write more than a few sentences.

When Miss Zelenski asked her class to write ten sentences about their relation to nature, Philip Todd said, "We live in a city," and others talked about indoor entertainment, video games, hanging out with friends in houses and apartments. "I hate nature because it interferes with sports," said Denzel. "How many of you have gone hiking in the woods?" Miss Zelenski asked. "How many have gone camping?" No more than a few in each case. The nature exercise was a nonstarter. They did better, however, responding to excerpts from such controversial texts as Amy Chua's boastful *Battle Hymn of the Tiger Mother*, which inflamed everyone with its view of punitive parenting.

And they were highly engaged in constructing public service announcements. They had watched a bunch of professionally created PSAs, for the environment and the like. They critiqued them: How effective were they as argument? To whom did they appeal? Miss Zelenski presented the "rhetorical triangle," derived from Aristotle, which consisted of the three modes that successful argument depended on: ethos (credibility, sense of right and wrong); pathos (emotion); logos (fact and logic). They split into groups and used their cell phones to download and create their own PSAs. The work was good, but Miss Zelenski went through their subject choices with a sigh. "Drugs, pregnancy, violence. Is there any more to say about these things?"

"This is what we know!" shouted Anika. She had lived with her father for a while after her parents separated, but her father had frightened her, and she moved back in with her mother and two young brothers. I visited them in their apartment about a mile from the school. Anika's family life was complicated. A few years earlier, her older brother, now in jail, robbed a jewelry store with a pellet gun, an event recorded and broadcast on local TV news. "It was . . . difficult to go to school the next day," she told me at home. When she lived with her father, her grades had declined, but, sitting next to her mother, she said, "I'm free now." She was doing better in school. An all-around athlete (volleyball, softball, track), she sang in a gospel choir and composed songs in a notebook, then recorded them in a home studio at the house of her sister's boyfriend. She wanted to be a doctor. English was less important to her than biology, but she liked Jessica Zelenski.

"I'm not good at the scaffolding," Miss Zelenski said to me several times, by which she meant the lesson plans created by the New Haven School

District. "I'm good at reading with them, pulling together information and responses." Jessica Zelenski shaped the air with her hands when she talked, acting out all the voices in a story, screwing up her face in woe, disgust, happiness. "In high school, I was erratic. I would read a book in one sitting and then not write what I was supposed to." She flung one arm across her chest, as if dismissing her high school years. "I flunked chemistry and biology, took summer classes and went to Southern"— Southern Connecticut State University, in New Haven. "I transferred to Northeastern in Boston because I liked Boston, finished up my BA there, and then got an MA in American Studies at the University of Massachusetts Boston." In her twenties, she worked for a year with teenagers who were "transitioning" out of the juvenile justice system into school and jobs; and then, for two years, with autistic kids and disabled adults. She began teaching at Hillhouse when she was thirty.

All through high school and college, she had waitressed. "I learned more of what I needed for teaching as a cocktail waitress than any other way," she said, laughing. "Some of the kids here are tough. Maybe ten percent, no more. They won't go to class, they won't listen. I've had kids who drank and smoked weed in school, kids who were descended from gang leaders in New Haven and threw their weight around. There was this boy, Frank, who popped a Molly"—Ecstasy—"right in front of me." Indignation was not part of Jessica Zelesnki's classroom arsenal— anger, maybe, but not indignation. Yet now she glared, furious and disbelieving. "He said, 'If you say anything, I'll slap the shit out of you.' Later he apologized and came back to class. He performed well, he's brilliant, but at the time I thought, 'If I'm gonna be this stressed, I've got to be getting more than $60,000.'"

I asked Miss Zelenski if she did sentence work with her students— grammar, syntax, paragraphing, and the rest of the skills that Mr. Leon at Beacon spent so much time developing with his class. She shrugged. "I want them to read as much as they can and get sentences and words in their head so they begin using them well. If they aren't reading, their language won't get any better." An eleventh-grade English teacher at

Hillhouse told me the same thing—the students' grammar would improve only if they read a lot. Reading a lot, you begin to think in sentences, or parts of sentences, and your writing begins to cohere.

As the year went on, into the winter and the new year, fiction was clearly what mattered most to Miss Zelenski's students. By January, they were reading at home, and some were eager to talk in class. When they filed in, they still milled around for a few minutes, but no one slept or slumped, and when Miss Zelenski raised her voice, they stopped talking and looked her way. They were beginning to be curious about the assigned texts—Kurt Vonnegut's 1961 story "Harrison Bergeron," for instance, still another dystopian satire. Vonnegut begins as follows:

> The year was 2081, and everybody was finally equal. They weren't only equal before God and the law. They were equal every which way. Nobody was smarter than anybody else. Nobody was better-looking than anybody else. Nobody was quicker or stronger than anybody else. All this equality was due to the 211th, 212th· and 213th Amendments to the Constitution, and to the unceasing vigilance of agents of the United States Handicapper General.

The Handicapper General was a woman named Diana Moon Clappers, who shotgunned anyone who was born—or tried to be—better than anyone else. She ruled over a society in which athletes and dancers were hobbled, beautiful people masked, intelligent men and women outfitted with a government-made radio that emitted screeching noises into their ears. Vonnegut was parodying the kind of fake democratic dogma that encourages leveling off and mediocrity, and the students were shocked. His mischievous outrage hit the Hillhouse students harder than it did Beacon students.

"If you're below average in something," Philip Todd asked, "do they bring you up?" which was something Vonnegut didn't address. "Why do they do that to the ballerinas?" The ballerinas were laden with sash-weights and bags of buckshot, and they wore masks. Philip seemed genuinely pained. The hero of the story was a seven-foot-tall boy, Harrison Bergeron, who was as powerful as Thor. The students were fascinated by the way he was burdened and diminished—his eyebrows shaved off, for instance, to make him ugly. "I guess I'd be handicapped," said Philip, who was well over six feet and handsome. He was joking, but the students were, in their own lives, diminished by poverty, by social disorder and isolation. All year long, they demanded fairness, and the more ambitious wanted to excel; they didn't want to be hampered.

In March, they read Hemingway's story "The Short Happy Life of Francis Macomber." The class loved the bitter and perverse tale; they were openly enthusiastic, and Miss Zelenski asked them to write a short paper in which they assumed, in a court hearing, the voice of one or another of the characters—Robert Wilson, the laconic and fearless British hunter and safari guide; Francis Macomber, a rich American sportsman who, in front of his wife, loses his courage in a lion hunt, and then finds it the next day when facing a huge, wounded buffalo; and Margaret Macomber, who has sex with Wilson in the night and shoots and kills her husband in a seeming accident an instant after he recovers his nerve. It was a story about treachery, a woman's contempt for a man who lacks conventional manliness and then turns predatory the minute he attains it. "Short Happy Life" was many other things—perhaps the greatest representation of wealthy whites at play in the late colonial period; a magnificent portrait of natural terrain and wild animals; a contrast between British cool professionalism and American emotionalism (Macomber can't stop oversharing).

One male student, speaking as Wilson, said bluntly, "Margaret shot her husband on purpose. She and I know it." And a girl spoke as Wilson, too: "She knew he was going to divorce her, so she killed him. . . . I taunted her about it because I knew she did it on purpose." Miss Zelenski read parts of a paper written by a boy in another of her tenth-grade classes. The paper began: "I Margaret Macomber plead innocent. . . . I felt like that buffalo was going to gore Francis. You think I was just going to sit there and watch him die?" But then, in midplea, she switches course: "Okay, okay! Yes, I shot him. I was afraid that Francis was going to leave me and I couldn't stand the thought."

At which point, Raymond stood up and shouted, "No, she's a bitch! She would never confess!"

Debate broke out in class over Margaret's motives. They were excited, but, soon after Raymond's outburst, class was over. Miss Zelenski said, "This was the best I've ever seen you. No one seemed to be squandering his time." She asked them to hand in what they had done, and she said they could come back to the room later in the day, get their paper, and finish it at home. Deadlines were less important to her than responsiveness.

In the spring, Miss Zelenski showed the students the movie *Shakespeare in Love* as a way of easing her class into reading a few of the sonnets. They enjoyed it, but when Miss Zelenski asked them their impression of Shakespeare the character, one girl said, "He old. Why isn't the movie in black-and-white?" This stunned me for a second, but I realized that she knew that there had been black-and-white movies, and black-and-white meant the past to her, and she was making connections, however strange.

After that, the class got off to a rocky start. Philip Todd read aloud Sonnet 18, "Shall I compare thee to a summer's day," in a delicate falsetto voice, and Miss Zelenski fired him as a reader. Many of the students had difficulty with the language, which was unfamiliar and odd for them, as it is for almost all American teenagers—the use of the second-person "thou," for instance, as a way of conveying intimacy. "Was this written in English?" one boy joked. Teaching Shakespeare was required by the New Haven School District, and Miss Zelenski had considered asking the students to read *The Tempest* but had chosen the sonnets instead. She asked them to go through the sonnet line by line, "translating" it into standard English. They guessed what the words of the poem might mean, and shouted out silly things. Again and again, Miss Zelenski said, "I need you to stop guessing. I know it's the first time with this language, but you're not thinking." After a few more derisive responses, she blew up. "Don't be proud of yourselves. Are you saying 'I'm not smart enough? I'm not trying?' I want you to make some sense of the difficult language, not to withdraw from it." And with that, as Anika, Malia, Denzel, Philip, Raymond, and the others looked on in disbelief, she stormed out.

She came back a few minutes later and apologized. Then she added, "I love you, but I want you to learn even more than I love you." Later, after class, she said to me, "They accept a lot from me because I've gone to bat for them. I fight for them within the school. You're asking them to open up. You have to give them something of yourself." Including anger, I thought. "If you're austere or utterly professional, the students don't like it. A few years ago, there was a white teacher who stood at the door and shook hands with everyone. The students hated her. If you want to be a total professional in manner, you won't be a success here."

After her apology to the class, they moved to Sonnet 130, "My mistress's eyes are nothing like the sun." The poem, an ambiguous (putting it mildly) homage, offers a series of extremely ungallant comparisons: "If snow be white, why then her breasts are dun; / If hairs be wires, black wires grow on her head." Miss Zelenski and the class went through the ritual of translation again, and after a while the students said that there was something false, something sarcastic in the poem. They were angered by it. "It's a lie," said Anika. The girls said that flattery or put-downs of any kind from a boy were always manipulative. But this was mocking flattery. The final couplet—"And yet, by heaven, I think my love as rare / As any she belied with false compare"—seems to refute and redeem everything that came earlier. The sonnet was possibly Shakespeare's mischievous parody of an Elizabethan love lyric.

If Sonnet 130 made the students angry, Sonnet 73, "That time of year thou may'st in me behold," which chronicled the poet's diminishing passion for a lover, moved them in its evocation of decline. They pulled apart the metaphors that linked the poet's diminishing vitality to the bareness of fall, the waning of light into darkness at day's end. I realized Miss Zelenski had picked the trio as a kind of progression—from Shakespeare's adoration of a mistress to ironic praise of an ugly woman to grief over a passion consumed by its own strength. At the beginning of classes about the sonnets, the students were sarcastic and bored, but, stung by Miss Zelenski, they stopped guessing and gave literal but accurate readings, and I thought: They've read some Shakespeare in tenth grade, which is more than Sean Leon's students can say. They weren't done with Shakespeare, and Shakespeare wasn't done with them.

The work on Shakespeare, however scrappy, helped them when, a few days later, Miss Zelenski asked the students to tackle the opening chapter of *Moby Dick*. She read them the verses from Genesis about Ishmael, the cast-out and wanderer: "He shall be a wild ass of a man, with his hand against everyone, and everyone's hand against him; and he shall live at odds with all his kin." They read lines from the opening paragraph to each other, over and over again.

> Whenever I find myself growing grim about the mouth; whenever it is a damp, drizzly November in my soul; whenever I find myself involuntarily pausing before coffin warehouses, and bringing up the rear of every funeral I meet; and especially whenever my hypos get such an upper hand of me, that it requires a strong moral principle to prevent me from deliberately stepping into the street, and methodically knocking people's hats off—then, I account it high time to get to sea as soon as I can.

Having read and discussed Shakespeare's "That time of year thou may'st in me behold / When yellow leaves, or none, or few, do hang / Upon those boughs which shake against the cold," they had no trouble unpacking "a damp, drizzly November in my soul." They were getting comfortable with metaphor. The actual meaning of the opening paragraph was a little harder. Anika saw a depressed man who was going to commit suicide on a ship. Denzel, who had a few days earlier moved to the window and gazed outside longingly—"There's a man riding around on a motorcycle when he should be working"—now nailed it: "He's going to sea to calm his ass down."

By late April, the students were waiting to speak, and were raising their hands. When they had to move around, for some classroom exercise—ten minutes of slow-motion chaos in September—they just got up and moved around. Miss Zelenski shouted a little less, and she had quiet personal conferences with students who wanted to talk something over. A number of kids who had chosen Elie Weisel in the Read Around now added Ishmael Beah's book as well—word had gotten around that it was exciting. Reports were coming in from the front lines on the chosen books. "Several times students have approached me privately," Miss Zelenski said to me. "Or even yelled out 'I really like this book!' They sounded surprised and even a little angry, as if I and everyone around them have been withholding the good stuff from them. Malia finished *A Thousand Splendid Suns*. She said she read for hours on the weekend because the book got so good she couldn't put it down." I knew this was true because Malia excitedly told me the plot of Khaled Hosseini's novel, with its abusive husband and father. When I suggested that her fascination with the book may have had something to do with her feelings about her own father, who was no more than "around" when she was a child, she gazed at me silently.

A little club had formed. Some of the students—the boys mostly—would skip lunch and hang out in the room. As Miss Zelenski chewed her way through a salad, Philip Todd and an athletic boy named Franklin Roberts, both over six feet, shyly poked around her desk, asking her questions, trading opinions on movies and on people in the school, going over their problems, likes and dislikes; they would tell her about their grades in other courses, and she would urge them to step up. Denzel grazed in the room, throwing in sweet and sour comments. In April, another of his friends had been shot and killed in gang warfare on the street. Again, he shrugged and averted his eyes when I asked him about it.

Jessica Zelenski said that something like the skipped-lunch club had been happening for years. "We can navigate within the adult world within the school, and we provide a resource that their parents may not. We love them, but we're not their mothers. So they speak to us about sensitive issues, and we can be supportive without making them feel insecure or calling them 'gay' as girls their own age might. We're educated aunties for the boys. The girls tend to have better support systems and be more social, so they outgrow us."

On May 9, when Anika shouted "I want to read!" followed by deep silence, the students achieved a kind of communion. They read voluntarily—that was the victory—but they also enjoyed reading in company, the lines of sympathy going out to one another, enfolding the characters and dilemmas they read about. They enjoyed not just the books but the act of reading together. You couldn't have asked more of any book club.

In class, they discussed the themes the books held in common. The talk was ragged but intense. Miss Zelenski led a discussion of the moral ambiguities and perversities surrounding disaster—the difference between bystanders and participants, for instance, in Elie Wiesel's *Night*. Miss Zelenski read them "The Good Samaritan" parable, from Luke, and they worked out the differences between witnesses and actual helpers. As I had noticed before, students came into tenth grade with an ardent and detailed belief in *fairness*. But the complications of morality—what they had understood when thinking about Mayella—extended the concept of fairness into a changed understanding of life. They puzzled over the fascinating pages of Ishmael Beah's book in which he and other boy warriors had been liberated from army service by UNICEF and put into a gentle rehab facility—only to wind up hating it. The boys missed the companionship of war, the adrenaline high of live fire. It was impossible to understand such things with a simple division into right and wrong.

That literature was marked by moral complexity was central to what Miss Zelenski wanted to convey to them. "Learning that there are two ideas when in the past there was only one," as she put it to me. She warned the students against reading literature purely as political advocacy. "A writer completely devoted to social injustice politicizes literature and weakens it," she said. She read the students some passages from Upton Sinclair's muckraking novel of 1906, *The Jungle*, with its disgusting scenes of the Chicago meatpacking trade—rats and men falling into the vats and getting ground up in Borax-speckled sausage meat. The students were appalled by the details. Some didn't want to hear more, but others shouted, "Keep reading!" Miss Zelensi told them that conditions were now much better for workers than in 1906, when there were no hospitals for immigrant labor. "Hospitals are for white people," a voice from the side said. "These people *are* white," Miss Zelenski replied. "They're just poor."

By this time the students were roused to the world's troubles in a way that they weren't (as far as I could see) at the beginning of the year. In class, they vented about the kidnapped schoolgirls in Nigeria; they were contemptuous of the baby-selling Irish nuns in Steven Frears's movie *Philomena*, which Miss Zelenski showed them. But she wanted more than outrage, and I remembered, from early in the year, her telling the class that she didn't welcome easy moralizing from them.

As part of their commitment on Read Around day, the students had to give presentations on social issues suggested by the books they chose. They had to teach the class, ask questions, keep order. Philip Todd the movie lover gave a presentation on media violence; it was clearly his obsession. "Why are we drawn to these stories of tragedy and atrocity?"

he mused, looming in his gentle way over the front of the classroom. He was saddened and puzzled. "Though all my life I've been really interested in violence. Why are we interested in serial killers?"

"Philip, you gotta take control," Miss Zelenski coached. "Don't ask. Tell them."

He didn't speak about books, but his obsession with movies was the strongest passion in the room. He showed them a bunch of movie clips—the frightening opening scene of *Inglourious Basterds*, scenes with Tom Cruise as a mangled vet in *Born on the Fourth of July*, and so on. He had put a number of questions on the board: "What was the injustice shown in this film? Was the clip effective? If not, how could it be more effective? Why do you believe that this happened? Would this happen in America now?" These were feature films, not documentaries or newspaper columns, and part of me rebelled at the thought of kids' judging them merely as persuasion. But the class was alive, and Philip showed more and more savage clips, until Miss Zelenski and the female students protested it was too much. "You're as much attracted to violence as repelled by it," I said to him, which was often the film critic's dilemma. He nodded and smiled and shook my hand.

Philip lived in a borderline neighborhood in Hamden, just north of New Haven, in a small, darkened house with three dens outfitted with screens, including a man cave in the basement with DVDs and Stephen King books stacked on a shelf. He downloaded films from various file-sharing outfits—all sorts of movies, including independent films and foreign films. Mostly, he watched them alone. Only one friend—a boy in the class—shared his tastes. Philip's gentle manner and movie-nerdish habits had led some of the other boys in the class to call him "Uncle Tom" and "Oreo." They accused him of "acting white" and turning into "an elitist." He told me this without bitterness.

His parents had been divorced since he was ten, and he lived with his mom. His father had odd jobs. "He drives a truck," and did "other things." He wanted to go to a place with a good film program, like

Wesleyan or NYU, but he didn't see how his mother could afford either school. Yale's tuition program would subsidize his attendance at a Connecticut public college or university, but none of the local schools had a decent film program. He was a great movie nut—as obsessed as any I had met—and I wondered if he would have the strength or the luck to make his way out of his cave into the professional world of moviemaking.

I wasn't able to see the other presentations, but Miss Zelenski gave me the highlights: "Malia and friends did oppression of women. It was more of a report, but it was very well done and engaging. Denzel joined a group in the fourth-period class and they did child labor in the U.S. and then elsewhere. They did their presentation Friday morning. Exams were over and students didn't even need to be in classes, yet these boys packed the house! They recruited students from all three of my classes and all of them actively participated. Denzel even had a great hook—asking us to hold up our iPhones and Nikes, then launching into readings and videos on child labor in China and elsewhere in Asia, where these things are made. Anika and friends, using video clips, had a very detailed lesson about child soldiers in Africa."

At the end of the year, it may not have been literature that the students were expounding, but they had learned to master one of literature's gifts, the ability to get out of themselves and to enter other people's lives. Azar Nafisi's book had bombed in Miss Zelenski's class, but her humanist principles of literary study had taken hold. Miss Zelenski had been working toward this end all year. She wanted the students to flourish. They needed information, they needed morally informed instruction in the ways of the world, they needed to be able to "read" themselves and other people. She didn't protect them or condescend to them by giving them easy assignments. Like Sean Leon with his largely middle-class students, Jessica Zelenski combined literature and ethical inquiry. The students were entering a forbidding economy; they needed to be armed with the intellectual and moral strengths that would enable them to

succeed—or at least survive. I don't think anyone could know whether
literature would be important to these students in the next year of school
or later in life. But they had made a beginning step into literature's pleasures and complications. Literature could be part of their strength.

The performance of Hillhouse students in standardized tests had never
been stellar, and it had been dropping in recent years. How were these
kids going to get through college? There had been rumblings of drastic
action all year at the school, and in the spring of 2014 the ax fell. The
Board of Education in New Haven and school superintendent Garth
Harries (who had worked for Mayor Bloomberg's administration in New
York) announced plans to break Hillhouse into three "academies," each
with a separate principal. Perceived as a failure, the school was being
broken up. Miss Zelenski was gloomy about the coming disruption—yet
another in the school's recent history of such changes. She stood at her
desk and raised her voice even though we were alone in her classroom.
"How dare you experiment with the real-life human kids? It's not fair."

Just after the long school year was over, however, Miss Zelenski and
her students got an unexpected lift. Ishmael Beah turned up in town.
The author of *A Long Way Gone* was giving a talk in New Haven, on
June 29, at Southern Connecticut State University, and Miss Zelenski
bought tickets for those who wanted to go.

The group spent time with Beah after his talk. "The kids were so nervous and starstruck," Miss Zelenski said. "I had to bite my fist to keep
quiet and not try to 'teach' them when he was talking." The girl who
had said "This doesn't interest me," and then read the book, came with
a friend. Anika, who became a fan of the book and did a presentation
on boy soldiers, was astonished by Beah's physical presence. "You've been
through so much," as she put it to me later, "and you are here today giving this talk!" Beah was precise, restrained, eloquent; he had a charming, boyish smile. He had survived hell; he had come *through*, and had

told his story in a book that reached people all over the world. The students took pictures of themselves with him—jubilant group shots and also individual shots of the smiling American-African author with Raymond and then with Denzel. The students had met a real writer whose book many of them had chosen to read. A writer and his book; they read it, and they met the author, and they were close to happiness.

CHAPTER THIRTEEN

MAMARONECK, SPRING: TENTH-GRADE ENGLISH

- ❧ Taste
- ❧ *Ta Dum*
- ❧ Mary Beth Jordan Risks Ridicule
- ❧ Soliloquy

If Mamaroneck began by dumbing down part of its curriculum, the goal in the end was to elevate it. As I came to understand in the spring, when I returned to the school, there were actually two kinds of reading ladders. There was the progression of increasing difficulty and quality, the kid who went from *I Hope They Serve Beer in Hell* to David Sedaris's stories and the girl I heard about who climbed a triumphal ladder, from *Rebecca* to *Jane Eyre* to *Pride and Prejudice*. But as well as pushing some of her kids upward, Miss Groninger asked her students, at the end of the year, to make a hierarchy among the work they had read, putting the hardest books on the top and the easiest on the bottom. That was a kind of laddering, too, and they had to explain their choices: What made one book harder than another? Was the hardest the best? Was difficulty a guarantee of quality? They wrote an essay—more fun for them, they agreed, than a standard book report—explaining their choices. They justified their taste. Suddenly they *had* taste in books, a new idea for many.

"They now know when it's an easy beach read," Annie Ward said to me, "and when it's something else," and I realized she was talking about cultivating what used to be called bookishness—a way of living, at least partly, *in* books. Bookish people never stopped exchanging opinions; they matched their friends or topped them, and for many reading a book was completed by talking it over. Today, much of book culture, as everyone in the publishing industry knew, flourished in reading groups, in informal gatherings of all sorts, in online chat rooms, on Goodreads and other websites. The English Department at Mamaroneck wanted to achieve in ninth- and tenth-grade students something like the morale of a good book club—what Miss Clain called "a social culture of reading." (That was also what Miss Zelenski's students achieved when they read together in silence.) What began as personal choice became an exercise of judgment. Nothing could be more obvious or natural, but how many teenagers talked that way about books? Nerdiness in teens usually bent toward technology. Mamaroneck was pushing against the habitual self-deprecating tone of so many American kids when they talked about anything in culture beyond pop. The school wagered that enjoyment of reading could conquer diffidence and self-parody.

But a question remained, at least for me. What was the intellectual relation between the core texts and the personal reading books—between, say, a Shakespeare play and Laura Hillenbrand's *Unbroken*, which I knew some of the students were reading? Yes, students might see the difference in quality between them, but apart from that how did core reading and personal reading connect with each other? Did they connect at all? Was there any cross-fertilization? Or did they just exist side by side? I wasn't sure how to answer these questions until I stepped into Mary Beth Jordan's tenth-grade classroom.

She was working through *Macbeth* with her students. They all read the play; then they acted out portions of it, plowing through act 5 in a large performing space. Lady Macbeth has died, and one boy, Sean, with a surprisingly baritonal voice, read Macbeth's last great soliloquy: "Life's but a walking shadow, a poor player / That struts and frets his hour upon the stage / And then is heard no more. It is a tale / Told by an idiot, full of sound and fury / Signifying nothing." He read with weighted emphasis; he had teen gravitas, maybe even a future as an actor. A moment later, wielding a plastic gray sword, he fought Macduff, played by a student named Evelyn. "I have no words," said Evelyn. "My voice is in my sword: thou bloodier villain / Than terms can give thee out!" Unfortunately, Evelyn had left her sword in the regular classroom, so the two passed a single weapon back and forth and took swipes at each other. When Sean fell in combat, Evelyn with a triumphant look dragged him off the stage by his feet. No matter how you do it, *Macbeth* never fails. I missed those words in Sean Leon's class.

The performance was actually preparation for the main event. I had been there a few days earlier, when the class discussed at length Shakespeare's use of soliloquies. "You're seeing the character raw," said Miss Jordan. "They're thinking on the spot." On big sheets of paper she printed out a number of famous soliloquies—passages from *Macbeth*, *Romeo and Juliet*, and *Hamlet* (which they would read the following year). Mary Beth Jordan had a class of twenty-eight students—twelve boys and sixteen girls. Three of the students were Hispanic, one Asian. They were mostly an eager and attentive group, except for a few boys in a stupor of half-sleep and a girl studying her fingernails (purple) as she giggled with a friend. Miss Jordan and the class did the usual analysis of poetic and dramatic devices—alliteration, imagery, metaphor, foreshadowing, and so on. But she also said she wanted to try out something special.

She read a soliloquy from act 1, scene 3 of *Macbeth*: "This supernatural soliciting / Cannot be ill, cannot be good." Shakespeare wrote it in iambic pentameter, the standard metric line: an unstressed syllable followed by a stressed syllable. As she read, a student, on cue, pounded out the rhythm on a tiny African drum: *ta Dum ta Dum ta Dum . . .* The effect was almost comical, but the class stayed with it. In order to do what Miss Jordan wanted next, they needed some feeling for the rhythm of the poetry.

She asked them to write a soliloquy of their own—not about murderous ambition or sound and fury or anything else having to do with the play. She said, "Write it in the voice of the leading character of the book you're reading." *The book you're reading*—the independent reading choice. "Write it in iambic pentameter and in blank verse, without rhymes, but don't worry too much about consistency. Follow the rules and break the rules." Shakespeare broke rules, too, she told them.

It was a tough assignment, and the class stirred uneasily. But Miss Jordan had a way of spurring them on. She took a crack at it herself. She was reading Malcolm Gladwell's recent book, *David and Goliath: Underdogs, Misfits, and the Art of Battling Giants*, and now she read aloud her own soliloquy based on her personal reading—not in David's voice but in Goliath's. She may have been new at this, having been teaching only two years, but she was game, and she told me later what was already apparent: if you want students to put themselves out for you, you have to do the same for them, even at the risk of ridicule. Taking a deep breath, Mary Beth Jordan's Goliath speaks:

> *The valley of Elah, it's ours today!*
> *As sycamore-sweet sands reveal our foe:*
> *Frail Isra'lites crouch, perched upon the hill*
> *So down and 'cross the plain I go—Why me?*
> *Though triple-armed I am, and towering, too,*
> *Too weary this old Philistine to brawl.*

That was the beginning. It ended with Goliath saying, "I did not see the slinger's shot . . . I am . . . *down!*" As she read the soliloquy, the accompanist hit the drum. *Ta Dum ta Dum ta Dum . . .*

There were some smiles but certainly no mockery. They had work to do, and, the following week, they came in with dramatic poetry in hand.

The iambs sounded. A student who had been reading Robert Louis Stevenson's *Strange Case of Dr. Jekyll and Mr. Hyde* soliloquized about Jekyll's transformation into his loathèd alter ego:

> *This hideous hag Hyde lives on in me;*
> *Jekyll the fate of innocent Duncan.*
> *The dark has started to overcome me,*
> *Indecency has grasped my empty soul.*
> *I have succumbed to primitive desires,*
> *Oh such great guilt to feel no guilt at all!*

They weren't supposed to mention anything from *Macbeth*, and this student had mentioned Duncan. Well, Miss Jordan had told them that breaking the rules was all right. "Oh such great guilt to feel no guilt at all!" was good, almost a Shakespearean paradox by way of Freud. Others wrote soliloquies based on Cormac McCarthy's grim shocker, *The Road* ("Why did the valley of death consume thee?"); on *Lord of the Rings*; on J. D. Salinger's *Franny and Zooey*. And then there was a soliloquy based on Hillenbrand's *Unbroken*, the tale of the American Olympic racer and Japanese prison-camp survivor Louis Zamperini, who competed in the Berlin Summer Games of 1936:

> *Running, the endless sprint against life's wind.*
> *From alleyways and city streets I come*
> *Running under the stars' light and the moon*
> *Over the sea a crowd awaits, Berlin*
> *The flame of wonder now afire, it's time*
> *To run a course before the world.*

That was quite good, too. Not all students did as well, but the assignment was a success: they had combined personal reading with Shakespearean prosody without dishonoring either. Some books, they knew, were better than others, but there were strengths in merely good books as well as in a masterpiece, and those qualities could be made to play upon each other. Part of the connection between classic texts and contemporary books was that they intermingled in the reader's mind, working on each other—usually in mysterious ways, this time in explicit ways. It was just a school assignment, no more than that, but Mamaroneck's goal, as always, was to create pleasure by connecting one book to another, the endless chain that made a reading life and that made a man and a woman, too.

CHAPTER FOURTEEN

BEACON, APRIL AND MAY: DOSTOEVSKY

- ➢ *Notes from Underground*
- ➢ Would He Talk to Us?
- ➢ If You Think, Must You Be Inert?
- ➢ Liberalism and Perversity
- ➢ Russian Musical Chairs

We had arrived at the climactic point—though not the end—of Sean Leon's reading list. The class was launching into Dostoevsky's *Notes from Underground,* a little book that would provide the fiercest of Mr. Leon's numerous trials of his students. It was not just the most difficult text, it was the most questionable as an assignment for tenth-graders—the most demanding, emotionally and intellectually. All along, pushing the students beyond their current understanding was part of his plan. I wondered if he was now pushing them too far.

"Dostoevsky is considered by many," he said, "to be the single greatest writer in Western civilization."

Sitting at the side of the room, I felt a twinge of misery. "What happened to Shakespeare?" I asked again. Mamaroneck's tenth-graders read Shakespeare, and so did Hillhouse students—at least a little. Most

Beacon students would read *Romeo and Juliet* and *Hamlet* and *Macbeth* and other plays as well as sonnets before they graduated. Mr. Leon wanted modern, or premodern, works only, though Shakespeare, as many have said, is both an Elizabethan and a contemporary—*our* contemporary. By this time, I was missing Shakespeare's presence in Mr. Leon's classroom as one might miss an old friend or lover.

Whatever Dostoevsky's standing in the Babe Ruth/Ty Cobb/Barry Bonds greatest-ever ratings game, many critics and intellectual historians have said this much: Dostoevsky's short novel *Notes from Underground*, published in 1864, marks the beginning of the modernist movement in literature. (Other candidates: Diderot's *Rameau's Nephew*, written in the 1760s but not widely read until the 1820s, and Flaubert's *Madame Bovary*, from 1856.) Certainly, a great many works, energies, moods have descended from *Notes*—some of Nietzsche's writings; perhaps Freud's theories of the unconscious and the neuroses (though Shakespeare was Freud's greatest teacher); perhaps Franz Kafka's "Metamorphosis"; definitely Ralph Ellison's *Invisible Man*, Saul Bellow's *Herzog*, and Philip Roth's *Portnoy's Complaint*; perhaps Martin Scorsese's *Taxi Driver* and some of Woody Allen's work, and much else. The book's influence was all around the students, haunting popular culture as much as high culture. There was Richard Hell, punk progenitor, definitely a guy with an intellectual bent, an Underground Man living in the East Village. And certainly the late Lou Reed of the Velvet Underground and many solo albums—Lou Reed, blowtorching his way through conventional sentiment. Larry David is a kind of perpendicular, elderly, well-paid Underground Man. Vile, funny, acidulous, self-conscious—we know this Underground Man, he is one of us.

"The text requires, even at eight in the morning, that we sort it out and take risks," Mr. Leon said. For the second time I marveled at the hour. I couldn't believe I was even there. At that moment, I couldn't handle *The Sound of Music*.

Mr. Leon spoke of Dostoevsky's nameless hero, a spiteful modern Hamlet living a barely respectable life in mid-nineteenth-century

St. Petersburg. "He's sarcastic, he holds ideas opposed to what we believe. Sometimes, he says things we *want* to say. Is he confused or contradictory?" Marina, always at the ready, said, "He's both sadistic and self-loathing, so his miserable circumstances make him happy." Yes, but his circumstances also make him *un*happy. His attitude toward everything is two-sided, even three-sided. He's always perverse:

> I, for instance, am horribly sensitive. I'm suspicious and easily offended, like a dwarf or a hunchback. But I believe there have been moments when I'd have liked to have my face slapped. I say this in all seriousness— I'd have derived pleasure from this, too. Naturally it would have been the pleasure of despair. But then, it is in despair that we find the most acute pleasure, especially when we are aware of the hopelessness of the situation. And when one's face is slapped—why, one is bound to be crushed by one's awareness of the pulp into which one has been ground. But the main point is that, whichever way you look at it, I was always guilty in the first place, and what is most vexing is that I am guilty without guilt, by virtue of the laws of nature. Thus, to start with, I'm guilty of being more intelligent than all those around me.

The Underground Man is unable, putting it mildly, to act in a straightforward way. He thinks that only fools act from instinct, without hesitation, and that intellectuals like himself must *necessarily* be inert. A self-regarding, miserable, witty man, then, who carries on as if he had a poisoned tooth in his head. Azar Nafisi wrote that literature "unsettled" us, forced us to "question what we took for granted." *Notes from Underground* pushed that notion to the outer limit and beyond. Dostoevsky blasts our concept of what a human being is capable of.

Dostoevsky worked on the book in 1863 and published it the following year in *Epoch*, the magazine edited by his brother Mikhail. From our vantage point, *Notes from Underground* feels like an anticipation of the colossus that came next, *Crime and Punishment* (1866). The two fictions share a solitary, restless, irritable hero and a background of St. Petersburg's dingy apartments and feverish streets and dives—an atmosphere of careless improvidence, neglect, even sordidness. It's the modern city in extremis. The text itself purports to be the writings of a retired midlevel government bureaucrat. A family bequest has allowed him to quit his job. Now forty, he lives in a "mousehole" with a servant he despises. He is writing a book—the book that we are reading. He addresses an imaginary audience he refers to as "you" or "ladies and gentlemen"— presumably a representative group of educated, westernized Russians. He alternately insults them and abases himself before them. They are people besotted, he believes, with Western ideas of progress and rationality—the ideologies of utilitarianism, socialism, evolution, the greatest good for the greatest number, and so on. After introducing himself, he rails, in his stop-and-start way, against the Crystal Palace, a vast London exhibition hall constructed in 1851 out of cast iron and glass, a structure considered for years the summa of industrial capitalism and modern technology. He reviles what the building represents—scientific rationality and any sort of predictive, mathematical model of human behavior.

"There was a belief in the nineteenth century," Mr. Leon said, "that everything could be charted, sorted—even us. But Dostoevsky said, 'You cannot sort me out.'" On the contrary, human beings are unfathomable, unknowable. Their behavior can't be determined, since they may act against self-interest, at least as other people define it.

> And what makes you so cocksure, so positive that only the normal and the positive, that is, only what promotes man's welfare, is to his advantage? Can't reason also be wrong about what's an advantage? Why can't man like things other than his well-being? Maybe he likes suffering just as much. Maybe suffering is just as much to his advantage as well-being. . . . And, personally, I even feel that it's shameful to like just well-being by itself. Right or wrong, it's very pleasant to break something from time to time.

"He suffers from excessive consciousness," Mr. Leon said, a remark I enjoyed a great deal, since in the past his aim had always been to increase and extend the consciousness of his students. The overlord Mustapha Mond in *Brave New World* had tried to destroy consciousness (except for his own), and the students, with Mr. Leon's encouragement, had seen him as an oppressor. But now, in *Notes from Underground*, consciousness was raised to "excess," and Mr. Leon said it caused suffering. He looked at his class, which seemed a little overwhelmed by these contraries. After some preliminaries, he asked a general question: "Would he be interested in talking to *us*?"

A slight rumble—it's a strange question—which ended when Marco said, "I don't think so."

"Meaning that you represent the ordinary man?"

"Yes, I don't know how to say what I want to say," he said with an anxious smile. But this was not always true. Marco had got better and better about saying what he wanted to say. Vanessa, however, was sure the underground man would be interested in talking to the class, since, she said, he always addresses *people*. But then Marina, often Vanessa's antagonist, said, "He would want to share *his* opinions. He wouldn't be interested in ours."

"Does anyone feel alienated, as he does?" Mr. Leon asked, and Nino answered, "I overthink things, so I can't take revenge." Revenge for *what?*, I thought. "I hate testing; I hate the SATs," he told me with great disgust when we talked again later. But no grounds for revenge existed there. He loved playing baseball, he loved music, he did magic tricks, he had many interests. He had never read much in the past, as he admitted to me, but he was recently reading more. He had developed a thing about Vonnegut. A loyal reader, with an obsession! And he had read recently *The Meaning of Everything*, Simon Winchester's account of how the Oxford English Dictionary was invented, and Mark Haddon's *The Curious Incident of the Dog in the Night-Time*. So allow him his mysterious talk of revenge. Readers are complicated people.

Other students nodded in agreement with his remark, and then stern

Adam, building on Nino, raised his hand and said, "I am easily offended, so if I carry out vengeance I feel awful that I have taken the easy way out," a remark almost worthy of Dostoevsky in its complexity. He was a Brooklynite, from the prosperous neighborhood of Carroll Gardens; his father ran day-care centers, his mother was an English teacher. He got into Brooklyn Tech, one of the elite math-and-science schools in the city, but, he told me, "I excel in math and science, so I thought I should study English and history," and decided to go to Beacon. In the beginning of the year, he had been shy about speaking in class. "I wasn't so sure of the ideas. And Marina talks so long, she made my point for me, and I put my hand down. Now, I like to be the center of the argument." Adam was tough on other people—tough on himself, too. Of all the students, he had the most imperious sense of his own value. "The books in English are important for seeing in what direction I'm going," he said.

We were under way, but still, the question of whether the malicious hero would talk to the students—and also whether they would want to talk to *him*—remained hanging, and I wondered why Mr. Leon had asked it. Jared Bennett, speaking a little more often now than at the beginning of the year, said, "Sometimes cynical viewpoints are good. You could have a really honest conversation. You could bend toward him. I could show my anger to him." So talking to the Underground Man would be liberating. And Vanessa added, "It would be like talking to my own head. Saying all the thoughts that I suppress."

Wait a second. Was this the plangent but guarded Vanessa we had heard all year long? Her remark was both an accurate description of what the Underground Man does—talking to his own head—and the work of a newly confident girl. Vanessa had stopped weeping; she was showing healthy signs of ego. As she spoke, someone outside the classroom—someone in the hall—shrieked, and Mr. Leon said, "Awesome!" which made the class laugh. But I was sure the word was meant for his student.

"Remember," Mr. Leon said, "that this is not Dostoevsky speaking but a voice he has created." That was the important point for literary study. A *voice*. As Mr. Leon emphasized, *Notes* is a canny work of literature, not a tract. Dostoevsky, he told them, probably agreed with many of his creation's opinions, but that was not the point, at least not for us, as readers. The Underground Man was the central and dominant character in a fiction. And what that voice indicated to us was that opinions were inseparable from personal strengths and weaknesses, even from personal pathology. That we are inevitably subjective is a tenet of modernism that runs right through literature and philosophy. We are also entirely inconsistent. The Underground Man taunts his listeners, apologizes, criticizes himself, then gets aggressive, then collapses again. He knows very well that he's trapped in the three-by-five cell of his own character.

"I commend you for fighting your way through this very difficult text," Mr. Leon said when we took the book up again.

"Fighting your way through" was the right phrase. Keeping them on track, Mr. Leon sent them assignments on the school's website—so many pages by next Monday, so many more by Thursday. They were reading it slowly, which is the only way you *can* read it. In class, they struggled with the pronunciation of Russian names, including Dostoevsky's name. It was their first brush with the infinite complications and satisfactions of Russian literature. Again, I thought of how young they were. I had read *Notes* four times in my life, and I couldn't possibly contain all of it in my head—Dostoevsky kept bursting the boundaries of his own created space, spilling over into wildness and whim. The book was unstable, the product of a disorderly genius. Laying it on fifteen-year-olds was outrageous.

But that was the point for Mr. Leon—hadn't I known that all year long? Hawthorne's "The Minister's Black Veil," Vonnegut's *Slaughterhouse-Five*? Too hard for tenth-graders. The students were balanced between childhood and adulthood; Mr. Leon was trying to push them into adulthood, and they resisted him and welcomed him at the same time. Fighting their way through, they had many questions and issues, but discussion settled on one issue alone: Did remarkable acumen like the Underground Man's lead only to inertia? "He's so intelligent," Mr. Leon said, "that he can't *be* anything, *do* anything." And he read aloud the beginning of part 1, chapter 6:

> If only my doing nothing were due to laziness! How I'd respect myself then! Yes, respect, because then I would know that I could be lazy at least, that I had at least one definite feature in me, something positive, something I could be sure of. To the question, "Who is he?" people would answer, "A lazy man." It would be wonderful to hear that. It would imply that I could be clearly characterized, that there was something to be said about me. "A lazy man." Why, it's a calling, a vocation, a career, ladies and gentlemen! Don't laugh, it's the truth. I'd be a member of the foremost club in the land, and my full-time occupation would be constant respect for myself.

Which was a splendid Russian joke that the students did not find particularly funny. A number of them said that the Underground Man's intelligence was limited. "Intellect is less about knowing things than understanding other people's opinions," said Maud. "He's unable to see what other people think," she said, which was a contemporary liberal-humanistic definition of intelligence, and about as far from Dostoevsky's temperament as you could get. Justin, looking up, added, "His intelligence has rid him of his sense of optimism," which was obviously true of Justin himself. When would Justin's gloom lift? "I don't have much respect for my family," he had said in a confessional moment. "And they don't have much respect for *me*." I looked at him with the eyes of an anxious uncle: he was out of shape, physically disconsolate, extremely bright; he needed friends, though it would take brave people to put up with his dark days.

Some of the students thought the Underground Man was spiteful because he had been sent off by relatives to a boarding school. "He never enjoyed family love, anyone's love," Maud said, and Nino added, "He's very sad, there's no one on his side, no one understands his real intentions." They were trying to rationalize the Underground Man's outlandish, cruel, and self-annihilating behavior; they redefined and penned up his chaos into their morally coherent notion of how things worked. Jane, the girl whom Mr. Leon had shocked when we were reading "The Minister's Black Veil" by saying "The whole time, it's been about *you*"—Jane now said, "The underground man is representative of a lot of different minorities. His rebellion can be generalized to what minorities face, and what we face as individuals. We don't fit in."

Liberals! Give them a ratty, arrogant, and malicious man, a worm outfitted with peacock feathers, and they will turn him into a persecuted minority. The Underground Man was a minority of one, persecuted by no one but himself. *Notes from Underground* was an antiliberal text in every sense of the word. The hero inveighs against rational planning, social improvement, "the greatest good for the greatest number." Human beings were perverse, he believed, they didn't want to be bettered. As for the students, they were kind, but they weren't quite zeroing in on Dostoevsky's creation. Mr. Leon didn't criticize their youth and goodness because, of course, he couldn't, even if he had wanted to. *Notes from Underground* was *his* assignment, and they were doing their best to hang in there.

"Why would Dostoevsky create a character in this way?" he asked, and Marina, who was wearing a leopard-skin shawl that day, aimed and fired—and hit herself. "We go through a process," she said, "and then we destroy ourselves. It's powerful to realize that you're being told something about yourself you don't want to hear. We mess things up for ourselves. I do think subconsciously as much as consciously. You struggle to make your life work, but you mess things up."

Which left the room silent. She was struggling for clarity in her own life, and no one wanted to intrude. A month earlier, in front of the class, she had said, "I'm leaving next year. I hate this school. I tried to kill myself. I've had people in this school tell me to kill myself, saying 'You bitch.' Everyone says I have an abrasive personality. But I have a reason for how I am."

She was a brilliant girl, self-willed, hard to argue with. For her, what mattered was that she was able to assert herself and take action, even if the action hurt her. She was a Dostoevskian creature right before us, a sister of the Underground Man. (Soon after this class, I pleaded with her to stay at Beacon as her best chance to get into a good college, but I got nowhere. You could say I was administered a Dostoevskian lesson in perverse will.) After a bit, Mr. Leon said, "This idea that you don't necessarily act in your own best interests struck me very hard when I first read Dostoevsky. Each man may choose to do things against his own interests because it preserves his personality."

At that moment, the question I had been asking for the entire year— who does he look like?—suddenly had an answer. The thin beard, the pronounced forehead, the penetrating stare. He was from Derry by way of Louisiana, he had some Italian in him, but his appearance was Russian—or at least my idea of what educated Russians looked like in nineteenth-century novels. He could have been Ivan and Alyosha Kara- mazov joined together, skeptic and saint. I remembered now that he had asked, in the Vonnegut classes, how God could allow the Dresden bomb- ing, which was not so different from Ivan's question to Alyosha: How could God allow the torture of children? He was forty, and his appear- ance had been shaped by his obsessions, which shaped soul and body. Yet Mr. Leon was as far from the Underground Man in temperament as could be imagined—relentless, definitely, but kindly and enormously useful to others. Practical, too. He could have been a plant manager, a banker, an executive, perhaps a wealthy and powerful man. He had the energy and concentration that produce success. Driving to his point, he asked, "Is Dostoevsky saying it's better to go through life as a man who doesn't think—the man of action? Or is it better to go through life as an Underground Man who thinks and thinks, and gets nothing done?"

Nino perked up, smiled, and said, "The man of action doesn't get anything done, either. Russia was a backward society, well behind other countries." A nifty remark, and Nino read a passage in which Dosto-evsky generalized about the Russian character. They were all doing that now, picking passages as a way of answering Mr. Leon's questions, read-ing the words aloud, often passionately—the mumbling was gone—and then saying whatever it was they wanted to say. Hasan, for instance, who had told me earlier that he read very little—Hasan was the media king, at 238 hours a week—spoke in detail about dueling and how it fit into Russian traditions. He probably picked that up somewhere on the Inter-net, which was fine. Hasan the nonreader was becoming a student. As they spoke, they went beyond impressions and settled on key moments—something Mr. Leon had trained them to do, starting with *Brave New World*. He would usually knit these remarks together, but this time, as once or twice before, he let his leading question go unanswered for the moment, and allowed the conversation to run free, a trainer watching his horses gallop across a field.

The students were actually sympathetic to the Underground Man, which was no surprise, for here was a man who, however unpleas-antly, had struck off chains, an individual not just *in* society but against it. Clare, ready with empathy, said, "He exposes himself, all his flaws, and it's okay to acknowledge them." They understood—though they didn't put it this way—that he was a hero of authenticity, that great uncomfort-able modern virtue, whose dictates, stringent as those of any religion, required that you acknowledge what's inside yourself, evil as well as good. This ferocious little book had a driving force: some of the students—Adam, Marina, Clare—were becoming more complicated people as they read it. Sitting there, I admired them a great deal.

For some weeks, Mr. Leon had been moving the students toward their final essays. At the end of the year, they would not take an exam. Instead, in Beacon style, they would put together the complicated project known as a PBA, the Performance Based Assessment. In tenth-grade English, the

PBA work was part essay (a compare-and-contrast paper), part creative effort of some sort (poem, video, collage, etc.), and part defense of the essay in a one-on-one session with Mr. Leon lasting fifteen minutes—private sessions, and outside my view.

"The first five to seven minutes you're presenting," he said. "It's a defense. I must see that you're prepared. Bring in note cards. Jump right into your thesis. I've read it, so take me through the thought process. Why you chose those two texts, why those arguments, what makes it a compelling argument." The students were very quiet. "The last eight minutes belong to me. I'm going to ask you questions, challenge your arguments. My job is not to expose you, but to give you a chance to flex your intellectual muscle. If you're nervous, that's normal. Take your time to work it out. Breathe, don't rush through your points. You can use your last minute, you can talk about your creative project."

They came in with the creative projects now—all based on one of the books, or perhaps two joined together. They made paintings or pencil drawings or collages; they created dioramas and placed them inside wooden or glass boxes, and pinned their poems to one side of the scene. Marisa made a large, fractured globe—a utopian society with people caught in wheels and gears on one side, and Big Brother, a plastic figure, watching from the other. Adam the moralist made a line drawing of a man reading the *Wall Street Journal* and lamenting his devotion to moneymaking (a journey theme); Jared Bennett created a collage in which the Underground Man had mirrored eyes like Orwellian disks; he wrote a poem in the Underground Man's voice that attacked those "oblivious that their lives are structured like a teacher's lesson plan," which could be considered a hostile way of summing up English 10G (Mr. Leon, however, beamed). Jane, alert to victims, made a painting of people behind bars. The poems were mainly devoted to existential themes—creation, paths, knowledge, imprisonment, escape.

Having given us rant, the Underground Man then offers experience. He recounts some strange incidents from his early life—his jealousies and grievances, his rage over an officer who treats him rudely in a tavern, and then a detailed account of a mortifying dinner party thrown by some old school classmates. The scene, in burlesque-catastrophic mode, is one of Dostoevsky's greatest. Our hero invites himself to the gathering, drinks a great deal, and insults everyone. He's accurate in his judgment of the four young men, a handsome doltish officer and three government bureaucrats like himself. They are just as unpleasant and shallow as he says. Still, he longs for their respect, and the more they refuse it, the more completely he wants it.

"He only likes the *idea* of a friend," Nino commented. "He's jealous and envious and worries about how other people see him." The students were making remarks of a psychological acuity that they couldn't have come close to at the beginning of the year. Lauren, whose name no one could remember on opening day, observed shrewdly: "When you criticize other people that hard, you desire to have what they have," which put abandonment in the light of Freudian psychology. And melancholy Justin, who, as he had revealed before, knew something about defending himself, added, "He's learned to hate people before they hate him." The more the year went on, the more I'd come to appreciate Justin's sullen clarity. Intellectual pride, I was sure, would carry him through his troubles.

At the end of the disastrous dinner party, the Underground Man winds up visiting a brothel and sleeping with a young prostitute, Liza, a smart, decent girl in desperate straits. At last, someone he can easily dominate! He lectures her, describing in punishing detail her likely end in illness and poverty, and then he holds forth absurdly on the joys of family life. He leaves his address, and suddenly there's some suspense: Will she come to him at home, make a man out of him? He needs her just as much as she needs him.

Mr. Leon had asked them to talk about certain issues raised by the text, with the appropriate quoted passages, and make presentations to the class. Adam led off as presenter. He was a slender, straight, unsmiling—

he had become a good Sean Leon student, as serious as an oak sapling. He did some exposition of the dinner party scene, read a passage, and asked what the Underground Man was talking about in his contempt for the other young men. The students mentioned his nonconformity and the hatred of materialism—the disgust he feels for the others, who were seeking promotions and status. Was the Underground Man a hero or not? Yes, he was a hero of a certain kind. Adam went on: "You need to go through desire, which leads to suffering, to get to consciousness." He was answering Mr. Leon's earlier question about too much conscious- ness leading to inertia. The Underground Man was not inert, Adam insisted. He suffered. Pushing a little further, Adam said, "We all need reasoning and the desire for things we can't have. Buddhists may want to remove desire to get to consciousness, but Siddhartha needs to *suffer* to get to consciousness, and so does the Underground Man," which neatly tied the two books together. Adam had certainly come close to Mr. Leon's point of view, which was a mixture of Christian soulfulness and existen- tialism. Consciousness was the goal, even in "excess." In class 10G, the Underground Man, however rancorous and self-defeating, had become a hero. The students found him fascinating.

Liza does come to the Underground Man's apartment, but it's hope- less. She wants to be with him, but he can't possibly give anything of himself. In the brothel, he had roused her hopes and then humiliated her, and now his uncontrollable contrariness—and his longing for misery—kills any possibility of love between them. But Mr. Leon, to my surprise, didn't consider the ending as terribly unhappy. He read the last page of the book, after Liza leaves. The Underground Man, having set all this down, claims a kind of moral victory:

All I did was carry to the limit what you haven't dared to push even halfway—taking your cowardice for reasonableness, thus making your- self feel better. So I may turn out to be more *alive* than you in the end. Come on, have another look at it. Why, today, we don't even know where real life is, and what it is, or what it's called! Left alone without literature [and here Mr. Leon added, "without the Internet and movies"], we immediately become entangled and lost—we don't know what to join, what to keep up with; what to love, what to hate; what to respect, what to despise!

Mr. Leon said, "Earlier he was pointing a finger at himself. Now he's talking directly to you, pointing a finger directly at *us*. If he were sitting in front of you, what would you say to him? Okay, write on this subject for fifteen minutes. Read him, *be* him. Write what he means and what it says about you." He was working toward something. After they had written down their thoughts, he said, "You're talking to the Underground Man. Someone is going to play him, and someone else is going to talk to him."

Now it was clear. He was going to bring the Underground Man into the room.

Nobody but me seemed particularly surprised. Quickly, they formed the tables into an inner rectangle, as they had for the Plath poetry session months ago. The inside of the rectangle would be a theater. Mr. Leon then appointed Clare—sweet-tempered Clare!—as the Underground Man, and Marina as the questioner, what he called "the Interlocutor." Earlier, he had asked them what the hero looked like. (Like *you*, I now thought to myself.) Well, here was the Underground Man, a lovely girl of fifteen or sixteen with a soft smile, and his questioner—the class's representative—a fiery girl of Puerto Rican and Dutch descent with decidedly strong opinions.

Marina (Interlocutor): "Why do you have so little faith in humanity? You attribute your poison to ourselves, your sickness to us."

Clare (Underground Man): "I like to watch, not to be part of society."

Marina (I): "If you had gotten to know humans—"

Clare (UM): "I've gotten to know humans."

Marina (I): "How can you say you weren't formed by society?"

Clare (UM): "I've chosen to seclude myself."

With a wave from Mr. Leon, Hasan jumped in as the Interlocutor. And Sean Leon jumped in as the second Underground Man. So now there were two of them in each role.

Hasan (I): "We choose our society and how to look at things. You're living through books."

Mr. Leon looked at Marina, the Interlocutor, and asked, "Are you living your life as you want or as society wants you to live?"

Marina (I): "Everyone is subject to society."

Mr. Leon (UM): "Living through a book is better. Is there any principle you would sacrifice yourself for?"

Marina (I): "I know who I am. I wouldn't sacrifice myself."

Jane now joined the above-ground party, Marco the underground party. Three on each side.

Marco (UM): "You say you don't hate your life. But you do."

Jane (I): "I live as I want. I do what I want."

Vanessa threw herself in as an additional underground person, which made the roster Underground Man four, Interlocutor three. The students played the roles, risking something of themselves every time they spoke. But *Vanessa* underground?

Vanessa (UM): "Why are you going to college? Are you doing it to earn a living—or because everyone wants you to?"

Hold on a second. We seem to have left fiction and mid-nineteenth-century St. Petersburg and have come close to Beacon students and their current concerns. But they were into it, and Mr. Leon showed no sign of calling it to a halt.

Jane (I): "I want to continue my education, to learn more."

Vanessa (UM): "Aren't you just reading a book in college, taking notes? You're not talking to a professor over coffee. You're fooling yourself."

Jane (I): "I'm not just taking notes. That's not what college is."

Mr. Leon (UM): "Poor Jane! You're really deceiving yourself, giving pat answers. You're saying what everyone else is saying about college. You call me sad, pathetic, but at least I'm leading my life as I want."

Marina (I): "Who are you to say society is wrong?"

Mr. Leon (UM): "I am pointing out that you are not living your life. I'm staying true to myself in a world that says I should be doing something else, chasing after money."

Marina (I): "I repeat, who are you to say that society is wrong?"

Mr. Leon (UM): "What are *you* going to do in two years?"

Marina (I): "Whatever the *fuck* I want to do!"

Everyone gaped at the two of them. Marina was livid, but Mr. Leon smiled at her. This was what he wanted. Excitement in the room, many students laughing nervously—what else was there to do but laugh? Seeing where this was going, Mr. Leon straightened things out a little. "It's intense. I'm just playing a role. I don't mean any of this," he said to everyone. The students drew a deep breath. He didn't mean it, but, at some level, he *did* mean it. He was challenging their college-marriage-bourgeois life track again. More and more students jumped in, on one side or another—Nino as the Underground Man and Vanessa, changing sides, as an Interlocutor. Also Jose, a very quiet boy, as another Interlocutor. The class had become a kind of mad Russian musical chairs. Students not on one side or the other were revving themselves up, going up and down on their toes, holding their sides or digging their hands through their hair.

Mr. Leon (UM): "Parents say they know what's best for you, but it's really best for them. They can say their daughter is going to Brown."

Vanessa (I): "College is breaking *away* from parents."

Mr. Leon (UM): "Why go to college? Do it for free on the streets."

Maud (I): "She [meaning Marina] needs to make a living to survive."

Mr. Leon (UM): "Survival in society means abandoning individuality."

Jose (I): "You just have poison in your head. You're a parasite."

Maud (I): "You were abandoned. Raised by relatives."

Mr. Leon (UM): "Yes, for the better! I'm going to continue leading my life. How much time do you spend in front of computers or on the cell phone? How much time do you spend with the people you love? They're going to die."

Jose (I): "I'm gonna spend time with them, and see them in heaven if I get there."

Suddenly, it was over. Time had run out. The exercise was over, and the Dostoevsky classes were over, too. It was a good place to end. Religion at last had its say in Jose's remark, and I remembered that in the class on *Slaughterhouse-Five*, Marco and Jose had not wanted to live in a godless universe in which there was no apparent moral order. Jose delivered us, for a second, out of a skeptical world.

As the tension broke, more laughter—a couple of students were almost doubled over—and some tears, too. They were all buzzing, even the students who didn't participate. Some fell into each other's arms; others surrounded Mr. Leon, ragging at him, and he came back at them, looking each one full in the face. The room was embroiled, and I couldn't hear what he was saying. He had brought his students into the state he wanted them in—living in the moment and defining themselves and saying what they lived for—and if the students didn't understand every facet of Dostoevsky's amazing little book (who *did*?), they had got the irritable spirit of it into their souls, which was a different but potent kind of understanding. The sweet, simple talk of an Underground Man deprived of love was now over.

Jared Bennett had been right: you could show your anger to the Underground Man; he would bring things out in *you*. And Vanessa was right, too: talking to him would be like talking to your own head. They had become the Underground Man or his antagonist, which was a way of forcing them to become stronger versions of themselves. But was it right that they asked each other personal questions? Yes, a population indifferent to literature needs to be shaken to life. They were excited by a novel, and not an easy novel, either, an antagonistic, often contradictory, emotionally demanding book. They assumed a role and defended themselves; they became, so to speak, modern people through one of modernism's most demanding and perverse masterpieces, and they would be less afraid in the future. If this wasn't character building, I didn't know what was.

Their next class was approaching, and they quickly left. The next class in *what*? Chemistry? Spanish? After all this tumult, how could they just leave and study irregular verbs: *tengo . . . tendré . . . tenía . . . tuve . . . tendría*? But they had to; they were students. Only Mr. Leon, who had another group coming in soon, remained in room 332. I looked over at him, and he seemed a little grave. But he must have been pleased. The tearful Vanessa had pulled herself together; so had Jose and Jane; Hasan had become a student; Adam was putting the year's reading together in his head. They had taken the emboldening step that could lead to the eager acceptance of intellectual effort.

Exhausted, I staggered down Beacon's narrow stairs. As always, shouting teenagers brushed past me, but their uproar felt like music and their tiny careless shoves like tender embraces.

BEACON, MAY AND JUNE:
SARTRE AND BECKETT

In 1944, when France was under German occupation, the philosopher Jean-Paul Sartre wrote a play with a famous line: "Hell is other people" (*L'enfer, c'est les autres*). Sartre's words, some will think, might be a good tag for a year as an adult spent in school, a year in English class. As I edged into my spot at the side of the room, I made that joke to myself, but then I took it back. I was surrounded by what I prized. On all sides of me lay speckled black-and-white school notebooks—the students' journals, which were filled with scrawls and block letters and graceful

script, sometimes in different color inks as well as pencil, the words spilling and surging into the margins. Mr. Leon had been reading, grading,
and handing back the journals all year long; the journals would go back
to the students again at the end of the class. Behind me on the table,
against the wall, lay piles of paperback books. Their pink and yellow and
purple Post-its had been removed (Sean Leon read those, too). The books
were out of action for the moment, lying ready, like stacked weapons, for
use in the future. *Brave New World, Siddhartha*, printed-out essays by
Orwell and Sartre, *Notes from Underground, The Alchemist*, and some
books assigned in other classes, Art Spiegel's *Maus*, Mark Haddon's *Curious Incident of the Dog in the Night-Time*, a pile of *Macbeth* paperbacks—
in all, the assorted materials (with a few extras) of a long year's reading,
a long year's work. The students worked hard; their teacher worked
hard. School! It can—sometimes—be the most worthy place in America.

No Exit is the best known of the theater works composed by the busy
Sartre, who wrote novels, criticism, and political tracts, as well as pen-
etrable and impenetrable philosophical texts. Mr. Leon assigned the
play—and also "Existentialism Is a Humanism," an essay Sartre wrote
in 1946—as a way of dramatizing the basic assumptions and ethics of
existentialism. In many ways, it was an odd assignment for tenth-graders,
but it was central to Mr. Leon's define-yourself mantra. And both Sartre
works, it turned out, were a warm-up for the last assignment of the
year, Samuel Beckett's *Waiting for Godot*, easily the most celebrated (and
mysterious) avant-garde theater work of the twentieth century. I wasn't
sure how the students were going to cope with it.

Mr. Leon asked them what they thought Sartre meant by the statement "Existence precedes essence"—the starting point of existentialism,
the foundational belief of a philosophy partly devoted to the destruction
of foundational beliefs. Luisa, cautious in the past, began by saying, "I
thought he was kinda like saying, you were there before you know what
you are gonna do," which, of course, was right, and Mr. Leon congratulated her on taking a risk. Ike allowed that "human life was like a painting in which the painter started slapping paint on and didn't know

where he was going," which was also right, and clever. A blank canvas but an active painter. The existentialists told us we were alone, there was no God, nothing out there that could be called metaphysical truth or natural law. We had to make ourselves up, create rules for ourselves through action. Mr. Leon, summing up Sartre's outlook, said, "What you dream of doing doesn't matter. What you could have done is nothing. What you *do* in life defines you—not what you felt about it, not what you thought about it." I recalled what he had said to Luisa earlier, that no one had ever lived her life before, and no one would live it after. "That's a wild idea," he said.

Luisa stared at him then, and she was staring now. They all were. "When you think of all the factors that come into play for you to be you," he said, "it's wildly inconceivable to think that you exist. Parents meeting, having sex, the sperm fighting to get to the goal . . . Then, with every step, you're taking a step on your own, and you're nothing more than the sum of your actions."

He was at it again, challenging them in their very being, and I experienced some of the foot-dragging hesitations I felt when we discussed *Siddhartha* and journeys, and he had said, "Be there." Everything he said that was true for them had to be true for me, too, and sitting where I was, surrounded by student journals, I wasn't sure that it *was* true. Sartre, writing at a time of French weakness, was pushing his readers toward self-defining acts—political activity, citizenly activity, morally heroic activity. Fine, but many of us would still say that we are also dreams, hopes, plans, evaded and rejected thoughts—slight wishes that don't go anywhere yet make up a good part of consciousness. What was the name of the famous Delmore Schwartz story? "In Dreams Begin Responsibilities." It was a line that Yeats had seized from somewhere and used as an epigraph for one of his collections. Yes, fantasies, anticipations, and desires that were not the mere vacancy of action but rather the quarry for action, not mere time-wasting but the source of renewal—all of that was part of identity, too.

For the second time, Mr. Leon's vitalist sentiments sparked a mild protest. Clare asked, "Isn't thinking an action?"—and before anyone could answer Vanessa said, "Thinking doesn't always transcend into action, and for me it's important that I think and feel. It's very important to think alone and not do," and I remembered her extraordinary remark to me earlier, "Being so obsessed with actions can lead to decay in yourself." As was clear in the Dostoevsky classes, Vanessa had become bolder, and she now spoke defiantly, as if issuing the truth of her being. She made a case for the contemplative view of life. She didn't want to be judged entirely by what she did.

But some of the others were very much bent on judgment. Marina insisted on personal responsibility. "You have the right to your own mind," she said. "We're not living in *1984*. There's no thought police, and you are free as long as you don't act out in an aggressive way." Adam, following up, insisted that we had the right, always, to judge other people, and hold them to account. Marina the self-willed; Adam the judge. Some of them, working from Sartre's existentialism, insisted on a no-excuses morality: you are free, your choices are your life, and you are completely responsible for choice and its consequences. They had heard Sean Leon (all year long) as well as Jean-Paul Sartre.

There was a nice irony here. Sartre was an atheist and a leftist, even an apologist for Soviet and Maoist tyranny. In his personal life, he was at times a scoundrel. Yet here were American teenagers enunciating ethical demands, derived from his ideas, that would not be out of place in a Republican Party platform. Nino, summing up, put it this way: "Even if there's a God who gives laws, that doesn't absolve you of the job of looking after yourself. This would be a good thing for atheists to say rather than arguing against God all the time."

Amen to that. Nino the wise.

Mr. Leon listened to their fervent comments, and then, as the class ended, he returned to his emphasis on action, but in a new way—he was, I thought, answering Vanessa and Clare's feelings that his definition of action was too narrow. He didn't want to leave it there. As before, he spoke of his family. "My stepfather moved us when I was very young, and we settled in Louisiana. There was a couple next door." The Washingtons. He had mentioned them before. "The husband let his wife know he loved her, every day. They danced every day, something especially important to me, since my mother and stepfather's marriage turned to shite."

He paused for a minute; he was moved by thoughts of his family, his boyhood in Louisiana, the disintegrating marriage—the neighborhood, too, which he missed. It was his constant obsession, made more insistent by the illness of his brother. As he had said before, he was considering going home—leaving Beacon and taking a job in Louisiana, so he could be near his family.

"Coming from an Irish-Catholic family," he said now, "and seeing my cousin murdered by the Brits in Derry, and our people treated like shite, we brought this idea of *action* with us. But Mr. Washington and his wife . . . *his* action was that he loved his wife and children. That idea of action was enormously empowering to me."

Sartre's play *No Exit* is literally a portrait of hell. Three dislikable people—a man and two women, adulterous, dishonest, murderous—have been delivered by Judgment to a sealed room. Eternally damned, they confront not fires and burning pits but one another. The room is without mirrors; their eyes are lidless, and they cannot sleep. As Sartre later explained, the line uttered by one of the characters, "Hell is other people," did not mean, as so many assumed, that relations with other people were hellish. It meant that one's judgment of oneself was reflected through other's people's perceptions. If those perceptions were twisted, life with them was misery. Each of the three people desperately want to impress the others—vanity, deception, and seduction are central to their lives—and they cannot.

For my money, the play was flavorless and uninteresting, but the class was intrigued by the fiction of a hell without physical punishment, and they chewed it over at length, going through each of the characters' crimes and defenses. They understood the trial of confronting other people without interruption, without relief, without the possibility of redemption. At Mr. Leon's invitation, they took turns standing at the board and expounding the play, posing questions as Mr. Leon listened. Latisha, the African American girl who was often reticent, fluently went through the three characters.

But Mr. Leon pushed their involvement further. He wanted the students to face one another in his own arena. First he tried a loosening-up exercise. He asked John to stand in the opening in the middle of the desks, and he asked Leonardo to stand facing him. "Whatever John does," he said, to Leonardo, "you have to mirror it." As John blinked, stuck out his tongue, reached for his side, and stood on one leg, grave Leonardo blinked, stuck out his tongue, and so on, and my mind, movie-soaked, went back to the famous bit in the Marx Brothers' *Duck Soup* (1933) in which Groucho and Harpo, identically dressed in a white nightshirt and cap, confront each other in a doorway, each thinking he's looking into a mirror but not sure, each smirking, dancing, trying to catch the other in un-mirrorlike behavior. An old vaudeville skit, I thought, was as good a way as any of getting to the mysteries of identity. Earlier in the year, in the compare-and-contrast exercise, Mr. Leon had brought out the students' differences, and now he was bringing out their similarities. Other pairs took the place of John and Leonardo—Marco and Clare, Lauren and Tina, who initially covered her face, as always. All year long, she had been strong when the students broke into groups, but quiet in class. Suddenly, she stuck her tongue out at Lauren. We were back in kindergarten. Education had returned to play, which is where it begins.

"Throw your inhibitions aside!" said Mr. Leon. "Someone announce a theme."

"Carnival!" came a voice from the corner. It was John, who began singing and air-juggling, at which point Marco, frowning, barged into the opening at the center of the class. "Hate Mr. Leon!" he said and staggered and roared like a wounded buffalo. For at least a moment,

Marco the clown was back. After quiet was restored, they read passages of the play aloud, the boys taking the two women's parts, the girls playing the man, and the classroom theater was alive. It didn't feel at all like hell. But all of this was a way of easing the students into *Waiting for Godot*.

When you try to read it cold, you run into trouble. Beckett's play opens this way:

ESTRAGON: Nothing to be done.

VLADIMIR: I'm beginning to come round to that opinion. All my life I've tried to put it from me, saying Vladimir, be reasonable, you haven't tried everything. And I resumed the struggle. So there you are again.

ESTRAGON: Am I?

VLADIMIR: I'm glad to see you back. I thought you were gone forever.

ESTRAGON: Me too.

VLADIMIR: Together again at last! We'll have to celebrate this. But how? Get up till I embrace you.

ESTRAGON: Not now, not now.

Two forlorn, quarrelsome, middle-aged gentlemen in worn-out clothes and bowler hats inhabit a rubbishy and largely featureless landscape (there is a single tree). Like Chaplin's tramp, Vladimir and Estragon have fallen in society, yet they try to maintain the social graces and something like self-regard. They have been waiting together for years—forever—for the promised appearance of Godot. (Beckett was Irish, and great Irish actors pronounce the word "GOD-oh.") The appearance of "Mr. Godot" is frequently heralded, but he never shows. In his place, he sends a sweet young boy, who says "Yes" when Vladimir asks if Godot will come tomorrow. The boy also says that Godot does "nothing."

As you read, the non sequiturs and repetitions, the jokes and tirades at times resemble old vaudeville and music-hall skits. Vladimir puzzles over the gospels: two thieves were crucified with Jesus, he points out, but of four Evangelists only one speaks of a thief being saved.

VLADIMIR: One out of four. Of the other three two don't mention thieves at all and the third says that both of them abused him.

ESTRAGON: Who?

VLADIMIR: What?

ESTRAGON: What's all this about? Abused who?

VLADIMIR: The Saviour.

ESTRAGON: Why?

VLADIMIR: Because he wouldn't save them.

ESTRAGON: From hell?

VLADIMIR: Imbecile! From death.

"Who's on first?" as the old Abbott and Costello routine goes. "What's on second?" and so on. This colloquy about the gospels in *Godot* suggests that making sense of life, forming an *interpretation*, is a hopeless task: four accounts of the same thing, and they didn't agree. Everyone has a different account of reality, of history, of the sacred truths. There is no law or certainty. Dialogue like this is despairing and funny—the comic side of impotence—but tough to read, page after page.

In class, the conversation was tentative at first.

"I was confused about what Vladimir and Estragon's relationship was," said Clare. "They don't remember what they did the day before. What time period does it take place in?" Which was a perfectly good but unanswerable question, since the time period is all eternity.

After the students' hard-won success with Dostoevsky and the eminently graspable *No Exit*, it seemed almost perverse of Mr. Leon to confront them with a text so tough to get a handle on. I felt a twinge of annoyance. What was the point of stripping them of their new powers? But Mr. Leon had taught the play before, and he obviously knew it was a killer to face on the page. After the opening stumbles, he renewed the classroom theater. Everyone would have to read aloud. John Gruen, standing, was Vladimir, and Nino, sitting before him, was Estragon. Together they did the beginning of the play, and that bit of theater turned out to be something to hear. The two boys, cranky as a long-married couple, read with more animation and color than any of the students had in the monotonal days of fall. Rather than just course through the words, they honored the pauses, the silences (Beckett's text is full of stage directions and instructions for the actors), letting the words claim the air for a moment. The thing came alive.

Infuriating and ungraspable on the page, *Godot* can be magnificent on the stage with actors who get into the vaudeville rhythms, the music and silence of its despair. The best production I had ever seen was mounted in New York in 2006 by Dublin's Gate Theatre company, and starred two actors, Barry McGovern (Vladimir) and Johnny Murphy (Estragon), who had been doing it together for eighteen years, a suitable arrangement for this play. (The filmed version of this production can be found on YouTube and in a mysteriously obscure Japanese-produced DVD.) The restricted physical space of the stage, concentrating our attention on what is known—on time passing, moment by moment, right before us—produces an extraordinary interrogation of what is unknown. Now over sixty years old, *Waiting for Godot* is a sharpened spear launched into God's silence, a protest against mystery and meaninglessness, a statement of the human condition as extreme in its way as *King Lear*.

Beckett himself oversaw different productions in Europe, in America, in prisons, but he refused to say what the play meant. About the obvious God question, however, I think many people might agree to the following, with or without Beckett's approval: *Godot* is very far from an atheist's tract. Salvation, damnation, the crucifixion, the end of time—all of these sacred currents run through the play, which could be described as a Christian work set after the fall of man and in the hollows of God's silence. "Christ have mercy on us," says Vladimir near the end. Mercy asked for but never received.

"We know at the beginning that Estragon slept in a ditch the night before," Mr. Leon said at the beginning of the next class. "Is this all an allegory? What does that mean, 'allegory'? At the beginning of the play, Estragon struggles to get his boot off. What does that represent?"

Jane mustered a definition of allegory in which "everything is symbolic of something else."

"Yes," Mr. Leon said, "but some things in the play are just *there*."

That was the miracle of *Godot*. The metaphysical conundrums are held in place by things that were just themselves. "Boots must be taken off every day, I'm tired of telling you that," Vladimir says to Estragon. Taking off boots, finding a way to pee (Vladimir has prostate problems), eating a carrot, the sheer repetition of daily routine—these things, stupid and stubborn as they are, give us something to hold on to. The play is grounded in common existence. Jared Bennett, of few, well-chosen words, said, "The natural world is always there." Yes, and physical need is always there. That's one reason the play is so much loved. Clare ventured that the carrot Estragon chews on represented life, but the carrot is also just a carrot. The entire play is balanced between a limitless view of human loneliness and pressing everydayness; the two elements are inseparable.

Midway through the first act, Lucky and Pozzo show up—Lucky, a slave, attached by a rope to his plump and overbearing master, Pozzo, who both brutalizes him and desperately needs him. Pozzo's magisterial bullying of Lucky—"Up pig!"—became, for the students, a kind of paradigm of power and the attractions of power. "Pozzo the king, Lucky the court jester," said Marco, and Hasan noted that the play was about "how human beings dominate each other." Clare, returning to the society-as-oppressor theme that had obsessed the students all year long, noted that "we're like Lucky, the slaves of society."

But Vladimir and Estragon were alarmingly free in some ways. Rousseau's chains—one of Mr. Leon's motifs—had fallen off. But free to do what? No action could possibly matter. "Society" was represented by Pozzo's assumption of power, but otherwise was no more than an echo, barely heard by naked men stripped of social roles. They were alone; reaching Godot was their only ambition. I remembered, from the first week, another of Nafisi's humanist principles: "In all great works of fiction, regardless of the grim reality they present, there is an affirmation of life against the transience of life, an essential defiance." Yes, defiance was there, even as Vladimir and Estragon, baffled and needy, endured silence and held to carrots and boots—they affirmed existence, *mere* existence. But Nafisi's principles sounded a little proper compared to the ferocity of Dostoevsky's and Beckett's work.

In class, the play flowed on; the students interpreted it by reading it aloud. I thought back to Mary Whittemore's classes on *The Scarlet Letter*, when indifferent and scornful students overcame their resistance to the novel by reading stretches of it publicly. Reading aloud was the essential beginning of understanding and interpretation. The students got inside of a *voice*—the author's voice, or the compulsions of some character. Marina took on Vladimir, and Nino took on Estragon; Hasan did Pozzo's role, and Latisha Lucky's. Each pair would read, and then appoint the next pair. Pair by pair, quartet by quartet, they entered the classroom theater. "Step out of your comfort zone," Mr. Leon said to some of the usually silent, and they did. They would act out a scene or two, then stop and interpret as much as they could, flagging larger themes, sorting out the characters. "Vladimir is more the intellectual, religious figure, Estragon the physical," said John. Hasan noted that "the four together could be Godot," which was a decent hunch, though many others thought that the enslaved Lucky, who remains silent until he bursts out in an enormous, tumultuous speech that passes (rather obscenely) through all of creation— Lucky might be Godot after all, Godot the silent, then Godot the master of creation. It was a good guess at the unknowable. After their initial puzzlement, the students turned interpretation into a high-stakes game.

They had great freedom to speculate because *Godot* was notoriously open-ended, subject to innumerable readings.

Time itself was at the dramatic and philosophic heart of the play, and Mr. Leon asked the students to "write about time. Write one sentence about time, just one sentence that captures your view of time." They went up to the board and used black marker on the whiteboard:

> *Time lasts forever, while I last for a second.*
> *Time doesn't exist. It is a human concept.*
> *I don't understand time because it is so removed from humanity.*
> *Time is impossible to freeze even when I want it to.*
> *I will be satisfied when time runs out.*
> *There will never be this exact moment in time again.*

I had to pinch myself to be sure I was in tenth grade. That these sentences existed at all was a challenge to conventional pedagogy. If *Godot* made extraordinary demands, it offered certain payoffs in speculative wonder, in imaginative and philosophical excitement that, say, *Death of a Salesman* would not have offered.

"I had an epiphany," Mr. Leon said, when they were done writing. "A time bank. It would be great at the end of my life if I hadn't spent too much time doing diddly on the computer. How much time did I spend talking to people I love? I find myself checking my phone, looking at my watch. I can't stop it. But time is something we draw on. We choose how to spend it."

In the time bank, I guessed, you could deposit and withdraw time, exactly what you can't do in life. But in life you could still choose how to spend the time you had. All year long, in class, Sean Leon created the sense of *presence*, of time passing, time that cannot be reclaimed or recalled. What happens in class—and by extension in the rest of the students' lives—is soul time, precious and unrecoverable. One way or another, he had been mourning lost time since September, but his urgency and grief had additional weight in the context of this play in which time moves both inexorably forward (day leads to night) and stands absolutely still.

At fifteen or sixteen, the students didn't know where their lives were going. They were waiting, too, and Beckett's portrait of limbo teased and infuriated them. "They need a direct relationship with God," said Nino. "They can't just wait." He was alarmed. "They are waiting for death, not doing anything with their lives." Clare added, "Estragon and Vladimir feel uncomfortable because of what they could be doing while they are waiting for Godot," and Jordan, so often Clare's intellectual soul mate, added, "If you go through it waiting for God, you'll accomplish nothing." Justin, with considerable disgust, added, "They are waiting like sheep for someone to save them."

Mr. Leon's vitalist demands and their own nature as teenagers, it turned out, ruled their responses to the play. College was before them, the rest of life. *They* wouldn't wait for God's appearance or revelation, they had to move forward, they were frightened of standing still. They were Americans. Even those like Justin who understood the play shrugged off its despair. The conversation was often ragged (what conversation about *Godot* wasn't?), but the students felt the freedom to take chances, speculate, contradict themselves. The struggle with the play's meaning had become, for them, the struggle to wrest meaning out of their own lives.

During the classes on Sartre and Beckett, the students brought in the essay part of their PBA—at least a decent first draft. Mr. Leon paired them up and asked each to edit the other's paper and eventually hand it back to the writer.

Marina came bursting in late. She held a handwritten draft. "I had to go to the cops yesterday to identify a girl who jumped me on the train," she announced. "There were thirteen girls in a lineup." She settled in, exchanged her paper with her neighbor. Her mysterious experience on the subway never came up again.

It was Mr. Leon's last time around for grammar and punctuation lessons. With great emphasis he instructed the student editors to circle misspelled titles; he asked them to circle the passive voice, contractions, and uses of the verb "to be"—the list of formal requirements and prohibitions he had been pushing all year, the basic rules without which neither intellectual clarity nor soul will reach any reader. "I want it down below ten," Mr. Leon said, meaning ten circles. Even in the alarming metaphysical territory of *Waiting for Godot*, he was insisting on form, consistency, and order.

He turned on some country music—a nod to student skills at multitasking, perhaps. Or simply a way of making a party out of drudgery. After fifteen minutes or so, the student editors finished their work and announced the total of circled offenses—from three, at the minimum, up to thirty-one. Then he instructed everyone to take the papers home over the weekend, turn them over, and write down what they thought the writers of the paper should be focused on, what they thought the weaknesses of the essay were. "Don't just criticize the flaws. Make constructive suggestions. You get graded on your editing effort. If you get heavy editing, and do little in return, that's poor form. If someone writes on your paper something you disagree with, that's okay, bring it to me and we'll talk it over."

The mutual edit job was one of his ways of binding the students together, something he had been doing as early as the opening weeks of the year: the Plath-inspired poetry readings, however anonymous, were certainly a move toward mutual warmth, even attachment. On several occasions, with his encouragement, they talked openly about themselves, particularly about their families. He wanted them to trust one another. But more than that, he wanted them to *see* one another—to have an acute perception of each person in the class. On the first day his emphasis on each student's identity set the tone. Throughout the year, a lot of this noticing—Clare is *this*, Adam is *that*—came through classroom responses to Vonnegut or Dostoevsky or Beckett. In the final weeks, however, Mr. Leon must have felt that there was some unfinished business. The books had churned up personal responses, and the conversations had left some unresolved tensions, apparently a few grievances. After provoking them all year long, Mr. Leon wanted something like harmony and reassurance. A good teacher's sense of honor—Mr. Leon's, Miss Zelenski's, what the students would call fairness—was likely the most palpable kind of morality that many of them had experienced in their lives.

The classroom theater would continue. He commandeered the form of *No Exit*. He arranged a confrontational scene. One student sat in the middle of the opening, and the others offered their observations of that boy or girl. It turned out to be a benevolent exercise. Jordan sat, and received compliments on her character. "She is judgmental but straightforward," Marina said. "She will say what she thinks."

Marina herself came next. She had beautiful eyes, but she was overweight, with frizzed hair, not as comfortable in her body as in her mind. "I had trouble with people in the school," she said. "It became hard to come to school. I got a call from the hospital saying my sister is dead; I went to school the next day and had people shit on me. If anyone in this room has anything against me, let go of it. I'm letting go of it."

Several students said they appreciated her honesty and her guts and felt nothing bad about her. Maud praised her.

"Do you feel consumed by anger and hatred?' Mr. Leon asked.

"At times. I try to love. I wouldn't reset my life, because that's what made me what I am. Redoing my relation with Dad, no, it's not possible."

Mr. Leon looked at her. "Freakin' warrior," he said admiringly, and I remembered their face-off in the Dostoevsky class. (She told me later she had never had a teacher she liked as much as him.) But despite this reconciliation, at least with other people in the class, there was no keeping Marina in Beacon. I remembered her remarks about knowing yourself and still messing up your life. She was leaving. Her own freedom to act was more important to her than the rationality of what she was doing. She may have taken the Underground Man and existentialism too literally.

And then came Justin, whose unhappiness had poured helplessly into the room all year, washing through his intelligent remarks about *Notes from Underground* and other works. As Justin sat before them, Nino said, "He's unemotional, but emotional underneath, scared of judgment, self-conscious, not materialistic, very intelligent," and Jared Bennett, sparing of words as always, looked straight at Justin and said, "You're insightful but beautifully cynical," at which point Justin wept, and he said, "What Nino said is true . . . It's not a self-hatred thing . . ." He trailed off, and there was a general laying-on of hands (spiritually, not physically), and the class ended.

When they returned for their final class, they exchanged their edited essays. For ten minutes or so, the pairs confabbed. The room was buzzing with excitement. A few were expounding ideas, holding papers, pressing forward like participants in some sort of trade conference, explaining, defending, clarifying, all of it a preparation for their eventual sessions with their teacher.

On this last day, Mr. Leon, in his red tie and gray shirt, was both buoyant and somber. Beckett in his twenties left Ireland and settled in France, where he set up as a poet, critic, and novelist. He went back to Ireland occasionally, but he lived most of his adult life in exile. In a way, Sean Leon was in exile, too. In fact, doubly in exile—first in the United States after his birth in Ireland, and then in New York after his family boyhood in Louisiana. His troubles were clear enough: What was his true home, Beacon or Louisiana?

"It's hard to watch someone you love fade away," he said of his brother. "In photographs sent to me, to hear it on the phone. To come into work . . . I loved every period. Take a moment and look around the room.

This is an extraordinary group of individuals. Every period was a high. It made life that much more wonderful."

With mock solemnity, he gave them a set of instructions and homilies:

"You are not as you imagine."

"The real trouble is things that have never crossed your minds."

"Do one thing every day that scares you."

"Don't congratulate yourself too much or betray yourself. Your choices are half determined by chance."

"Friends come and go."

"Live in California, but leave before it makes you soft."

"Live in New York, but leave before it makes you hard."

He would see them again when they came in to defend their papers, but the year's classes were over.

They had done the following: They had thought about literature in a general way, citing Azar Nafisi's solidly humanist definitions of what literature could do. They had mulled over Rousseau's man-in-chains declaration, considering all year the problem of authority, the solitary individual, and society. They encountered the malicious nature of one such society in a Faulkner story, and puzzled over the sense of sin as judgment in Hawthorne; confessed anonymously to family unhappiness in short bitter poems after reading some of Sylvia Plath's work; learned to avoid "to be" and the passive voice as their teacher pressured them to live and write actively; endured a digital fast that left many of them unstrung as well as unplugged; encountered the most dangerous aspects of modernity in Huxley and Orwell; created, in the Alanis Project, satire, spoof, and parody; considered life as a journey in Coelho's and Hesse's fictions (and discovered that there was no single key but, ideally, a span of one intense moment after another); saw, in Vonnegut's subversive war-and-peace novel, that comedy and tragedy were inseparable; faced the destruction of identity in Viktor Frankl's death-camp memoir and death itself in the passing of a teacher, Mr. Goldman; entered Dostoevsky's

emotionally enlarged universe of self-knowledge, self-contempt, and defiance (all mixed together) and stepped in and out of self-defining roles;
discovered that hell was (and was not) other people and that life was both
over in a flash and went on endlessly, a metaphysical conundrum in
which men and women faced eternity alone but ate carrots and took off
boots every day. They had gone from a powerful, straightforward gothic
tale by Faulkner to two of the most difficult works in modernism's thorny
canon.

Hasan, the media king, became a student; Vanessa stopped her tears
and insisted on the primacy of her own thinking; brilliant Marina
defined herself with dramatic flair and took responsibility for a possibly
self-destructive act; Adam went from silence to intellectual pride; Clare
from silence to intellectual empathy; Marco ceased being the class clown
and spoke seriously and then became a risk-taking clown again; Nino
turned himself into an ambitious solitary reader; Leonardo, whose eyes
were dead when literature was discussed, moved from indifference to preliminary engagement; Lauren, whose name no one could remember
on opening day, began making shrewd remarks; and others changed
in similar ways over the year.

Mr. Leon talked about structure, metaphor, and theme, and took the
class through point-by-point analysis of the texts, but the most powerful part of his class was devoted to the spiritual value of literature and
the moral instruction of teenagers at a crucial moment in their lives. He
gave them difficult texts, and pessimistic texts, too, and he reached out
to what seemed to come naturally to American teenagers, a fascination
with the darker side of life. He took that interest and turned it from pop
culture to literature, and he ministered to their souls. He introduced
them to modernist literature in all its miseries and glories. If they were
lucky and ambitious, aesthetic bliss, in Nabokov's phrase, would be theirs
some day. But first they were aroused by reading serious things.

"There are reasons to engage them now," he said to me in the depths
of PD O'Hurley's when the school year was over. "We break the texts
down down structurally, but, in this society, critical thought has been

numbed by media and politics, and thinking critically about the world and themselves is far more important. These are life issues. They all engage. It's very powerful for them."

Everyone milled around at the end of the last class, and some of the students were unwilling to let go. They were located in that time, in that place, in the fifteenth and sixteenth years of their lives, in a single English class, in a shabby building on West 61st Street in Manhattan. In a few years, Beacon will have left the building; the school was getting a big new home on West 44th Street with a sizable gym, increased lab space, more classrooms. No one could say what would happen to any of the students in the future, but it was unlikely that they would be afraid of any book, and unlikely as well that they would go through life thinking that literature couldn't possibly matter to them.

AFTERWORD

- Sean Leon
- Marina Rodriguez
- Jessica Zelenski
- Denzel Jefferson
- Raymond Brown
- Philip Todd
- What Students Want and Need
- Teachers

I met with Sean Leon again about a year after school had ended, this time in an Upper West Side restaurant called Le Monde. (We were both sick of PD O'Hurley's, which, in any case, closed soon after our meeting at Le Monde.) The past year had been rough for him. He had gone home to Louisiana and had tended to his older brother in his last days; then he took a semester off from Beacon to be with his mother and the rest of his family. For a time, he told me, he seriously considered leaving Beacon altogether and teaching instead in New Orleans, about two hours from home in Opelousas. He sent out résumés, and an offer came from Benjamin Franklin High School, the best public high school in New

Orleans, a magnet school for gifted children with an ethnic enrollment similar to Beacon's.

"Good school," he said with a grimace. "But I finally turned them down. Do you know why? Test prep. And I would have to teach literature out of a textbook. I couldn't create my own reading lists." Beacon's withdrawal from the national testing regimens combined with Ruth Lacey's guarantee of freedom to her teachers had provided the most powerful arguments, in the end, for staying at Beacon.

"All over the country, it's test, test, test! Beacon is a school where content drives instruction. Teaching the content is the key to getting kids college ready. Critical discussion, asking questions of yourself, your society, asking the big questions!"

He was passionate, and other people at Le Monde looked our way. "That approach has to be embraced at grade-school and middle-school levels," he said. "The arts and critical thinking shouldn't be just on the side but woven into every humanities course."

He went on for some time, and I realized that we had slightly different goals for the education of fifteen-year-olds. He wanted active, vital beings, active language, a sense of the preciousness of every instant— every second was soul time—combined with love of family and friends. I certainly had no objection to any of that, but I also wanted ego strength, the authority and dignity of an ego trained by experience and reading, a stable center in the midst of economic and media flux. They were different but related goals, and I knew I would miss terribly the sound of his hard, lively, defining voice. In the spring of 2015, I went back to Beacon for a visit and stood outside his classroom just out of sight, listening as he taught a tenth-grade class. The voice was the same.

The young woman who stepped out of the elevator at my office had beautiful skin and eyes; she was slender in leather jacket and jeans, a diamond stud at her nose and throat. As she had said she would, Marina

Rodriguez left Beacon at the end of sophomore year. She enrolled at a public school called City As School, which encouraged kids to hold jobs in the city while they were studying—hardly a new routine for Marina, who held three jobs while going to Beacon. But she was socially uncomfortable at Beacon; the students outside of Mr. Leon's class didn't take to her challenging ways. Her sense of her own will, her selfhood, was at stake. She had to leave. In the intervening three years, the smart fifteen-year-old, burdened with books, purse, stuff, everything flying all over the place, had changed remarkably. She had lost weight; she dressed well; her hair was sleek and beautiful. But nothing had been easy.

"I worked my ass off at City As School and graduated in one year," she said. Sixteen at graduation, she got into New York University, but without enough support to make it possible for her to attend. For the next year she interned at a New York courthouse, a clothing company, a public school, and worked at Jamba Juice and Juice Press. At this point, at eighteen, she was trying to get licensed as a beautician and also as a fitness instructor. "Billionaires have seven different incomes. I am going to build as many skills as possible so I'm never without a job."

After a year of working full-time, she entered the Borough of Manhattan Community College (BMCC), a two-year branch of the City University, and she hated it. The school had over twenty thousand students, it was overburdened and disorganized, she said, the student services poor. "No one talks in class, no one reads. It's dead in there. They wait for me to talk. It's a drag." At the same time, she worked as an assistant general manager at the Lucille Roberts Gym, a women's exercise salon at Fifth Avenue and Union Square. She was as decisive as ever, looking straight at me as she talked, but her manner had softened. She no longer spoke as if every sentence was a challenge issued to the world.

All through the three years, her family situation remained dismal. She left her father, and, for two years, lived with her painter mother, inhabiting a walk-in closet in a tiny apartment filled with paintings, brushes, books. "Living there this last year while going to college was very tough. I was stagnant. I had to leave." She now lived with two friends in the Bushwick neighborhood of Brooklyn, one of the borough's rapidly gentrifying neighborhoods.

Pushing defeat and unhappiness into the past, leaving and moving on—that was Marina Rodriguez's identity. She had defined herself as vigorously as Sean Leon might have dreamed. I saw her as a kind of self-willed urban adventurer, tough as any young man making his way in business or in the service. She loved Sean Leon's class (her eyes warmed when we talked about it), but she had no regrets about quitting Beacon, even though, in practical terms, it was a mistake: if she had stayed, Beacon's college office would likely have found her the support she needed at a first-rate college. But she would have felt defeated if she had stayed, and her sense of herself could not bear defeat.

What now? She could quit BMCC and college altogether, remain at the Lucille Roberts Gym, and probably settle into a good salary there as an administrator. She had grown into a shrewd, very savvy, very pulled-together woman, and she could be a great business success if she wanted to be. But she was also intellectually hungry and contemptuous of ordinary lives, ordinary jobs. In all, I had never met anyone more suited for university education. She dreaded the second year at BMCC, but she said she would stay and finish up. A student again, she had begun reading good stuff for the first time since Sean Leon's class. "That was the most satisfying thing about going back." I read some of her written work from BMCC, and it was strong. Yet she needed to get out of where she was in her life. My guess: she would finish up at the school she hated, apply again to a four-year college, and move on and up, always on and up.

I returned to Hillhouse in the late spring of 2015 and dropped in on Jessica Zelenski. She had recently won a teaching award, and the New Haven School District had asked her to sit on a curriculum committee, a definite honor. But she was tired, she was angry, she glared and stomped. She had multiple sections of tenth-grade English in 2014–15, ninety-five students in all, and she was exasperated in a way that I didn't remember from the year before. The breaking of Hillhouse into three academies, she felt, had cut off both teachers and students from a community that was a good part of the school experience in the past.

The day I visited, one of her tenth-grade sections was writing short responses in class to both Susanna Kaysen's 1993 memoir *Girl, Interrupted* and Ann Patchett's early story, "All Little Colored Children Should Play the Harmonica." She moved quickly from student to student, going over passages, posing questions. "Success and happiness are not the same thing. What does that mean in terms of the story?" she asked three students who were sitting together. Then she would turn to me and offer a running public commentary on the class, praising one student or another. "Willie says the things that other people just think. He's very empathic, talks about feelings." And she had an extraordinary fifteen-year-old, Tyriq, who finished his work quickly and ran to a computer at the side of the room, looking up anything on the Internet that interested him, a student with ravenous curiosity.

Yet in her whole time at Hillhouse—fourteen years—she had never been unhappy in the way she was now. I asked her if she would consider leaving. Would she take, for instance, a job in an upper-middle-class Connecticut community? She stared at me. "No, never upper-middle class. Working class only." Then she paused. "I always thought this is where I was going to make my career. I need grieving time. I can't just leave."

Later that week, she sent a note describing what another English teacher had told her years ago: "His seniors were writing their life stories and a student wrote that I had saved her life earlier with our mutual love of reading. Her mother had recently died, and she and her five siblings and alcoholic father had uprooted and moved to New Haven following her mother's death. She was playing mother to the whole family but never breathed a word of this for a few years—never to me, either. But when I heard what she wrote, I was happy to have found a kindred spirit, especially such a young one. That's my most important 'teaching' moment and it has nothing to do with skills."

During the same visit to Hillhouse I tried to see Denzel Jefferson. His mother Shiniqua Jefferson, a paraprofessional at the school, button-holed me in the hallway outside Miss Zelenski's classroom—she knew I was looking for her son. A short, powerful woman with a long braid of reddish hair and many bracelets, she told me she was driving Denzel out of town on the weekends to basketball games—he played in Amateur Athletic Union teams. "I'll wear ten-dollar shoes," she said in the hall-way, "so he can wear two-hundred-dollar shoes and not sell drugs to pay for them. What I don't want to spend money on is a bail bondsman and a lawyer." She laughed loudly, and students walking by smiled—she was a familiar, in-your-face presence in school. "I've had my turn. You know? You gotta pay. Anything that gets him out of the inner-city ghetto is good."

I found Denzel a bit later. He was fit; his long, sorrowful face had turned handsome; he looked straight at me rather than turning away. He told me he would take college-prep courses at Gateway Community College in New Haven in his senior year. He wanted to go where his sister went, Virginia State, but the out-of-state tuition was $24,000, and he wasn't sure his mother could afford it.

I asked him about his friends. His face turned sorrowful again, but then he smiled. The situation had passed beyond simple grief. "In the last eighteen months, I've lost four friends," he said. Two more had died in the year since I last saw him. "It's ridiculous. You go out to play basketball with friends, a couple of weeks later one of them gets shot. Ridiculous."

I asked him how he saw himself in ten years. "I would like to have a good job," he said, "and be able to take care of whatever I have to take care of. I want to be a normal black man and live as long as I can."

I looked up Raymond Brown, too. He still had a furtive grin and spoke in a whisper. The year before, when he'd told me his Trinidadian father was in jail, he'd said he didn't know why. Now Raymond told me he had been convicted for drug possession. After three years in Corrigan-Radgowski Correctional Center in northern Connecticut, his father had recently brought a court case to appeal the conviction, but he had lost and was now being deported back to Trinidad. Raymond didn't know when he would see him again. His kid brother was now twelve, and they continued to play basketball near their house in the Tre; Raymond kept him away from older neighborhood kids. "I don't want him trying things he shouldn't," he said.

He said he liked to write for himself, but only in long uninterrupted periods, not in school. He was keeping a journal of his life.

A year after Miss Zelenski's class ended, Philip Todd, then seventeen, sent me a draft of his college-application essay, which turned out to be an account of his birth and stealthy development as a moviegoer. He didn't have the money to see new films, and, in any case, the availability in New Haven (outside of Yale) of anything besides mass-market hits was limited. Some college town! Anyway, Philip did what other movie-hungry kids did, he downloaded films from the Internet and squirreled them away. Then he turned systematic.

"I made it my goal to hunt for the best directors," he wrote in his essay. "I studied Quentin Tarantino, Clint Eastwood, Martin Scorsese, David Lynch, Paul Thomas Anderson, Danny Boyle, Steven Spielberg and of course the master himself Stanley Kubrick. When I had exhausted the 'must-see' classics, I turned to independent, older films from the '80s and '90s. When I couldn't fall asleep, I tiptoed downstairs to watch films like Terrence Malick's *A Thin Red Line* or Gus Van Sant's *Drugstore*

Cowboy. . . . I'd get my laptop and turn the audio down low so that each film is a whisper inviting me to its world."

Phil's secret habits—and unorthodox tastes—required a certain bravery to maintain. An urban, working-class African American boy, very dark, easily six feet two, he rejected the clichés of macho culture, and some of his friends in Miss Zelenski's class had called him "Uncle Tom" and "Oreo." But he stuck to his passion, an opening to art that was also an opening to the world. The movies of the eighties and nineties, he told me, had led him to the music of the same period. Maybe he'd eventually get to fiction and journalism, too. As I knew from a year earlier, he wanted to go to a college with good film program. Yale with its Promise initiative would pay his tuition at local colleges and universities, but none of them had the courses he needed, and he hadn't figured out yet how to get serious support from Wesleyan or NYU, which had exactly what he wanted. At the end of his junior year, Philip Todd needed persistence and luck to make a life out of what he loved.

Proust described his childhood reading of novels as "a dream more lucid and abiding than those that come to us in sleep," but none of us can compare to Proust—or to Nabokov—as a reader. My reporting suggests, however, that certain passionate commitments in teachers (and certain temperamental gifts) can arouse tenth-graders, pull them away from screens and social networking and the other obsessions of teenage life—at least for a while—pull them into enjoyment of reading, maybe into complicated literary texts, and possibly drive them into asking serious questions about their lives. All of which lays the groundwork for a lifetime interest in reading, in bookishness, even in literature as one of the great pleasures. The groundwork, not the certainty. As I have said before, you have to begin somewhere.

Teens are entering a media-Internet world of infinite choices, manifold but chaotic, decentered, even incoherent. But if there's little or no authority anywhere in the public atmosphere of assertion and counter-assertion, they can at least try to gain a little authority of their own. They can hope for the dignity of knowing something, understanding something. They can know math and the sciences; and they can also know things that, by their very nature, are unquantifiable but help create three-dimensional human beings. Children, elementary reason would suggest, need that chance more than anyone, and to abandon children and teenagers to the tumult of screens and to lessen the value of literature and the humanities in favor of the STEM subjects, as many powerful men reforming education now want to do, is almost certainly a mistake and very possibly a disastrous mistake. Again: Did we need so many STEM graduates? Many of them entering a glutted market can't find jobs or, if they do find them, are quickly replaced in midcareer by younger men and women willing to work at lower pay. For this dubious end we were changing the nature of education, downplaying the humanities, shunting to the side literature, the arts, and much else.

Perhaps no one can say definitively how much teenagers gain or lose by obsessively playing games, obsessively using social media and the Internet (evidence exists on both sides of the case), but we can be sure they lose an enormous amount by not reading very seriously. The ability to understand the world and other people can't be created on screens alone. The ability to recognize lies and stupidity can't be created there either. When he received the Nobel Prize for Literature, in 2010, Mario Vargas Llosa said this: "We would be worse than we are without the good books we have read, more conformist, not as restless, more submissive, and the critical spirit, the engine of progress, would not even exist." That's a witty negative claim: We would be "worse" than we are. Thinking back on your life as an adult, you might remember when you became a little less worse than before.

But here's the practical question: How do you build the appetite Mario Vargas Llosa is talking about? Through *books*, in one form or another, in hard copy or on an e-reader. But teens rarely have any idea what books they're looking for. Sure, students could go to websites that tell them about the books most relevant to them, the good books, the best books, the super-great books. But how many kids do that? And whom should they trust—some impersonal authority? What everyone else is reading? Such guides on the Internet may simply register what's popular. My loving parents read three or four newspapers every night and all through the weekends. Initially, before I had any taste of my own, teachers, librarians, and friends pushed me toward good things. Teachers, especially. Most of us need teachers immersed in literature, history, and science to get us going anywhere worth going to.

At Mamaroneck, the administration and the English Department were trying to create hunger for books—and then better books—as a value in itself. In their gently insistent way, they had declared war on student laziness, evasiveness, ignorance. They wanted students to perform in school and on standardized tests; they also wanted to turn them into vibrant men and women. Mamaroneck's goals were both practical and utopian at once. And at Beacon, Sean Leon was building and saving souls, though not with improving lessons and heroic stories (at least not conventionally heroic), but in the modern way, with a demand for intellectual bravery and boldness, candor, authenticity, and clarity. At the same time, he insisted on family and religion (whatever his own faith or loss of faith) and love of friends. He was a radical in spirit, a conservative in values. Both he and the Mamaroneck teachers were trying to create students with enough internal authority to make their way in a dangerous world.

Lionel Trilling, in his essay "On the Teaching of Modern Literature" (written in 1961, initially collected in *Beyond Culture*), noted that formalism as a practice—the study of literature as a structure of words—is illuminating and powerful, but it's not enough for him or for us. (This essay was written well before deconstruction and theory replaced the "New Criticism" that Trilling was reacting to.) We have to ask, Trilling said, the modern question: "Is it true? Is it true for me?" In other words, we have to pose moral and spiritual as well as formal questions and try to arrive at some sort of answers. But can students now ask "Is it true? Is it true for me?" in college courses, where the study of literature is often conducted by professionals immersed in the New Historicism, in post-deconstruction, in one arcane method or another of criticism and inter-pretation? In any case, many literature professors would insist that "Is it true?" has little meaning as a question, "truth" having bitten the dust as a delusion or at best as unknowable.

In high school, you can ask such questions with a directness, a fierceness even—certainly with a lack of embarrassment—that would be impossible in university courses. "Is it true for me?" is particularly a ques-tion that adolescents—at least the serious-minded ones—love to ask. Obviously Sean Leon knows that. His own preoccupations link up with the turmoil that fifteen-year-old students are going through. Literature is his obsession, and he wants it to be their obsession. What he values most is the students' emotional connection to whatever they read. Later, in college or on their own, they might learn to love literature as art, the structural freedom and power of poetry and fiction, the sound of language—they might enjoy what Nabokov has called "aesthetic bliss." Enjoyment is the goal and reward that trumps all others. But to get to that moment the ability to read seriously at all must be created.

If teenagers' bliss at fifteen is Facebook or texting or gaming; if read-ing seriously goes against their inclination; if the "deep reading" circuits have to be replanted, or planted for the first time, then becoming seri-ous readers at all is something of a triumph for them and their teachers, perhaps as much a victory as learning to read in the first place.

Both Sean Leon at Beacon and Jessica Zelenski at Hillhouse hit their students where they lived. They didn't shy away from adolescent obses-sions; they didn't try to turn students into adults by assigning "improv-ing" work in the Victorian style. They found them where they were as fifteen-year-olds, which did not mean underestimating them. Anything but. American teenagers are preoccupied with justice—not in the legal sense, necessarily, but in the sense of fairness, especially fair treatment of *them* as still powerless members of the society. They also want to find some purpose in life. Challenge a mumbling or ironically self-deprecating American fifteen-year-old, and you will find someone looking for answers or at least ready to ask questions.

Yes, they want a way of earning a living, of fitting in and having a good life, but they want a way of being, too. Basic ethical and philosophical questions of right and wrong, acting and doing, belief and skepticism, acquiescence and critical thinking fascinate them, and nothing is more effective than reading literature for churning up such questions. Zadie Smith, one of the most exciting contemporary novelists and essayists, put it this way: "It seems that if you put people on paper and move them through time, you cannot help but talk about ethics, because the ethical realm exists nowhere if not here: in the consequences of human actions as they unfold in time, and the multiple interpretive possibility of those actions. Narrative itself is the performance of that very procedure" (*Guardian*, October 3, 2003). In other words, one of contemporary literature's actual makers, disputing advanced literary theory of the last forty years, believes that fiction has some vital and complicated relation to reality, a relation that makes ethical issues inescapable. Conversations that uncover the moral issues lodged in narrative have a good chance of meaning something special to fifteen-year-olds. My apocalyptic tremblings at the end of the digital fast at Beacon had long subsided. Fifteen-year-olds will read seriously when inspired by charismatic teachers alert to what moves adolescents.

If teachers initially accommodate student interests and emotions, the ambitious ones move them up and out. For instance, the dark side runs right through pop culture—as spectacle, as wonder, as the thrill of the forbidden. In evil, there is vitality, or at least gaudy self-assurance, and American teenagers know that and wonder over it. Instead of fighting their absorption, Mr. Leon and Miss Zelenski nurtured and deepened student fascination by turning it toward art. They assigned fictions and memoirs chronicling extreme experience, the loss of identity, the exhilarations and tragedies of living out at the edge. They gently broke down protective narcissism, launching the students into the grown-up world of moral difficulty, contingency, money, family love, loss, and death. They did not emphasize craft, technique, the historical circumstances in which the books were composed. That was for later. Instead, they wanted students to have an actual experience when they read. And the students, for the most part, weren't offended by work that was hard for them. On the contrary, they were flattered.

Curious and ambitious teens always read things that are too hard for them and fail to understand half of what they read. But frustration only makes them eager to find out more. The acceptance of initial failure is built into avid natures. But ordinary kids may also feel haunted by what they don't quite understand—haunted if it moves them in some way. Even in a classroom assignment, they don't have to understand everything in a book in order to be excited by it, awed by it. They will enjoy the ego boost of having read something difficult. Overmastered at first, they will move toward mastery of themselves.

I saw this at Beacon when an eleventh-grade class, taught by Daniel Guralnick, read one of the great books of American literature, Ralph Ellison's *Invisible Man*. The novel dramatizes the situation of a young black man in the twentieth century as a binary pair of impossible choices: if you fight all the time, you destroy yourself physically; if you give in all the time, you destroy yourself spiritually. Could the narrator (he has no name) find a way out of this double choke hold? Born in the South, he gets tossed out of a black college, struggles to get a job in New York, undergoes shock therapy in which he comes close to losing his identity altogether. He recovers, and begins a tumultuous time in Harlem as an organizer and soapboxer for the authoritarian "Brotherhood" (Ellison's mocking version of the Communist Party). He gets razzed by black nationalists, vamped by wealthy white women, caught up in a bizarre and spectacular riot. He undergoes one jolting encounter after another as he looks for himself among the ambitious, the mad, the defeated. *Invisible Man*, published in 1952, moves back and forth between stern realism and fantasia, between the vernacular traditions of black America (slave songs, blues, street put-ons) and the most advanced literary techniques. It was exhausting and exhilarating—almost baffling at times, and also an American masterpiece.

At one level, it was a "social novel" about race and identity, and Mr. Guralnick and his class certainly didn't duck the racial issue. But if you read it just for what it says about race, you were only half reading it. "There's something much bigger here than any message," Daniel Guralnick said. "It's art." Again and again, Guralnick, a marathon runner in a T-shirt, informal yet stringent in his demands on students, convinced his class that by studying a work of art, they would find out things they needed to know, both about literature and themselves, something that had likely eluded them up until then. They were primed. Earlier in the year, they had read stories by Poe, Twain, and Melville, novels by Fitzgerald and Hemingway, and much else—it was an eleventh-grade course in American literature. Yet *Invisible Man* was complex and many-voiced, and at times the students had trouble understanding what Ellison was up to. Mr. Guralnick eased them into the difficulties, taking them through strange passages in which the narrator slips into dreams and fantasies and bluesy speculation. They read the book for structure, image, and language, tracing the life of the text through its surging metaphors and descriptive and rhetorical abundance. As they drew near the end, the students were surging themselves, in time with the book, seeing the hero's struggle for selfhood as a series of lost illusions—and possible illuminations.

The benefits of interpreting a difficult book were literary and more than literary. A structural reading of *Invisible Man* necessarily traced the hero's fortunes. In his early twenties, Ellison's hero has the recurring experience of being thrown into some task without even rudimentary explanation of what in the world he is supposed to do. He can't read the codes—the way to succeed in one situation after another—and most strangers seem eager to see him fail. That hostility was a young person's common fear—the fear that no one in the world would make room for *his* ego, *his* right to succeed. The students got close to the hero as he struggled, for in their own lives they needed to read the codes, too. By seeing how the narrative was put together, and what the structural elements actually meant, they would be forced, willy-nilly, to understand their own experience—linking the different parts of their lives together by linking the different parts of the novel together.

You make a self by matching yourself against the text. When you respond to the text fully, understanding how it is constructed, and what the parts mean, you come into being. This was hardly a narcissistic exercise; the students couldn't do what they did without the provocation of an exceedingly complicated work of literature and an ardent teacher who believed in the book as art. Pop literature, skillfully composed by formula, wouldn't offer as rich a field of reference and action.

Difficult books are one kind of challenge that students can meet if they're pushed. And reading a long book, too, if it goes like a shot. Reading a long narrative makes teenagers proud. It gives them the full span of a life, a family, a war, whatever it is the book is devoted to. It develops reading stamina in the way that track practice builds lung power and muscle.

In Mary Beth Jordan's tenth-grade section at Mamaroneck High School, the class read John Steinbeck's *East of Eden* (1952), an epic family novel (640 pages), burly in its heavy-limbed movements yet also delicate in its innumerable notations of weather, terrain, trees, plants, rocks, and bushes. (Steinbeck had written, among other things, an agronomist's four-season handbook to his beloved Salinas Valley in California—much about eucalyptus and gum, lupins and poppies.) At Mamaroneck, *East of Eden* was a core reading, not an independent choice, and a lot of it, in truth, made me wince. A Cain and Abel fable, constructed with Old Testament clay, it gorged on such things as land, inheritance, sex, violence;

it featured a ludicrous female creation, Kate, a cross between Jezebel and the Whore of Babylon. Was the book loam or depleted soil? Both, perhaps. It was old-fashioned and literary in many of the wrong ways—portentous and Bible-haunted and full of Steinbeck's sagacity, much of it a wheeze.

But Steinbeck's narrative power pulled me along, and it pulled a lot of the students along, too. Much of it was about young people growing up, making choices (often bad ones). Miss Jordan, working on it for over a month, discussed theme and plot and metaphor; she required papers as part of a complicated project; she got the students to write speeches in the voice of one of Steinbeck's characters; and she broke the class into groups, made students become experts in one aspect or another of the novel which honored the Mamaroneck ideal of reading as a social culture, not just a solitary experience. They read *East of Eden*, and they acted upon it, as medium as well as a text. They mixed their labor with it, and many of them conquered the length with a little burst of self-esteem.

In all the classes I attended, teachers put themselves out in order to get students to put *them*selves out. This meant more than the obvious things—that a teacher has to be intellectually serious, responsive to everyone, and also in her person the spirit of justice. I repeat: For many kids, a good teacher may be the most palpable form of honor they will ever experience. For the moment, the students have an authority in their lives that they can depend on. All familiar enough—it's the heart of teaching—but even more than that is required to sustain a fifteen-year-old's absorption in literature. At Beacon, Sean Leon was there for his students—between classes and after school, when he camped in an empty basement room and saw kids who had problems or questions. The eleventh-grade teacher Mary Whittemore turned herself into a version of Hester Prynne. Margaret Groninger, at Mamaroneck, read above and beyond the course load in order to produce the "book talks" that lay at the center of the independent reading initiative. At Hillhouse, Jessica Zelenski stood up for the kids within the school and coaxed and teased

and shouted in class, even storming out when her students weren't trying hard enough, only to come back and apologize. She loved them,
and by the end of the year they started reading, they performed for her.

Teenagers, distracted, busy, self-obsessed, are not easy to engage—
not by their teachers or by their parents. To keep them in the game, the
teachers I watched experimented, altered the routine, changing the physical dimensions of the class. They kept kids off balance in order to put
them back in balance. They demanded more of students than the students
expected to give. They talked candidly, acknowledging that they were
neither perfect nor invulnerable. They were more experienced, certainly,
than students; they were guides, leaders, dispensers of knowledge and
justice, but also people subject to the ups and downs, the happiness
and mishaps, that the students were subject to. They demonstrated that
it was possible to do that without losing authority. In fact, in media-
sozzled America, where skepticism is the prevailing mode of thought,
candor may be a way of gaining authority. Teaching is about building
trust. Acknowledgment of one's own humanity is one powerful way of
building it.

As I knew at the beginning of my reporting and reading, there is no
perfect syllabus, no perfect set of classroom conversations, and certainly
no perfect model for how understanding, assurance, and daring should
be enlarged in teenagers. Intellectual ability and "emotional intelligence"
are built through an innumerable number of small steps. If we think of our
own lives, we will remember how gradually, through so many moments,
through so many stupidities, errors, and evasions—seeming failures—
we moved ahead and got anyplace worth going to. Education is labori-
ous and intermittent. Strength may come in sleep, in dreams, in fantasy.
But after children leave their parents' arms, school is still the necessary
place for knowledge and soul to spring into life, and good teachers are
still the loving instigators of that miracle.

Reading Lists

SEAN LEON
The Beacon School, Tenth Grade

Khalid Hosseini: *The Kite Runner* (summer)

William Faulkner: "A Rose for Emily"

Nathaniel Hawthorne: "The Minister's Black Veil"

Sylvia Plath: "Daddy," "Lady Lazarus"

Aldous Huxley: *Brave New World*

George Orwell: "Politics and the English Language," *1984*

Paulo Coelho: *The Alchemist* (trans. Alan R. Clarke)

Herman Hesse: *Siddhartha* (trans. Hilda Rosner)

Kurt Vonnegut: *Slaughterhouse-Five*

Viktor E. Frankl: *Man's Search for Meaning* (trans. Ilse Lasch)

Fyodor Dostoevsky: *Notes from Underground* (trans. Andrew R. McAndrew)

Jean-Paul Sartre: *No Exit* (trans. Stuart Gilbert)

Samuel Beckett: *Waiting for Godot* (trans. Samuel Beckett)

JESSICA ZELENSKI
James Hillhouse High School, Tenth Grade

Ursula Le Guin: "The Ones Who Walked Away from Omelas"

Sandra Cisneros: "Woman Hollering Creek"

Harper Lee: *To Kill a Mockingbird*

Public Service Announcements

Time magazine articles

William Shakespeare: Sonnets

Kurt Vonnegut: "Harrison Bergeron"

Ernest Hemingway: "The Short Happy Life of Francis Macomber"

Choice of:

Ishmael Beah: *A Long Way Gone*

Amy Tan: *The Joy Luck Club*

Elie Wiesel: *Night* (trans. Stella Rodway)

Khaled Hosseini: *A Thousand Splendid Suns*

MARY BETH JORDAN
Mamaroneck High School, Tenth Grade

Jeannette Walls: *The Glass Castle* (summer)

Elie Wiesel: *Night*

William Shakespeare: *Macbeth*

John Steinbeck: *East of Eden*

Kurt Vonnegut: "Harrison Bergeron"

Alice Walker: "The Flowers"

John Cheever: "Reunion"

George Saunders: "Sticks"

Poetry by Percy Bysshe Shelley, Robert Frost, T. S. Eliot, Theodore Roethke, Maxine Kumin

Choice of:

George Orwell: *1984*

Ray Bradbury: *Fahrenheit 451*

And Choice of:

Stephen King: *The Body*

Khaled Hosseini: *The Kite Runner*

Independent Reading Choices

All year long

MARY WHITTEMORE
The Beacon School, Eleventh Grade

Jeffrey Eugenides: *Middlesex* (summer)

Ralph Waldo Emerson, Henry Thoreau, Walt Whitman: Excerpts

Nathaniel Hawthorne: *The Scarlet Letter*

F. Scott Fitzgerald: *The Great Gatsby*

Toni Morrison: *The Song of Solomon*

Ken Kesey: *One Flew Over the Cuckoo's Nest*

Tim O'Brien: *The Things They Carried*

Leslie Marmon Silko: *Ceremony*

Junot Diaz: *The Brief Wondrous Life of Oscar Wao*

DANIEL GURALNICK
The Beacon School, Eleventh Grade

Washington Irving: "Rip Van Winkle"

Nathaniel Hawthorne: "The Birthmark"

Edgar Allen Poe: "The Cask of Amontillado"

Mark Twain: "The Celebrated Jumping Frog of Calaveras County"

Henry James: *Daisy Miller*

Stephen Crane: "The Open Boat"

Charlotte Perkins Gilman: "The Yellow Wallpaper"

Truman Capote: *In Cold Blood*

F. Scott Fitzgerald: *The Great Gatsby*

Ernest Hemingway: *The Sun Also Rises*

Ralph Ellison: *Invisible Man*

Beacon Students' College List

When they graduated in 2014, the students of English 10G, Mr. Leon's class, went to the following colleges and universities:

Borough of Manhattan Community College

Boston University

Clark University

Cornell University

CUNY Brooklyn College

CUNY Hunter College

CUNY John Jay

CUNY Queensborough

Hamilton College

Hampshire College

Lawrence University

Middlebury College

Mount Holyoke College

New York University

Northeastern

NYC College of Technology

Occidental College

Rochester Institute of Technology

Smith College

SUNY Albany

SUNY Binghamton

SUNY Geneseo

SUNY New Paltz

Syracuse University

University of Hartford

University of Tampa

University of Wisconsin

Vassar College

Williams College

BIBLIOGRAPHY

This is a work of reporting, reading, and criticism. As I worked on it, I tried to hold to my initial resolve not to read pedagogy, teaching manuals, and other forms of professional education research. This wish turned out to be foolish. At times, out of curiosity and need, I was drawn to the work of educators and psychologists, also to the work of critics, teachers, and journalists, many of them passionate and knowledgeable in ways that I benefited from. I cite here those works that I found most useful.

Allington, Richard L. *What Really Matters Is Fluency.* Upper Saddle River, NJ: Pearson, 2008.

Alter, Robert. *The Pleasures of Reading in an Ideological Age.* New York: W. W. Norton, 1989.

Bellow, Saul. *It All Adds Up: From the Dim Past to the Uncertain Future.* New York: Viking Penguin, 1994.

Bloom, Harold. *How to Read and Why.* New York: Simon & Schuster, 2000.

Bruni, Frank. "Read, Kids, Read." *New York Times*, May 12, 2014.

Common Sense Media. "Children, Teens, and Reading." May 12, 2014, https://www.commonsensemedia.org/research/children-teens-and-reading.

Dickstein, Morris. "Ralph Ellison, Race, and American Culture." *Raritan*, Spring 1999. Reprinted in John F. Callahan, *Ralph Ellison's Invisible Man.* New York: Oxford University Press, 2004.

Fadiman, Anne. *At Large and at Small*. New York: Farrar, Straus and Giroux, 2007.

Fernald, Anne, Virginia A. Marchman, Adriana Weisleder. "SES Differences in Language Processing Skill and Vocabulary Are Evident at 18 Months." *Developmental Science*, March 2013.

Finnegan, William. *Cold New World: Growing Up in a Harder Country*. New York: Random House, 1998.

Freedman, Samuel G. *Small Victories: The Real World of a Teacher, Her Students, and Their High School*. New York: HarperCollins, 1990.

Gallagher, Kelly. *Readicide: How Schools Are Killing Reading and What You Can Do About It*. Portland, ME: Stenhouse, 2009.

Gardner, Howard. *Truth, Beauty, and Goodness Reframed: Educating for the Virtues in the Age of Truthiness and Twitter*. New York: Basic Books, 2011.

Gladwell, Malcolm. "Most Likely to Succeed." *New Yorker*, December 15, 2008.

Gopnik, Adam. "The Information." *New Yorker*, February 14, 2011.

Green, Elizabeth. *Building a Better Teacher: How Teaching Works (and How to Teach It to Everyone)*. New York: W. W. Norton, 2014.

Hacker, Andrew. "The Frenzy About High-Tech Talent." *New York Review of Books*, July 9, 2015.

Heckman, James. *Giving Kids a Fair Chance*. Boston: MIT Press, 2013.

Hardwick, Elizabeth. *American Fictions*. New York: Random House, 1999.

Hart, Betty, and Todd R. Risley. *Meaningful Differences in the Everyday Experiences of Young American Children*. Baltimore: Brookes, 1995.

Hirsch, E. D., Jr. *The Knowledge Deficit*: *Closing the Shocking Education Gap for American Children*. New York: Houghton Mifflin, 2006.

Kidder, Tracy. *Among Schoolchildren*. New York: Houghton Mifflin, 1989.

Kittle, Penny. *Book Love: Developing Strength, Stamina, and Passion in Adolescent Readers*. Portsmouth, NH: Heinemann, 2013.

Konnikova, Maria. "Being a Better Online Reader." *New Yorker*, July 16, 2014 (interview with Maryanne Wolf).

Kristof, Nicholas. "Do Politicians Love Kids?" *New York Times*, November 19, 2014.

———. "Starved for Wisdom." *New York Times*, April 16, 2015.

Lesser, Wendy. *Why I Read: The Serious Pleasure of Books*. New York: Picador, 2014.

Levi, Primo. *If This Is a Man* (trans. Stuart Woolf). New York: Little, Brown,

1991. Also available in *The Complete Works of Primo Levi, Volume I*. New York: Liveright, 2015.

————. *The Drowned and the Saved* (trans. Raymond Rosenthal). New York: Simon & Schuster, 1998. Also available in *The Complete Works of Primo Levi, Volume III* (trans. Michael Moore). New York: Liveright, 2015.

Nafisi, Azar. *Reading Lolita in Tehran: A Memoir in Books*. New York: Random House, 2003.

National Endowment for the Arts. *To Read or Not to Read: A Question of National Consequence*. Washington, DC: 2007, http://arts.gov/sites/default/files/To Read.pdf.

OECD iLibrary. *The ABC of Gender Equality in Education: Aptitude, Behaviour, Confidence*. OECD Publishing, 2015, http://dx.doi.org/10.1787/9789264 229945-en.

Packer, George. "Cheap Words." *New Yorker*, February 17, 2014.

Patchett, Ann. "Triumph of the Readers," *Wall Street Journal*, January 17, 2009.

Patterson, Leonardo, and Ethan Fosse (eds.). *The Cultural Matrix: Understanding Black Youth*. Cambridge, MA: Harvard University Press, 2015.

Pew Research. "A Snapshot of Reading in America in 2013." http://www .pewinternet.org/2014/01/16/.

————. "Teens, Social Media & Technology Overview 2015." http://www .pewinternet.org/2015/04/09/.

Quenqua, Douglas. "Is E-Reading to Your Toddler Story Time, or Simply Screen Time?" *New York Times*, October 12, 2014.

Ravitch, Diane. *The Death and Life of the Great American School System: How Testing and Choice Are Undermining Education*. New York: Basic Books, 2010.

————. *Reign of Error: The Hoax of the Privatization Movement and the Danger to America's Public Schools*. New York: Alfred A. Knopf, 2013.

Rich, Motoko. "Study Finds Reading to Children of All Ages Grooms Them to Read on Their Own." *New York Times*, January 8, 2015.

Richtel, Matt. "Growing Up Digital, Wired for Action." *New York Times*, November 21, 2010.

Rosenwald, Michael S. "Serious Reading Takes a Hit from Online Scanning and Skimming, Researchers Say." *Washington Post*, April 6, 2014 (interview with Maryanne Wolf).

Rushkoff, Douglas. *Present Shock: When Everything Happens Now.* New York: Current, 2013.

Sanneh, Kelefa. "Don't Be Like That." *New Yorker*, February 9, 2015.

Smith, Zadie. "Love, Actually." *Guardian*, October 31, 2003.

Strauss, Valerie. "Author Works to Prevent Reading's 'Death Spiral.'" *Washington Post*, March 24, 2008.

Talbot, Margaret. "Talking Cure." *New Yorker*, January 12, 2015.

Trilling, Lionel. *Beyond Culture.* New York: Viking, 1965.

———. *Sincerity and Authenticity.* Cambridge, MA: Harvard University Press, 1972.

Turkle, Sherry. *Alone Together: Why We Expect More From Technology and Less From Each Other.* New York: Basic Books, 2011.

Turner, Kristen Hawley, and Troy Hicks. *Connected Reading: Teaching Adolescent Readers in a Digital World.* Urbana, IL: National Council of the Teachers of English, 2015.

Wallace, David Foster. *Consider the Lobster and Other Essays.* New York: Little, Brown, 2005.

Wieseltier, Leon. "Among the Disrupted." *New York Times*, January 7, 2015.

Wolf, Maryanne. *Proust and the Squid: The Story and Science of the Reading Brain.* New York: HarperCollins, 2007.

Zakaria, Fareed. *In Defense of a Liberal Education.* New York: W. W. Norton, 2015.

ACKNOWLEDGMENTS

This book was a difficult undertaking, and I am grateful for the ardent support of Steve Rubin, president and publisher of Henry Holt and Company, and for the unfailing judgment and skill of Gillian Blake, Holt's editor in chief. Gillian read the manuscript at every stage; I benefited greatly from her many suggestions, her sense of drama and detail. Gillian's assistant, Eleanor Embry, provided needed help at key moments. Chris O'Connell, senior production editor, saw the manuscript through its many stages to completion.

The entire project might never have come off without the canny advocacy and editorial suggestions of my agent and friend, Kathy Robbins. Much thanks as well to Kathy's reader, Rachelle Bergstein. My wife, Susan Rieger, participated in the shaping and detail of the book in every way. Gilad Edelman gave invaluable aid in New Haven. I would also like to thank Paul Bass (editor) and Melissa Bailey (reporter) at the *New Haven Independent*.

Jonathan Cole, John Mitchell Mason Professor of the University at Columbia University, contributed stern and friendly advice, fueled by his extensive knowledge of education in this country. Carol Sanger came up with the main title, for which much thanks. At the *New Yorker*, David Remnick, Henry Finder, Hilton Als, and Kelefa Sanneh gave needed advice. Peter Blauner, Jane Booth, Joel Doerfler, Daniel Okrent, and Cathleen

Schine read part or all of the manuscript and made helpful comments. James Shapiro fired me up and also read parts of the manuscript. Sam Abrams, as I relate in the introduction, approached me on the street; the book was born in that moment. In many conversations afterward, Sam, now director of the National Center for the Study of Privatization in Education at Teachers College, offered his inexhaustible knowledge of primary and secondary education.

At the Beacon School, principal Ruth Lacey and assistant principal Harry Streep opened up the school's classrooms and halls and answered my many questions. I am grateful to Beacon English teachers Mary Whittemore and Daniel Guralnick, who allowed me to sit in their English classes, and especially grateful to Sean Leon, who instructed me (as well as the students of English 10G) through a long school year. Beacon's students bore my inquisitive gaze, answered inquiries in the hallways and the lunchroom, and generously gave their opinions and feelings about many things. I would also like to acknowledge the help of teachers Dale Lally, Brian Letiecq, and Sarah Fink and librarian Ann Hanin.

The James Hillhouse High School also opened its doors and classrooms. I am indebted to principal Kermit Carolina, who welcomed me in, and to Jessica Zelenski, who provided many moments of passionate teaching, warmth, and decency. Her students in Period 3 English were interested in my interest in *them*, and answered my many questions about their lives and experiences. I would also like to thank teachers Ben Nelkin and Kevin Barbaro, librarian Mary McMullen Jones, and assistant principal John Nguyen for providing necessary information.

Principal Elizabeth Clain, at Mamaroneck High School, fervently expounded the school's reading initiative and introduced me to Robert Shaps, superintendent of schools in the Mamaroneck School District, and to Annie Ward, assistant superintendent for curriculum and instruction in the district, both of whom clarified many issues related to the initiative. Margaret Groninger, head of the English Department, and Mary Beth Jordan, both tenth-grade teachers, allowed me into their classrooms and shared their enthusiasm for Mamaroneck's experiment. My thanks go to all of them and to Mamaroneck's students.

INDEX OF AUTHORS AND WORKS

ABOUT THE AUTHOR

DAVID DENBY is the author of *Great Books*, an acclaimed account of returning to college and reading the Western classics during the curriculum wars; *American Sucker*; *Snark*; and *Do the Movies Have a Future?* He is a staff writer and former film critic for *The New Yorker*, and his reviews and essays have appeared in *The New Republic*, *The Atlantic*, and *New York* magazine, among other places. He lives in New York City with his wife, writer Susan Rieger.